René Descartes

Meditations, Objections, and Replies

René Descartes

Meditations, Objections, and Replies

Edited and Translated by
ROGER ARIEW AND DONALD CRESS

Hackett Publishing Company, Inc.
Indianapolis/Cambridge

For SAA

For further information, please address:

Hackett Publishing Company, Inc.
P.O. Box 44937
Indianapolis, IN 46244-0937

www.hackettpublishing.com

Cover design by Abigail Coyle
Text design by Chris Downey
Composition by Agnew's, Inc.
Printed at Edwards Brothers, Inc.

Library of Congress Cataloging-in-Publication Data

Descartes, René, 1596–1650.
  [Meditationes de prima philosophia. English]
  Meditations, objections, and replies / René Descartes ; edited and translated by
Roger Ariew and Donald Cress.
      p.   cm.
  Includes bibliographical references and index.
  ISBN 0-87220-799-4 (cloth) — ISBN 0-87220-798-6 (pbk.)
  1. First philosophy.   2. Metaphysics—Early works to 1800.   I. Ariew, Roger.
II. Cress, Donald A.   III. Title.

B1853.E5A75   2006
194—dc22   2005057430

ISBN-13: 978-0-87220-799-8 (cloth)
ISBN-13: 978-0-87220-798-1 (pbk.)

CONTENTS

INTRODUCTION

The Meditations and the Objections and Replies

René Descartes did not just publish six Meditations; he presented his work to a select group of scholars before official publication so that their comments and his replies would be issued in a single volume with the Meditations. Thus the edition of 1641 was not the *Meditations* alone but a compendium: introductory essays that set the new text in relation to questions already raised about the *Discourse on Method* four years earlier, the six Meditations themselves, and then the objections of other scholars, together with the author's replies to those objections. To see the *Meditations* clearly for what they are, therefore, we need to look at all of the materials Descartes saw fit to publish, and especially the *Objections* and the *Replies;* in addition, we need to understand who the people were to whom Descartes was offering his work for criticism and the reasons they had for their appraisal of his arguments, as well as his reasons for replying as he did. In working toward such an understanding, we may find not only where Descartes and his critics fit into the intellectual environment of a tumultuous time, but also ways in which his own thought developed as he was articulating his responses.

The chief person who managed the circulation of the text of the *Meditations* to most of its first critics was Descartes' friend Marin Mersenne, a member of the Catholic order of Minims, who from his cell in the convent of the Minims in Paris served as the center and informal coordinator of a wide and diverse intellectual circle. Descartes was in constant correspondence with his monastic friend from his retreat in the Netherlands. However, it was the *Meditations* plus the *First Set of Objections and Replies* that Mersenne received for further circulation. To start the ball rolling, Descartes asked his friends Jan Albert Bannius and Augustinus Alstenius Bloemaert to write some objections; they, in turn, asked the Dutch priest Caterus (Johan de Kater) to do so. Caterus' *First Set of Objections* together with Descartes' *Replies* and the manuscript of the *Meditations* were sent to France to be printed, Descartes leaving Mersenne to organize the rest, telling him that he would be "glad if people make as many objections as possible and the strongest they can find" (AT III, 297). Thus five more sets of objections were obtained, making six altogether in the first edition; a seventh set followed in the second edition of 1642. The objectors could be listed as follows:

I. Caterus, with remarks addressed by him to his friends Bannius and Bloemaert, to be conveyed to Descartes. Descartes seems to treat this set of objections as part of the text of the *Meditations,* referring on a couple of occasions to the *Second Set* as the first (AT III, 293 and 328). He even discusses inserting the *Objections* and *Replies* within the text of the *Meditations,* though he vehemently rejects the move: "I do not consider it in any way appropriate, or even possible, to insert in my Meditations the reply to the objections that can be made to them. For that would interrupt their sequence, and would even remove the force of my arguments, which depend principally on the ability to turn one's thought away from sensible things, from which most of the objections would be drawn" (AT III, 267). Thus, he tells Mersenne: "I have put those of Caterus at the end, in order to show the place where others could also be, if any arrive" (AT III, 267). The *First Set of Objections* exemplifies Descartes' relations to the Scholastics of the period. In his objections Caterus concentrates on the theological aspects of Descartes' metaphysics. Five major topics emerge for the discussion: Whether ideas need a formal cause for their existence; God as self-caused; that we have the idea of an infinite being; the ontological argument for God's existence; and the real distinction between mind and body.

II. "Theologians and philosophers," described in the French edition of 1647 as "collected by Mersenne." This set of objections places Descartes directly in Mersenne's circle, that is, in debates characteristic of the developing sciences of the time. They cover a wide range of issues, such as the immortality of the soul and what we call the Cartesian circle, and contain a request (possibly inspired by the astrologer Jean-Baptiste Morin) to reformulate the contents of the *Meditations* in geometrical fashion. This last demand results in Descartes producing an appendix, "Arguments Proving the Existence of God and the Distinction of the Soul from the Body, Arranged in Geometrical Fashion," a geometric arrangement of the *Meditations* with definitions, postulates, axioms or common notions, and propositions (together with their demonstrations).

III. Thomas Hobbes, described in 1647 as "a famous English philosopher." Hobbes, like Gassendi, author of the fifth set of objections, has little sympathy with Cartesian doubt, which he finds exaggerated and at best a reheated version of old skeptical arguments. He rejects Descartes' method and dualism, insisting instead on the empirical basis of all our ideas and the dependence of the mind to the body. Descartes had little patience with these objections; the tone of his replies is sometimes sharp and personal; as he says to Mersenne: "having read at leisure the last writing of the Englishman, I find completely confirmed the opinion I had of him when I wrote to you two weeks ago. I think it would be best that I never have anything more to do with him, and consequently that I avoid answering him. For if his temperament is what I judge it to be, we would not be able to exchange views without becoming enemies. . . . Unless I am mistaken, he is a man who seeks to acquire a reputation at my expense and by unsavory means" (AT III, 320).

IV. Antoine Arnauld, a theology doctorate student at the Sorbonne, whose objections were addressed to Mersenne as intermediary. Descartes was pleased with Arnauld's objections, which he found "the best of all" because

Arnauld "had grasped the sense of what he had written better than anyone" (AT III, 331). The *Fourth Set of Objections* exhibits the profound kinship, and at the same time the differences, between Descartes and the Augustinian tradition (what is shortly to become the Port-Royal group and Jansenism in general). The topics discussed involve the real distinction between mind and body and our knowledge of substances; the souls of animals; material falsity; God as self-caused; the "Cartesian circle"; whether anything can be in the mind of which we are unaware; and the explanation of the sacraments of the Eucharist.

V. Pierre Gassendi, philosopher and historian. *The Fifth Set of Objections*, like the *Third*, places the Cartesian enterprise in relation to materialist or Epicurean movements of the day. While Gassendi is no materialist, this is the stance he takes in the objections, mocking Descartes by calling him "O Mind," which causes Descartes to call him "O Body." The debate between Descartes and Gassendi was long and contentious, Descartes becoming even angrier with Gassendi when the latter published *Disquisitio Metaphysica*, a separate edition with rejoinders. For the 1647 French edition of the *Meditations*, Descartes asked his translator Claude Clerselier to omit Gassendi's objections and to substitute instead a letter produced by his friends, in which he would answer a selection of Gassendi's strongest arguments. The letter, translated here, discusses standard objections against each Meditation, ending up with what Descartes calls "the objection of objections," that everything we are able to understand and conceive is but imaginations and fictions of our mind that can have no subsistence.

VI. A group described in 1647 as "various theologians and philosophers," once more collected by Mersenne, together with an appendix containing the arguments of "a group of philosophers and geometers." The debate centers about such topics as the cogito; the kind of knowledge an atheist can possess; whether God can deceive; the status of the eternal truths; and human freedom as indifference of judgment.

VII. The Jesuit mathematician Pierre Bourdin. Descartes deplored the fact that there were no Jesuits among the objectors, feeling that their approval, if given, would carry much weight: "Since he [Bourdin] is a member of a society which is very famous for its learning and piety, and whose members are all in such close union with each other that it is rare that anything is done by one of them which is not approved by all, I confess that I did not only 'beg' but also 'insistently demand' that some members of the society should examine what I had written and be kind enough to point out to me anything which departed from the truth" (AT VII, 452). In the 1640s the Jesuit order controlled a significant portion of French collegiate education and Descartes thought that the Jesuits, his old teachers, were so well regulated by their order that they usually acted as a corporate body; as Descartes said: "since I understand the communication and union that exists among those of that order, the testimony of one of them alone is enough to allow me to hope that I will have them all on my side" (AT II, 50). Eventually Bourdin, whom Descartes disliked for his criticism of Descartes' theories of subtle matter, reflection, and refraction, sent him a voluminous packet of objections. Descartes received these in January 1642, when his Dutch publisher Elzevier was already printing the second edition of the *Meditations.* So Descartes had them printed in the second edition, with his replies interspersed within the objections. Since the printer was slow to complete the volume, Descartes also added a long letter to the provincial of the Jesuits in the Île de France, Father Jacques Dinet, in which he complained of Bourdin's methods and suggested that the Jesuit Order should dissociate itself from him.

The Introductory Essays

As we have said, Descartes prefaced his *Meditations* with introductory essays: the *Letter of Dedication* to the Doctors of the Sorbonne, *Preface to the Reader,* and *Synopsis of the Meditations.* A passage from the *Preface to the Reader* can illuminate the setting for the *Meditations.* Descartes refers to the two issues of God and the human soul from the title of the *Meditations,* which he discusses in the *Letter of Dedication* to the Doctors of the Sorbonne as "two issues that are chief among those that are to be demonstrated with the aid of philosophy rather than theology" (AT VII, 1); he says: "I have already touched briefly on the issues of God and the human mind in my *Discourse on Method. . . .* The intent there was not to provide a precise treatment of them, but only to offer a sample and to learn from the opinion of readers how these issues should be treated in the future. For they seemed to me to be so important that I judged they ought to be dealt with more than once" (AT VII, 7). Descartes then refers to his offer, at the end of Discourse VI, to respond to criticisms. He asserts that there were only two objections worth noting and replies briefly to them "before undertaking a more precise examination of them" (AT VII, 7). Thus the *Discourse* does not just provide an early version of the *Meditations;* it constitutes the setting for the work and it provokes two preliminary objections that must be answered initially and then more fully in the *Meditations.* As Jean-Luc Marion asserts, "contrary to a widespread legend, Descartes is neither here nor elsewhere anything like a solitary, or even autistic, thinker, soliloquizing, in the manner perhaps of a Spinoza."[1] Marion details the steps taken by Descartes (between 1637 and 1640) to answer the two objections made by Pierre Petit to the metaphysical portion of the *Discourse,* objections the *Meditations* attempts to answer more

1. Jean-Luc Marion, "The Place of the *Objections* in the Development of Cartesian Metaphysics," in *Descartes and His Contemporaries: Meditations, Objections, and Replies,* ed. Roger Ariew and Marjorie Grene (Chicago: University of Chicago Press, 1995), pp. 10–1.

fully. Marion concludes that "not only would it be illegitimate to read the *Meditations* in abstraction from the *Objections and Replies,* with which they intentionally form an organic whole, but it would also be wholly illegitimate to read them otherwise than as replies to the objections evoked by the *Discourse.*"[2]

Marion is right to insist that we should think of Part IV, the metaphysical portion of the *Discourse,* and the *Meditations* as forming a "responsorial schema" of objections and replies. Even the first sentence of the *Meditations* sends the reader back to another time, outside the frame of the *Meditations:* "Several years have now passed since I first realized how numerous were the false opinions that in my youth I had taken to be true, and thus how doubtful were all those I had subsequently built on them." The first series of thoughts from Meditation I is set in a historical, autobiographical past, Descartes having realized that he had to "raze everything to the ground and begin again from the original foundations," if he wanted to establish anything firm and lasting in the sciences. As Descartes asserts, he waited until he reached a point in his life that was so timely that no more suitable time for undertaking these plans of action would come to pass (AT VII, 17). But if the first sentence of the *Meditations* sends us to the *Discourse,* the *Discourse* itself, like the *Meditations,* also sends us outside itself. The first sentence of the metaphysical portion of the *Discourse* states "I do not know whether I ought to tell you about the first meditations I engaged in there; for they are so metaphysical and so out of the ordinary that perhaps they will not be to everyone's liking" (AT VI, 31). The "there" referred to by Descartes is the Netherlands, to which Descartes moved in 1628 or 1629; so in 1637, Descartes tells us: "it is exactly eight years ago that this desire"—that is, the desire to begin to reject totally the opinions that had once been able to slip into his head and to seek the true method for arriving at the knowledge of everything of which his mind would be capable (AT VI, 17)—made him resolve to "take my leave of all those places where I might have acquaintances, and to retire here," to the Netherlands (AT VI, 30–1). But Descartes places the origin of that desire further back about nine years from 1628, to the famous stove-heated room in 1619, in Germany, near Ulm: "Nevertheless, those nine years slipped by before I had as yet taken any stand regarding the difficulties commonly debated among learned men, or had begun to seek the foundations of any philosophy that was more certain than the commonly accepted one" (AT VI, 30).

Thus the project of the *Meditations* began with a resolve to examine all the truths for the knowledge of which human reason suffices,[3] which, according

---

2. Ibid., p. 20.

3. What in Rule 8 is called "the most noble example of all," a task that should be undertaken at least once in one's life by anyone who is in all seriousness eager to attain excellence of mind (AT X, 395).

to Descartes, he carried out nine years later, circa 1629, having spent the first nine months of his stay in the Netherlands working on metaphysics: "Now I am of the opinion that all those to whom God has given the use of this reason are obliged to use it chiefly to try to know him and to know themselves. It is in this way that I have tried to begin my studies. . . . The first nine months I was in this country I worked at nothing else, and I believe you have already heard me say that I had planned to put something of this in writing. But I do not consider it appropriate to do so until I have first seen how my physics will be received" (AT I, 143–4). We know little about Descartes' lost "small metaphysical treatise," other than that it was written in Latin, unfinished, and that it concerned the existence of God and that of our souls.[4] Descartes at the time also worked simultaneously on his physics (*The World*) and optics (*Dioptrics*). All of this changed after the condemnation of Galileo in 1633. Although Descartes thought of including some of the older material in a new Latin edition of the *Discourse* (AT I, 350), he seems to have started seriously to think of a new presentation of his metaphysics only in 1639.[5] Thus began in earnest the *Meditations,* together with new rounds of *Objections* and *Replies.*

Are the Meditations Self-Contained?

So far, we have been developing the view that the introductory essays and *Objections* and *Replies* allow us to see the development in Descartes' thought. We should, however, consider whether this is the best way to approach Descartes' text. A standard line of interpretation for Descartes' *Meditations* treats the work as an attempt to construct a self-consistent unity, a geometrical whole whose structures can be revealed or whose elements can be shown as interconnected, a totality, however, that cannot fruitfully be analyzed by psychological or historical methods. The *Meditations,* it is asserted, resembles Euclid's geometry, and to understand a given geometrical system it is necessary to grasp its demonstrations and its sequences. According to Martial Gueroult, interpreters who "see in Descartes only a biographical succession, and not a rational linkage . . . merely observe the simple chronological sequence of topics. . . . This is evidently a way of doing things that is repugnant to the spirit and letter of Descartes' doctrine."[6] Gueroult is prob-

---

4. "Perhaps I may one day complete a little *Treatise on Metaphysics,* which I have begun when in Friesland, in which I set out principally to prove *the existence of God and of our souls* when they are separate from the body, from which their immortality follows" (AT I, 182).

5. *To Mersenne,* November 13, 1639, AT II, 622; see also *To Mersenne,* March 11, 1640, AT III, 35–6, July 1640, 102–3, and *To Huygens,* July 30, 1640, AT III, 126.

6. Martial Gueroult, *Descartes' Philosophy Interpreted According to the Order of Reasons,* vol. 1, p. xx. For the order of topics being contrary to Descartes' intention, Gueroult cites a letter to Mersenne (AT

ably the most noted interpreter who held such an internal, nondevelopmental reading of the *Meditations,* though many commentators in the Anglo-American tradition might appropriately be thought to accept this kind of approach. Gueroult treats Descartes' doctrine as "a single bloc of certainty, without any cracks, in which everything is arranged such that no truth can be taken away without the whole collapsing."[7] To support this interpretation, he cites various passages from Descartes' corpus: one from a 1642 letter to Mersenne, "I see that it is easy to make mistakes about the things I have written, for truth being indivisible, the least thing that is taken away from it or added to it, falsifies it" (AT III, 544); another from the *Seventh Set of Objections and Replies:* "for truth consists in what is indivisible" (AT VII, 548); and a third from an earlier letter to the Jesuit Vatier, "All my opinions are joined together in such a way and so strongly dependent on one another that one could not appropriate any for oneself without knowing all of them" (AT I, 562). For Gueroult, Descartes is "a thinker of granite," a "powerful, solid, and geometrical monument, like a Vauban fortress."[8]

Gueroult's view does have textual support; it seems to be an integral part of Cartesian rhetoric. In fact, there is yet one more passage in which Descartes asserts that his views are so interdependent that they cannot be separated or changed. Early on, when he was finishing his treatise *The World,* he found out that the censors of Rome had condemned Galileo because of his defense of the motion of the earth, an opinion deemed false and inconsistent with the sacred scriptures.[9] Descartes says to Mersenne in a 1634 letter: "Now I shall tell you that all the things I explained in my treatise, which included that opinion about the motion of the earth, were so completely dependent on one another, that the knowledge that one of them is false is sufficient for the recognition that all the arguments I made use of are worthless" (AT I, 285). This presents Descartes with a dilemma: he cannot give up the motion of the earth without abandoning his whole system, but the motion of the earth, which he thinks has been supported by "very certain and very evident demonstrations," has been prohibited by the Church; he hesitates: "I know very well that it could be said that everything the Inquisitors of Rome have decided is not for all that automatically an article of faith, and that it is first necessary for the Council to pass on it." But he decides:

III, 266–7) in which Descartes asserts, "to proceed by topics is only good for those whose reasons are all unconnected; . . . it is impossible to construct good proofs in this way."

7. Gueroult, *Descartes,* vol. 1, p. 5.

8. Gueroult, *Descartes,* vol. 1, p. xx.

9. One can distinguish between the motion of the earth (as false and foolish in philosophy) and immobility of the sun (as formally heretical), but it would not be necessary in this context, since Descartes does not make use of such a distinction and the Church declaring the proposition false is sufficient to cause a serious problem for Descartes.

"I am not so much in love with my own opinions as to want to make use of such exceptions, in order to have the means of maintaining them. . . . I would not for anything in the world maintain them against the authority of the church" (AT I, 285). So he stops the publication of *The World*.[10] But this does not prevent him, later on, from publishing the *Principles of Philosophy*— *The World* having been taught to speak Latin, as he says[11]—which contains a discussion of the heretical proposition. In fact, Descartes has no problem ultimately keeping most of his system together with the *negation* of the condemned proposition, deciding that "strictly speaking the earth does not move, any more than the planets" (*Principles* III, art. 28) and "no motion should be attributed to the earth even if motion is taken in the loose sense, in accordance with ordinary usage" (art. 29).

So, although Descartes does at times claim the complete dependence of his principles on each other such that none of them can be changed without the whole set collapsing, it is also obvious that he did make such changes (even to principles he claimed could not be changed). In fact, it is even clear that Descartes at times understood that he was making changes to his doctrine and at times wanted others to know that he was doing so. Descartes' project itself seems to belie the treatment of the system as a single bloc of certainty: Why bother with other people's objections if they had no real possibility of altering the doctrine objected to? Were the objections not going to be taken seriously by Descartes?

Descartes was keenly aware of the problem. After receiving Arnauld's objections to the *Meditations,* he wrote to Mersenne on March 18, 1641, "I am sending you at last my reply to Arnauld's objections, and I ask you to change the following things in my metaphysics, thus letting it be known in this way that I have deferred to his judgment, and so that others, seeing how ready I am to follow his advice, may tell me more frankly what reasons they have for disagreeing with me, if they have any, and may be less stubborn in wanting to oppose me without reason" (AT III, 334). Descartes then proceeded to list six separate corrections, which he insisted should be put between brackets "so that it can be seen that they have been added" (AT III, 335). The requested corrections were indeed accomplished, though, despite Descartes' request, they were not inserted between brackets.

The intended bracketed changes by Descartes were minor, but were in effect *corrections* to the *Meditations* and intended to be displayed as such. Other changes were not so minor; some of them were acknowledged as changes and others not. One does not have to delve too deeply into the *Meditations, Objections,* and *Replies* to understand that some central Cartesian

10. For more on *The World* and its historical context, see Stephen Gaukroger, *Descartes: an Intellectual Biography,* Chap. 7.

11. *To Huygens,* January 31, 1642, AT III, 782.

doctrines, such as God as "positive" cause of himself (*causa sui*)[12] and God's free creation of the eternal truths, do not occur explicitly in the *Meditations* but are to be found in the *Objections* and *Replies*. In his article, "Méditer, Objecter, Répondre," Jean-Marie Beyssade enumerates many additions, corrections, and changes to the doctrine of the *Meditations* brought about by the *Replies* to the *Objections*.[13] As additions, Beyssade lists fragments of theology, such as the pages on the Eucharist in the *Fourth Replies,* and fragments of philosophy, such as the developments concerning God's freedom and the creation of the eternal truths in the *Sixth Replies.* He mentions as well the doctrine of God as self-cause in the *First Replies* to Caterus and quotes a passage about it in which Descartes himself announces that he is adding something new: "In fact, I will also add here something I have not put in writing before, namely, that it is not even a secondary cause at which one arrives, but certainly that cause in which there is enough power to conserve something existing outside it and *a fortiori* conserves itself by its power, and thus is derived from itself" (AT VII, 111).[14]

While additions are frequent, corrections are more rare. Other than those from the March 18, 1641 letter referred to above, Beyssade cites an interesting case of successive corrections, within the *Objections and Replies,* concerning the doctrine of God as self-cause.[15] In the *Fourth Set of Objections,* Arnauld apparently criticized some formulations of the *First Set of Replies,* which Descartes had appended to the *Meditations* with Caterus' *Objections* before having Mersenne distribute the set to others for further objections. A March 4, 1641 letter to Mersenne shows Descartes asking Mersenne to correct a text of the *First Set of Replies,* which he indicates was already corrected on the initial copy: "I must also ask you to correct these words, which come in my reply to the penultimate objection made by the theologian [Caterus]" (AT III, 329); he then tells Mersenne which text to suppress and which to substitute. And he adds "but please correct it in all the copies in such a way that none will be able to read or decipher the words. . . . For many people are more curious to read and examine words that have been erased than any others, so as to see how the author thinks he has gone wrong, and to discover there some grounds for objections, attacking him in the place which he

---

12. The terminology is standard and comes from Caterus. God as cause of himself is usually taken negatively, meaning "not from another," and not positively, meaning giving existence to himself (AT VII, 95). Descartes seems to reply that he considers God as efficient cause of himself taken positively: "When these people say that something is 'derived from itself,' they are in the habit of understanding only that it has no cause. . . . But there is another rendering, a positive one, which has been sought from the truth of things and from which alone my argument proceeds" (AT VII, 109–10).

13. Jean-Marie Beyssade, "Méditer, Objecter, Répondre," *Descartes, Objecter et Répondre,* ed. Jean-Marie Beyssade and Jean-Luc Marion (Paris: PUF, 1994), pp. 21–38.

14. Ibid., pp. 33–4.

15. Ibid., pp. 34–6.

himself judged to be the weakest" (AT III, 330). Descartes speculates that the obvious erasure is why Arnauld paid so much attention to the question of God as self-cause: "I remember that my first draft of this passage was too crude; but in the later version I amended and refined it to such an extent that, had he merely read the corrections, without stopping to read the words that were crossed through, he would perhaps have found nothing at all to say. For I do believe that everything is in fact quite in order. You yourself, when you read the passage the first time, wrote to me saying that you found it crudely expressed, but at the other end of the letter you remarked that after reading a second time you found nothing to object to. I attribute this to your having paid attention, on your first reading, to the words that are only lightly crossed through there, whereas on the second reading you took note only of the corrected version" (AT III, 330–1). Thus Mersenne dutifully corrected for a second time a passage Descartes corrected once before, but this time in such a way that the act of correction would not be so obvious.[16]

Beyssade relates a couple of other interesting items in the broader category of changes.[17] He refers to the synthetic exposition of the *Meditations* in the *Second Replies* as a substantial change from its canonical analytic exposition.[18] But he also mentions the ontological argument Descartes provides for Caterus in the *First Replies*. The question can be raised whether this ontological argument is the same as the one given in the Fifth Meditation. Descartes understands that he introduced a change but explains the matter thus: "All of these points are readily apparent to one who pays careful attention, and they differ from what I have previously written only in the manner of their explanation, which I have deliberately altered so that I might suit a wide variety of minds" (AT VII, 120).

We could continue and delve more deeply into other changes Descartes made but did not acknowledge, some of which perhaps he might not have been aware of, such as the apparent transformation of his definition of material falsity from the *Meditations* through the *Objections and Replies* to its abandonment in the *Principles*.[19] But we need not to go that far: there are a number

16. For more on the development of the concept of self-cause, see Jean-Luc Marion, "Entre analogie et principe de raison: la *causa sui*," *Descartes, Objecter et Répondre,* pp. 305–34.

17. Beyssade, "Méditer, Objecter, Répondre," p. 36.

18. At the end of the *Second Set of Objections,* Mersenne asked Descartes to set out the argument of the *Meditations* in geometrical fashion (AT VII, 28). Descartes responded that he had already done so, drawing a distinction between the order and the mode of demonstration, in the geometrical style of writing, and then further distinguishing the mode of demonstration into one that proceeds by way of analysis and the other synthesis (AT VII, 155–6). Thus according to Descartes, the *Meditations* was written as an analytical exposition, but could be produced as a synthetic exposition, which is what Descartes begins to provides in the Appendix to the *Second Set of Replies* (AT VII, 160–71).

19. Descartes introduced the possibility, in the Third Meditation, that his idea of cold may be materially false insofar as it "represents what is not a thing as a thing" (AT VII, 43–4). There he might

of obvious deliberate alterations that should be mentioned, setting aside the question of whether these also entail changes in Descartes's doctrine.

Descartes revised the subtitle of his work between the two Latin editions: originally entitled *Meditationes de prima philosophia* (*Meditations on First Philosophy*), it was subtitled "in qua Dei existentia et animae immortalitatis demonstatur (in which the existence of God and the immortality of the soul are demonstrated)" in the first edition and "in quibus Dei existentia, et animae humanae a corpore distinctio, demonstratur (in which the existence of God and the distinction between the human soul and body are demonstrated)" in the second.[20]

Moreover, taking Mersenne's advice, Descartes did not publish the last seven paragraphs of his *Replies* to Arnauld, concerning the Eucharist, in the first Latin edition; as he says, he censored himself at Mersenne's urging, so that he would not have any difficulty in getting the approbation of the Sorbonne theologians for his work.[21] Descartes explained the matter more fully

---

have had in mind the possibility that cold is merely the privation of the quality of heat, and thus it is not the thing or quality that the idea represents it to be. This sort of falsity would be called material since it derives from the idea itself rather than, as in the case of formal falsity, from a judgment concerning the idea. Arnauld objected that an idea cannot be materially false, since an idea cannot fail to represent what it does in fact represent (AT VII, 207). In response, Descartes explained the material falsity of an idea by emphasizing not so much the fact that that idea represents a privation as a quality, but more the fact that the idea is obscure and confused (AT VII, 234–5). The exchange may have prompted Descartes to drop the notion of material falsity, which is not present in his later writings. There is a considerable secondary literature on this subject, much of it precipitated by Margaret D. Wilson, who in her *Descartes* argues that Descartes' reply to Arnauld is inconsistent with his doctrine in Meditation Three.

20. The 1647 French translation subtitle generally follows the 1642 edition, though there are minor changes, both in the title and in the subtitle of the work, each containing an extra significant adjective not found in the Latin versions. The 1647 edition reads "*Les Meditations Metaphysiques de René Descartes touchant la premiere philosophie,* dans lesquelles l'existence de Dieu, et la distinction réelle entre l'âme et le corps de l'homme, sont demonstrées."

Adrien Baillet, in the abridgment to his biography of Descartes—*La vie de M. Des Cartes* (Paris, 1691; reprinted Paris: La Table Ronde, 1946)—asserts that *immortalitas* in the first subtitle was a misprint for *immaterialitas:* "Mas il faut remarquer que ce fut contre l'intention de l'auteur qu'on laissa glisser le mot d'immortalité au lieu de celui d'immatérialité" (p. 171). Others argue that the subtitle was Mersenne's responsibility and his mistake. Neither hypothesis seems likely. It is true that Descartes says to Mersenne on November 11, 1640, "I am finally sending you my work on metaphysics, which I have not yet put a title to, in order to make you its godfather and leave you the power to baptize it" (AT III, 238–9; see also AT III, 235), but Descartes does suggest titles and subtitles to Mersenne (AT III, 235, 238, and 297). I find convincing the following passage from a Descartes letter to Mersenne of December 24, 1640: "As for what you say, that I have not said a word about the immortality of the soul, you should not be surprised. For I could not prove that God cannot annihilate it, but only that it is of a nature entirely distinct from that of the body, and consequently it is not bound by nature to die with it" (AT III, 265–6; see also AT III, 272). It is Mersenne who seems to have queried Descartes about the appropriateness of the subtitle with respect to the contents of the *Meditations* and Descartes who appears to be defending it.

21. "I very much approve your having pruned what I put at the end of my Reply to Arnauld, especially if this can help us to get formal approval for the book" (AT III, 341).

in a letter to Constanijn Huygens: "Father Mersenne has pruned two or three pages from the end of my replies to the *Fourth Objections,* concerning the Eucharist, because he feared that the Doctors would be offended in that I proved there that their opinion concerning that point did not agree as well as mine with the Scriptures and the Councils" (AT III, 772). None of this prevented him from restoring the paragraphs in the second Latin edition, when there was no need for the approbation of the Doctors of the Sorbonne.[22]

An interesting case of a suspected change in Descartes' doctrine operates subtly through the *Meditations, Objections,* and *Replies,* but Descartes in *Principles of Philosophy* ultimately acknowledges it to be a genuine change. As the subtitle to the 1642 edition of the *Meditations* indicates, a major result of the work is the distinction between the human soul and body. Presumably, Descartes thinks that he has proven the distinction to be a real distinction, as the title of the Sixth Meditation[23] and the subtitle to the 1647 French translation indicate, not merely a modal distinction or a distinction of reason.[24] One would assume that Descartes would have worked up accounts of real distinction, modal distinction, and distinction of reason to support this important result. But when Caterus queried him, in the *First Objections,* about his proof of a real distinction, he responded in a muddled fashion. Caterus stated: "He [Descartes] seems to prove the distinction (if that is what it is) between the soul and the body by the fact that they can be conceived distinctly and separately. Here I leave the very learned gentleman with Duns Scotus, who declares that, for one thing to be conceived distinctly and separately from one another, it suffices that there be a distinction which he calls 'formal and objective,' which he claims to be midway between a real distinction and a distinction of reason" (AT VII, 100).

Descartes answered: "As far as the formal distinction is concerned, which

---

22. The approbation, together with the right to publish, can be seen on the title page of the 1641 edition of the *Meditations*—"Cum Privilegio, et Approbatione Doctorum"—but it is missing from the title page of the other editions. The approbation of the Sorbonne is also missing from the 1647 title page, but one can find the indication "Avec Privilege du Roy" there. Whether or not Descartes actually received the approbation of the Sorbonne is a disputed issue. For the positive case, see Jean-Robert Armogathe, "L'approbation des *Meditationes* par la faculté de théologie de Paris (1641)," *Bulletin Cartésien XXI, Archives de Philosophie* 57 (1994): 1–3.

23. The subtitles to the *Meditations* were added late by Descartes, that is, after January 28, 1641; see AT VII, 297.

24. A real distinction is one that holds between two substances; as Descartes says, "we can conclude that two substances are really distinct one from the other from the sole fact that we can conceive the one clearly and distinctly without the other" (*Principles,* art. 60) A modal distinction holds between the mode and the substance of which it is the mode or between two modes of the same substance. The two things modally distinct are not really distinct, since we can clearly conceive a substance without the mode that differs from it; reciprocally, we cannot have a perception of the mode without perceiving the substance (art. 61). Finally a distinction of reason holds between a substance and some one of its attributes or between two such attributes of the same substance; the two things distinguished by reason are neither really nor modally distinct (art. 62).

the very learned theologian draws from Duns Scotus, I declare briefly that a formal distinction does not differ from a modal distinction, and that it applies only to incomplete beings, which I have carefully distinguished from complete beings. Moreover, it surely suffices for a formal distinction that one thing be conceived distinctly and separately from another by an act of abstraction on the part of the intellect inadequately conceiving the thing, yet not so distinctly and separately that we understand each one as something existing in its own right and different from every other thing" (AT VII, 120). Descartes proceeded to illustrate his thought with the distinction between the motion and the shape of the same body, ultimately dealing with the distinction between justice and mercy, which Caterus had brought up as an example. Sometime later, prodded by the use Arnauld made of his distinctions,[25] it must have dawned on Descartes that he was confusing formal, modal, and distinction of reason. When he finally set out formally his theory of distinctions in the *Principles,* Descartes stated in the article on distinction of reason: "I recollect having elsewhere conflated this sort of distinction with modal distinction (near the end of the *Reply to the First Set of Objections* to the *Meditations on First Philosophy*), but then it was not necessary to treat accurately of these distinctions, and it was sufficient for my purpose at the time simply to distinguish them both from the real" (Principles I, art. 62). That may be right, but still this episode imparts the distinct impression that the Cartesian doctrine was in the process of formation.

All in all, Descartes' bloc of certainty looks more like a sedimentary rock, a geological stratum with cracks and fissures, able to be read in historical terms.[26]

---

25. See AT VII, 200 ("For our distinguished author admits in his reply to the theologian . . . ") and AT VII, 218 ("Further he recognizes no distinction between the states of a substance and the substance itself except for a formal one . . . ").

26. There is a temptation to treat Gueroult's internal methodology at the level of a historiography. But Gueroult is clear that his method is intended to be subordinate to developmental approaches. As he puts it, "Historians have two techniques at their disposal for this [discovering the enigma proposed to them by the work of the great geniuses]: textual criticism itself and analysis of structures. For Descartes' philosophy, textual criticism (problem of sources, variations, evolutions, etc.) has been amply practiced: the remarkable work of Gilson, Gouhier, Laporte, and others are known by all. On the other hand, the analysis of structures has been little attempted" (*Descartes,* vol. 1, p. xviii). So Gueroult proposes for himself the work of discovering the structures of the *Meditations,* what he also calls the laying bare of the architectonic elements. As we have said, he finds support for this endeavor in Descartes' own writings; it is not as if his method is imported into the texts, but it is derived from them in the same manner those who favor developmental approaches derive their evidence. Thus, Gueroult, using "textual criticism," discovers that "analysis of structures" is needed in this case at this time. He concludes: "it seems that once the requirements of historical critique are satisfied, the better method is truly the analysis of structure of the work" (*Descartes,* vol. 1, p. xix). There can be no genuine conflict between developmental views and Gueroult's laying bare of the architectonics of the *Meditations;* of course, we can always disagree with any of Gueroult's results, including his internal method.

Selected Bibliography

There are over 3,500 items listed in Gregor Sebba's annotated Cartesian bibliography, *Bibliographia Cartesiana: A Critical Guide to the Descartes Literature 1800–1960* (The Hague: Martinus Nijhof, 1964). The post-1960 Descartes literature is even more extensive; another 4,400 items are listed in Jean-Robert Armogathe, Vincent Carraud, and Massimiliano Savini, *Bibliographie cartésienne (1960–1996)* (Lecce: Conte, 2003).

The standard edition of Descartes' works is the 11-volume *Oeuvres de Descartes,* edited by Charles Adam and Paul Tannery, begun in the 1890s and given a second, expanded edition in the 1970s (student edition, [Paris: Vrin, 1996]). Volume VII contains the *Meditations, Objections, and Replies* in Latin and Volume IXa contains their French version. At present the Adam and Tannery edition (AT) can be supplemented in two directions: first by the searchable database edited by André Gombay et al., *Oeuvres complètes de René Descartes* (Charlottesville, VA: InteLex, 2001. http://www.pastmasters2000.nlx.com) and second by the Conte Editore exact reprints of the works of Descartes, which give readers the look and feel of the originals—and in particular *Meditationes de prima philosophia, In quibus Dei existentia, et animae humanae à corpore distinctio, demonstratur* (Amsterdam, 1642; reprint, Lecce: Conte, 1992).

The most comprehensive English-language edition of Descartes' works is the 2-volume *Philosophical Writings of Descartes,* edited and translated by John Cottingham, Robert Stoothoff, and Dougald Murdoch (Cambridge: Cambridge University Press, 1984–91). Volume 2 contains the almost complete English translation of *Meditations, Objections, and Replies.*

There are a number of relatively new English-language biographies of Descartes, including: Stephen Gaukroger, *Descartes: An Intellectual Biography* (Oxford: Oxford University Press, 1995); Geneviève Rodis-Lewis, *Descartes: His Life and Thought* (Ithaca, NY: Cornell University Press, 1995); Richard Watson, *Cogito, Ergo Sum: The Life of René Descartes* (Boston: Godine, 2002); and Desmond N. Clarke, *Descartes: A Biography* (New York: Cambridge University Press, 2006).

As for Descartes' philosophy, one can begin its study with something like Gary Hatfield's guidebook to the *Meditations, Descartes and the Meditations* (London: Routledge, 2003) or a well designed collection of commissioned articles on Cartesian topics, such as John Cottingham's *Cambridge Companion to Descartes* (Cambridge: Cambridge University Press, 1992) and Stephen Gaukroger's *The Blackwell Guide to Descartes' Meditations* (London: Blackwell, 2005). The relations between Descartes and the objectors to his *Meditations* are studied by the various contributors to the collection of essays edited by Roger Ariew and Marjorie Grene, *Descartes and His Contemporaries: Meditations, Objections, and Replies* (Chicago: University of Chicago Press, 1995). A selection of background primary texts for the *Meditations* is given in *Descartes'*

Meditations: Background Source Materials, edited and translated by Roger Ariew, John Cottingham, and Tom Sorell (Cambridge: Cambridge University Press, 1998).

Here are a few other selected discussions of Descartes' philosophy:

Ariew, Roger. *Descartes and the Last Scholastics.* Ithaca, NY: Cornell University Press, 1999.

Curley, Edwin M. *Descartes Against the Skeptics.* Cambridge, MA: Harvard University Press, 1978.

Frankfurt, Harry. *Demons, Dreamers and Madmen: The Defense of Reason in Descartes' Meditations.* Indianapolis: Bobbs-Merrill, 1970.

Garber, Daniel. *Descartes Embodied: Reading Cartesian Philosophy through Cartesian Science.* Cambridge: Cambridge University Press, 2001.

Grene, Marjorie. *Descartes.* Minneapolis: University of Minnesota Press, 1985.

Gueroult, Martial. *Descartes' Philosophy Interpreted According to the Order of Reasons.* Translated by Roger Ariew et al. (2 vols.). Minneapolis: University of Minnesota Press, 1984.

Marion, Jean-Luc. *On Descartes' Metaphysical Prism: The Constitution and Limits of Onto-theo-logy in Cartesian Thought.* Chicago: University of Chicago Press, 1999.

Wilson, Catherine. *Descartes's Meditations: An Introduction.* Cambridge: Cambridge University Press, 2003.

Wilson, Margaret. *Descartes.* London: Routledge, 1978.

Acknowledgments

Meditations translated by Donald Cress: René Descartes, *Meditations on First Philosophy,* 3rd ed. (Cambridge: Hackett Publishing Company, 1993); *Objection and Replies* (except for the *Letter Serving as a Reply to Gassendi*), newly translated by Donald Cress or from René Descartes, *Philosophical Essays and Correspondence,* edited by Roger Ariew (Cambridge: Hackett Publishing Company, 2000). *Announcement Regarding the Fifth Set of Objections and Letter Serving as a Reply to Gassendi,* translated by Roger Ariew.

Chronology of Descartes' Life and Works

1596   born in Touraine at La Haye on March 31
1607–15   studies at the Jesuit college of La Flèche in Anjou
1616   receives M.A. in law from the University of Poitiers in November
1618   enlists in the Netherlands in the army of Prince Maurice of
           Nassau; has a chance encounter with Isaac Beeckman; composes
           first work, on musical theory
1619   travels in Germany; has three strange dreams, November 10, that
           set him on the right course of life; works on *Rules for the Direc-
           tion of the Mind,* which he leaves unfinished in 1628
1620   notes that he "began to understand the foundations of a wonder-
           ful discovery"
1621   returns to Paris but also takes an extended trip to Italy in the
           next few years
1624   trial of the libertine poet Théophile de Viau and condemnation
           of anti-Aristotelian theses posted by the alchemists and atomists
           Etienne de Clave, Jean Bitaud, and Antoine Villon
1628   leaves for the Netherlands
1629   begins a small treatise in metaphysics (now lost); begins working
           on the essays *Meteors* and *Dioptrics* and the treatise *The World*
           (with its lengthy chapter on man)
1633   Galileo condemned for defending the motion of the earth; stops
           the publication of *The World*
1635   birth of his daughter, Francine, in July, baptized August 7 (dies
           September 1640)
1637   publishes *Discourse on Method* with *Dioptrics, Meteors,* and *Geometry*
1641   publishes *Meditations on First Philosophy* with *Objections*—sets by
           Caterus, Thomas Hobbes, Antoine Arnauld, Pierre Gassendi, and
           two sets collected by Marin Mersenne—and his *Replies*
1642   publishes the second edition of the Meditations with a new set
           of *Objections* by the Jesuit Pierre Bourdin and his *Replies,* plus
           the *Letter to Father Dinet*
1643   the University of Utrecht prohibits the teaching of the new
           philosophy (reaffirmed in 1645); starts a correspondence with
           Princess Elisabeth of Bohemia
1644   briefly returns to France for the first time; publishes *Principles of
           Philosophy*
1647   publishes French translations of the *Meditations* and *Principles,* plus
           Notes against a Program
1648   –   the University of Leyden prohibits the teaching of his works
1649   leaves for Sweden in the fall; publishes *Passions of the Soul*
1650   dies at Stockholm on February 11

[Letter of Dedication]

To those Most Wise and Distinguished Men,
the Dean and Doctors of the Faculty of Sacred Theology of Paris
René Descartes Sends Greetings

So right is the cause that impels me to offer this work to you, that I am confident you too will find it equally right and thus take up its defense, once you have understood the plan of my undertaking; so much is this the case that I have no better means of commending it here than to state briefly what I have sought to achieve in this work.

I have always thought that two issues—namely, God and the soul—are chief among those that ought to be demonstrated with the aid of philosophy rather than theology. For although it suffices for us believers to believe by faith that the human soul does not die with the body, and that God exists, 2 certainly no unbelievers seem capable of being persuaded of any religion or even of almost any moral virtue, until these two are first proven to them by natural reason. And since in this life greater rewards are often granted to vices than to virtues, few would prefer what is right to what is useful, if they neither feared God nor anticipated an afterlife. Granted, it is altogether true that we must believe in God's existence because it is taught in the Holy Scriptures, and, conversely, that we must believe the Holy Scriptures because they have come from God. This is because, of course, since faith is a gift from God, the very same one who gives the grace that is necessary for believing the rest can also give the grace to believe that he exists. Nonetheless, this reasoning cannot be proposed to unbelievers because they would judge it to be circular. In fact, I have observed that not only do you and all other theologians affirm that one can prove the existence of God by natural reason, but also that one may infer from Sacred Scripture that the knowledge of him is easier to achieve than the many things we know about creatures, and is so utterly easy that those without this knowledge are blameworthy. For this is clear from Wisdom, chapter 13 where it is said: "They are not to be excused, for if their capacity for knowing were so great that they could think well of this world, how is it that they did not find the Lord of it even more easily?" And in Romans, chapter 1, it is said that they are "without excuse." And again in the same passage it appears we are being warned with

Selections on pp. 1–50 reprinted from *René Descartes: Meditations on First Philosophy,* 3rd ed., translated by Donald Cress (Indianapolis: Hackett Publishing Company, 1993). Reprinted by permission of the publisher with minor changes by permission of the translator.

the words:"What is known of God is manifest in them," that everything that can be known about God can be shown by reasons drawn exclusively from our own mind. For this reason, I did not think it unbecoming for me to inquire how this may be the case, and by what path God may be known more easily and with greater certainty than the things of this world.

3   And as to the soul, there are many who have regarded its nature as something into which one cannot easily inquire, and some have even gone so far as to say that human reasoning convinces them that the soul dies with the body, while it is by faith alone that they hold the contrary position. Nevertheless, because the Lateran Council held under Leo X, in Session 8, condemned such people and expressly enjoined Christian philosophers to refute their arguments and to use all their powers to demonstrate the truth, I have not hesitated to undertake this task as well.

Moreover, I know that there are many irreligious people who refuse to believe that God exists and that the human mind is distinct from the body—for no other reason than their claim that up until now no one has been able to demonstrate these two things. By no means am I in agreement with these people; on the contrary, I believe that nearly all the arguments which have been brought to bear on these questions by great men have the force of a demonstration, when they are adequately understood, and I am convinced that hardly any arguments can be given that have not already been discovered by others. Nevertheless, I judge that there is no greater task to perform in philosophy than assiduously to seek out, once and for all, the best of all these arguments and to lay them out so precisely and plainly that henceforth all will take them to be true demonstrations. And finally, I was strongly urged to do this by some people who knew that I had developed a method for solving all sorts of problems in the sciences—not a new one, mind you, since nothing is more ancient than the truth, but one they had seen me use with some success in other areas. Accordingly, I took it to be my task to attempt something on this subject.

4   This treatise contains all that I have been able to accomplish. Not that I have attempted to gather together in it all the various arguments that could be brought forward as proof of the very same conclusions, for this does not seem worthwhile, except where no one proof is sufficiently certain. Rather, I have sought out the primary and chief arguments, so that I now make bold to propose these as most certain and evident demonstrations. Moreover, I will say in addition that these arguments are such that I believe there is no way open to the human mind whereby better ones could ever be found. For the urgency of the cause, as well as the glory of God, to which this entire enterprise is referred, compel me here to speak somewhat more freely on my own behalf than is my custom. But although I believe these arguments to be certain and evident, still I am not thereby convinced that they are suited to everyone's grasp. In geometry there are many arguments developed

by Archimedes, Apollonius, Pappus, and others, which are taken by everyone to be evident and certain because they contain absolutely nothing which, considered by itself, is not quite easily known, and in which what follows does not square exactly with what has come before. Nevertheless they are rather lengthy and require a particularly attentive reader; thus only a small handful of people understand them. Likewise, although the arguments I use here do, in my opinion, equal or even surpass those of geometry in certitude and obviousness, nevertheless I am fearful that many people will not be capable of adequately perceiving them, both because they too are a bit lengthy, with some of them depending on still others, and also because, first and foremost, they demand a mind that is quite free from prejudices and that can easily withdraw itself from association with the senses. Certainly there are not to be found in the world more people with an aptitude for metaphysical studies than those with an aptitude for geometry. Moreover, there is the difference that in geometry everyone is of a mind that usually nothing is put down in writing without there being a sound demonstration for it; thus the inexperienced more frequently err on the side of assenting to what is false, wanting as they do to give the appearance of understanding it, than on the side of denying what is true. But it is the reverse in philosophy: since it is believed that there is no issue that cannot be defended from either side, few look for the truth, and many more prowl about for a reputation for profundity by arrogantly challenging whichever arguments are the best.

And therefore, regardless of the force of my arguments, because they are of a philosophical nature I do not anticipate that what I will have accomplished through them will be very worthwhile unless you assist me with your patronage. Your faculty is held in such high esteem in the minds of all, and the name of the Sorbonne has such authority that not only in matters of faith has no association, with the exception of the councils of the Church, been held in such high regard as yours, but even in human philosophy nowhere is there thought to be greater insightfulness and solidity, or greater integrity and wisdom in rendering judgments. Should you deign to show any interest in this work, I do not doubt that, first of all, its errors would be corrected by you (for I am mindful not only of my humanity but also, and most especially, of my ignorance, and thus do not claim that there are no errors in it); second, what is lacking would be added, or what is not sufficiently complete would be perfected, or what is in need of further discussion would be expanded upon more fully, either by yourselves or at least by me, after you have given me your guidance; and finally, after the arguments contained in this work proving that God exists and that the mind is distinct from the body have been brought (as I am confident they can be) to such a level of lucidity that these arguments ought to be regarded as the most precise of demonstrations, you may be of a mind to make such a declaration and publicly attest to it. Indeed, should this come to pass, I have no doubt that all the errors that have ever been entertained regarding these issues would shortly be erased from the minds of men. For the truth itself will easily cause other men of intelligence and learning to subscribe to your judgment. Your authority will cause the atheists, who more often than not are dilettantes rather than men of intelligence and learning, to put aside their spirit of contrariness, and perhaps even to defend the arguments which they will come to know are regarded as demonstrations by all who are discerning, lest they appear not to understand them. And finally, everyone else will readily give credence to so many indications of support, and there no longer will be anyone in the world who would dare call into doubt either the existence of God or the real distinction between the soul and the body. Just how great the usefulness of this thing might be, you yourselves, in virtue of your singular wisdom, are in the best position of anyone to judge; nor would it behoove me to commend the cause of God and religion at any greater length to you, who have always been the greatest pillar of the Catholic Church.

7   ## Preface to the Reader

I have already touched briefly on the issues of God and the human mind in my *Discourse on the Method for Conducting One's Reason Well and for Seeking the Truth in the Sciences,* published in French in 1637. The intent there was not to provide a precise treatment of them, but only to offer a sample and to learn from the opinions of readers how these issues should be treated in the future. For they seemed to me to be so important that I judged they ought to be dealt with more than once. And the path I follow in order to explain them is so little trodden and so far removed from the one commonly taken that I did not think it useful to hold forth at greater length in a work written in French and designed to be read indiscriminately by everyone, lest weaker minds be in a position to think that they too ought to set out on this path.

In the *Discourse* I asked everyone who might find something in my writings worthy of refutation to do me the favor of making me aware of it. As for what I touched on regarding these issues, only two objections were worth noting, and I will respond briefly to them here before undertaking a more precise explanation of them.

8   The first is that, from the fact that the human mind, when turned in on itself, does not perceive itself to be anything other than a thinking thing, it does not follow that its nature or *essence* consists only in its being a thinking thing, such that the word *only* excludes everything else that also could perhaps be said to belong to the nature of the soul. To this objection I answer that in that passage I did not intend my exclusion of those things to reflect the order of the truth of the matter (I was not dealing with it then),

but merely the order of my perception. Thus what I had in mind was that I was aware of absolutely nothing that I knew belonged to pertain to my essence, save that I was a thinking thing, that is, a thing having within itself the faculty of thinking. Later on, however, I will show how it follows, from the fact that I know of nothing else belonging to my essence, that nothing else really does belong to it.

The second objection is that it does not follow from the fact that I have within me an idea of a thing more perfect than me, that this idea is itself more perfect than me, and still less that what is represented by this idea exists. But I answer that there is an equivocation here in the word "idea." For "idea" can be taken either materially, for an operation of the intellect (in which case it cannot be said to be more perfect than me), or objectively, for the thing represented by means of that operation. This thing, even if it is not presumed to exist outside the intellect, can nevertheless be more perfect than me by reason of its essence. I will explain in detail in the ensuing remarks how, from the mere fact that there is within me an idea of something more perfect than me, it follows that this thing really exists.

In addition, I have seen two rather lengthy treatises, but these works, utilizing as they do arguments drawn from atheist commonplaces, focused their attack not so much on my arguments regarding these issues, as on my conclusions.[1] Moreover, arguments of this type exercise no influence over those who understand my arguments, and the judgments of many people are so preposterous and feeble that they are more likely to be persuaded by the first opinions to come along, however false and contrary to reason they may be, than by a true and firm refutation of them which they hear subsequently. Accordingly, I have no desire to respond here to these objections, lest I first have to state what they are. I will only say in general that all the objections typically bandied about by the atheists to assail the existence of God always depend either on ascribing human emotions to God, or on arrogantly claiming for our minds such power and wisdom that we attempt to determine and grasp fully what God can and ought to do. Hence these objections will cause us no difficulty, provided we but remember that our minds are to be regarded as finite, while God is to be regarded as incomprehensible and infinite.

But now, after having, to some degree, conducted an initial review of the judgments of men, here I begin once more to treat the same questions about God and the human mind, together with the starting points of the whole of first philosophy, but not in a way that causes me to have any expectation

9

---

1. One of the objectors to which Descartes is referring is Pierre Petit (c. 1594–1677), a French engineer and mathematician; the other is unknown. For an analysis of Petit's objections and Descartes' replies, see Jean-Luc Marion, "The Place of the *Objections* in the Development of Cartesian Metaphysics," in *Descartes and His Contemporaries,* eds. Roger Ariew and Marjorie Grene, pp. 7–20.

of widespread approval or a large readership. On the contrary, I do not advise anyone to read these things except those who have both the ability and the desire to meditate seriously with me, and to withdraw their minds from the senses as well as from all prejudices. I know all too well that such people are few and far between. As to those who do not take the time to grasp the order and linkage of my arguments, but will be eager to fuss over statements taken out of context (as is the custom for many), they will derive little benefit from reading this work. Although perhaps they might find an occasion for quibbling in several places, still they will not find it easy to raise an objection that is either compelling or worthy of response.

But because I do not promise to satisfy even the others on all counts the first time around, and because I do not arrogantly claim for myself so much that I believe myself capable of anticipating all the difficulties that will occur to someone, I will first of all narrate in the *Meditations* the very thoughts by means of which I seem to have arrived at a certain and evident knowledge of the truth, so that I may determine whether the same arguments that persuaded me can be useful in persuading others. Next, I will reply to the objections of a number of very gifted and learned gentlemen, to whom these *Meditations* were forwarded for their examination prior to their being sent to press. For their objections were so many and varied that I have dared to hope that nothing will readily occur to anyone, at least nothing of importance, which has not already been touched upon by these gentlemen. And thus I earnestly entreat the readers not to form a judgment regarding the *Meditations* until they have deigned to read all these objections and the replies I have made to them.

Synopsis of the Following Six Meditations

In the First Meditation the reasons are given why we can doubt all things, especially material things, so long, that is, as, of course, we have no other foundations for the sciences than the ones which we have had up until now. Although the utility of so extensive a doubt is not readily apparent, nevertheless its greatest utility lies in freeing us of all prejudices, in preparing the easiest way for us to withdraw the mind from the senses, and finally, in making it impossible for us to doubt any further those things that we later discover to be true.

In the Second Meditation the mind, through the exercise of its own freedom, supposes the nonexistence of all those things about whose existence it can have even the least doubt. In so doing the mind realizes that it is impossible for it not to exist during this time. This too is of the greatest utility, since by means of it the mind easily distinguishes what things belong to it, that is, to an intellectual nature, from what things belong to the body. But because some people will perhaps expect to see proofs for the immortality of the soul in this Meditation, I think they should be put on notice here that I have attempted to write only what I have carefully demonstrated. Therefore the only order I could follow was the one typically used by geometers, which is to lay out everything on which a given proposition depends, before concluding anything about it. But the first and principal prerequisite for knowing that the soul is immortal is that we form a concept of the soul that is as lucid as possible and utterly distinct from every concept of a body. This is what has been done here. Moreover, there is the additional requirement that we know that everything that we clearly and distinctly understand is true, in exactly the manner in which we understand it; however, this could not have been proven prior to the Fourth Meditation. Moreover, we must have a distinct concept of corporeal nature, and this is formulated partly in the Second Meditation itself, and partly in the Fifth and Sixth Meditations. From all this one ought to conclude that all the things we clearly and distinctly conceive as different substances truly are substances that are really distinct from one another. (This, for example, is how mind and body are conceived). This conclusion is arrived at in the Sixth Meditation. This same conclusion is also confirmed in this Meditation in virtue of the fact that we cannot understand a body to be anything but divisible, whereas we cannot understand the mind to be anything but indivisible. For we cannot conceive of half a mind, as we do for any body whatever, no matter how small. From this we are prompted to acknowledge that the natures of mind and body not only are different from one another, but even, in a manner of speaking, are contraries of one another. However, I have not written any further on the matter in this work, both because these considerations suffice for showing that the annihilation of the mind does not follow from the decaying of the body (and thus these considerations suffice for giving mortals hope in an afterlife), and also because the premises from which the immortality of the mind can be inferred depend upon an account of the whole of physics. First, we need to know that absolutely all substances, that is, things that must be created by God in order to exist, are by their very nature incorruptible, and can never cease to exist, unless, by the same God's denying his concurrence to them, they be reduced to nothingness. Second, we need to realize that body, taken in a general sense, is a substance and hence it too can never perish. But the human body, insofar as it differs from other bodies, is composed of merely a certain configuration of members, together with other accidents of the same sort. But the human mind is not likewise composed of any accidents, but is a pure substance. For even if all its accidents were changed, so that it understands different things, wills different things, senses different things, and so on, the mind itself does not on that score become something different. On the other hand, the human body does become something different, merely as a result of the fact that a change in the shape of some of its parts has taken place. It follows from these considerations that a body can very easily perish, whereas the mind by its nature is immortal.

In the Third Meditation I have explained at sufficient length, it seems to me, my principal argument for proving the existence of God. Nevertheless, since my intent was to draw the minds of readers as far as possible from the senses, I had no desire to draw upon comparisons based upon corporeal things. Thus many obscurities may perhaps have remained; but these, I trust, will later be entirely removed in my *Replies to the Objections.* One such point of contention, among others, is the following: how can the idea that is in us of a supremely perfect being have so much objective reality that it can only come from a supremely perfect cause? This is illustrated in the *Replies* by a comparison with a very perfect machine, the idea of which is in the mind of some craftsman.[2] For, just as the objective ingeniousness of this idea ought to have some cause (say, the knowledge possessed by the craftsman or by someone else from whom he received this knowledge), so too, the idea of God which is in us must have God himself as its cause.

In the Fourth Meditation it is proved that all that we clearly and distinctly perceive is true, and it is also explained what constitutes the nature of falsity. These things necessarily need to be known both to confirm what has preceded as well as to help readers understand what remains. (But here one should meanwhile bear in mind that in that Meditation there is no discussion whatsoever of sin, that is, the error committed in the pursuit of good and evil, but only the error that occurs in discriminating between what is true and what is false. Nor is there an examination of those matters pertaining to the faith or to the conduct of life, but merely of speculative truths known exclusively by the means of the light of nature.)[3]

In the Fifth Meditation, in addition to an explanation of corporeal nature in general, the existence of God is also demonstrated by means of a new proof. But again several difficulties may arise here; however, these are resolved later in my *Replies to the Objections.* Finally, it is shown how it is true that the certainty of even geometrical demonstrations depends upon the knowledge of God.

Finally, in the Sixth Meditation the understanding is distinguished from the imagination and the marks of this distinction are described. The mind is proved to be really distinct from the body, even though the mind is shown to be so closely joined to the body that it forms a single unit with it. All the

---

2. See *Replies I,* AT VII, 103 et seq.

3. The parenthetical passage was added by Descartes following upon Arnauld's objections (see AT VII, 215–6). Descartes asked Mersenne to make the changes and to enclose them in brackets, "so that it can be known that I have deferred to his judgment, and so that others, seeing how ready I am to take advice, would tell me more frankly whatever reasons they might have against me, and be less stubborn in wanting to contradict me without reason," AT III, 334–5.

errors commonly arising from the senses are reviewed; an account of the ways in which these errors can be avoided is provided. Finally, all the arguments on the basis of which we may infer the existence of material things are presented—not because I believed them to be very useful for proving *16* what they prove, namely, that there really is a world, that men have bodies, and the like (things which no one of sound mind has ever seriously doubted), but rather because, through a consideration of these arguments, one realizes that they are neither so firm nor so evident as the arguments leading us to the knowledge of our mind and of God, so that, of all the things that can be known by the human mind, these latter are the most certain and the most evident. Proving this one thing was for me the goal of these Meditations. For this reason I will not review here the various issues that are also to be treated in these Meditations as the situation arises.

Meditations on First Philosophy in Which the   *17* Existence of God and the Distinction between the Soul and the Body Are Demonstrated

MEDITATION ONE: Concerning Those Things That Can Be Called into Doubt

Several years have now passed since I first realized how numerous were the false opinions that in my youth I had taken to be true, and thus how doubtful were all those that I had subsequently built upon them. And thus I realized that once in my life I had to raze everything to the ground and begin again from the original foundations, if I wanted to establish anything firm and lasting in the sciences. But the task seemed enormous, and I was waiting until I reached a point in my life that was so timely that no more suitable time for undertaking these plans of action would come to pass. For this reason, I procrastinated for so long that I would henceforth be at fault, were I to waste the time that remains for carrying out the project by brooding over it. Accordingly, I have today suitably freed my mind of all cares, secured *18* for myself a period of leisurely tranquillity, and am withdrawing into solitude. At last I will apply myself earnestly and unreservedly to this general demolition of my opinions.

Yet to bring this about I will not need to show that all my opinions are false, which is perhaps something I could never accomplish. But reason now persuades me that I should withhold my assent no less carefully from opinions that are not completely certain and indubitable than I would from those that are patently false. For this reason, it will suffice for the rejection of all of these opinions, if I find in each of them some reason for doubt. Nor therefore need I survey each opinion individually, a task that would be endless. Rather, because undermining the foundations will cause whatever has been built upon them to crumble of its own accord, I will attack straightaway those principles which supported everything I once believed.

Surely whatever I had admitted until now as most true I received either from the senses or through the senses. However, I have noticed that the senses are sometimes deceptive; and it is a mark of prudence never to place our complete trust in those who have deceived us even once.

But perhaps, even though the senses do sometimes deceive us when it is a question of very small and distant things, still there are many other matters concerning which one simply cannot doubt, even though they are derived from the very same senses: for example, that I am sitting here next to the fire, wearing my winter dressing gown, that I am holding this sheet of paper in my hands, and the like. But on what grounds could one deny that these hands and this entire body are mine? Unless perhaps I were to liken myself to the insane, whose brains are impaired by such an unrelenting vapor of black bile that they steadfastly insist that they are kings when they are utter paupers, or that they are arrayed in purple robes when they are naked, or that they have heads made of clay, or that they are gourds, or that they are made of glass. But such people are mad, and I would appear no less mad, were I to take their behavior as an example for myself.

This would all be well and good, were I not a man who is accustomed to sleeping at night, and to experiencing in my dreams the very same things, or now and then even less plausible ones, as these insane people do when they are awake. How often does my evening slumber persuade me of such ordinary things as these: that I am here, clothed in my dressing gown, seated next to the fireplace—when in fact I am lying undressed in bed! But right now my eyes are certainly wide awake when I gaze upon this sheet of paper. This head which I am shaking is not heavy with sleep. I extend this hand consciously and deliberately, and I feel it. Such things would not be so distinct for someone who is asleep. As if I did not recall having been deceived on other occasions even by similar thoughts in my dreams! As I consider these matters more carefully, I see so plainly that there are no definitive signs by which to distinguish being awake from being asleep. As a result, I am becoming quite dizzy, and this dizziness nearly convinces me that I am asleep.

Let us assume then, for the sake of argument, that we are dreaming and that such particulars as these are not true: that we are opening our eyes, moving our head, and extending our hands. Perhaps we do not even have such hands, or any such body at all. Nevertheless, it surely must be admitted that the things seen during slumber are, as it were, like painted images, which could only have been produced in the likeness of true things, and that therefore at least these general things—eyes, head, hands, and the whole

body—are not imaginary things, but are true and exist. For indeed when   *20*
painters themselves wish to represent sirens and satyrs by means of especially
bizarre forms, they surely cannot assign to them utterly new natures. Rather,
they simply fuse together the members of various animals. Or if perhaps
they concoct something so utterly novel that nothing like it has ever been
seen before (and thus is something utterly fictitious and false), yet certainly
at the very least the colors from which they fashion it ought to be true. And
by the same token, although even these general things—eyes, head, hands
and the like—could be imaginary, still one has to admit that at least certain
other things that are even more simple and universal are true. It is from these
components, as if from true colors, that all those images of things that are in
our thought are fashioned, be they true or false.

This class of things appears to include corporeal nature in general, together
with its extension; the shape of extended things; their quantity, that is, their
size and number; as well as the place where they exist; the time through
which they endure, and the like.

Thus it is not improper to conclude from this that physics, astronomy,
medicine, and all the other disciplines that are dependent upon the consideration of composite things are doubtful, and that, on the other hand, arithmetic, geometry, and other such disciplines, which treat of nothing but the
simplest and most general things and which are indifferent as to whether these
things do or do not in fact exist, contain something certain and indubitable.
For whether I am awake or asleep, 2 plus 3 make 5, and a square does not
have more than 4 sides. It does not seem possible that such obvious truths
should be subject to the suspicion of being false.

Be that as it may, there is fixed in my mind a certain opinion of long   *21*
standing, namely that there exists a God who is able to do anything and by
whom I, such as I am, have been created. How do I know that he did not
bring it about that there is no earth at all, no heavens, no extended thing,
no shape, no size, no place, and yet bringing it about that all these things
appear to me to exist precisely as they do now? Moreover, since I judge that
others sometimes make mistakes in matters that they believe they know
most perfectly, may I not, in like fashion, be deceived every time I add 2
and 3 or count the sides of a square, or perform an even simpler operation,
if that can be imagined? But perhaps God has not willed that I be deceived
in this way, for he is said to be supremely good. Nonetheless, if it were
repugnant to his goodness to have created me such that I be deceived all the
time, it would also seem foreign to that same goodness to permit me to be
deceived even occasionally. But we cannot make this last assertion.

Perhaps there are some who would rather deny so powerful a God, than
believe that everything else is uncertain. Let us not oppose them; rather, let us
grant that everything said here about God is fictitious. Now they suppose that
I came to be what I am either by fate, or by chance, or by a connected chain

of events, or by some other way. But because deceived and being mistaken appear to be a certain imperfection, the less powerful they take the author of my origin to be, the more probable it will be that I am so imperfect that I am always deceived. I have nothing to say in response to these arguments. But eventually I am forced to admit that there is nothing among the things I once believed to be true which it is not permissible to doubt—and not out of frivolity or lack of forethought, but for valid and considered arguments. Thus I must be no less careful to withhold assent henceforth even from these beliefs than I would from those that are patently false, if I wish to find anything certain.

22

But it is not enough simply to have realized these things; I must take steps to keep myself mindful of them. For long-standing opinions keep returning, and, almost against my will, they take advantage of my credulity, as if it were bound over to them by long use and the claims of intimacy. Nor will I ever get out of the habit of assenting to them and believing in them, so long as I take them to be exactly what they are, namely, in some respects doubtful, as has just now been shown, but nevertheless highly probable, so that it is much more consonant with reason to believe them than to deny them. Hence, it seems to me I would do well to deceive myself by turning my will in completely the opposite direction and pretend for a time that these opinions are wholly false and imaginary, until finally, as if with prejudices weighing down each side equally, no bad habit should turn my judgment any further from the correct perception of things. For indeed I know that meanwhile there is no danger or error in following this procedure, and that it is impossible for me to indulge in too much distrust, since I am now concentrating only on knowledge, not on action.

Accordingly, I will suppose not a supremely good God, the source of truth, but rather an evil genius, supremely powerful and clever, who has directed his entire effort at deceiving me. I will regard the heavens, the air, the earth, colors, shapes, sounds, and all external things as nothing but the bedeviling hoaxes of my dreams, with which he lays snares for my credulity. I will regard myself as not having hands, or eyes, or flesh, or blood, or any senses, but as nevertheless falsely believing that I possess all these things. I will remain resolute and steadfast in this meditation, and even if it is not within my power to know anything true, it certainly is within my power to take care resolutely to withhold my assent to what is false, lest this deceiver, however powerful, however clever he may be, have any effect on me. But this undertaking is arduous, and a certain laziness brings me back to my customary way of living. I am not unlike a prisoner who enjoyed an imaginary freedom during his sleep, but, when he later begins to suspect that he is dreaming, fears being awakened and nonchalantly conspires with these pleasant illusions. In just the same way, I fall back of my own accord into my old opinions, and dread being awakened, lest the toilsome wakefulness which

23

follows upon a peaceful rest must be spent thenceforward not in the light but among the inextricable shadows of the difficulties now brought forward.

MEDITATION TWO: Concerning the Nature of the Human Mind: That It Is Better Known than the Body

Yesterday's meditation has thrown me into such doubts that I can no longer ignore them, yet I fail to see how they are to be resolved. It is as if I had suddenly fallen into a deep whirlpool; I am so tossed about that I can neither touch bottom with my foot, nor swim up to the top. Nevertheless I will work my way up and will once again attempt the same path I entered upon yesterday. I will accomplish this by putting aside everything that admits of the least doubt, as if I had discovered it to be completely false. I will stay on this course until I know something certain, or, if nothing else, until I at least know for certain that nothing is certain. Archimedes sought but one firm and immovable point in order to move the entire earth from one place to another. Just so, great things are also to be hoped for if I succeed in finding just one thing, however slight, that is certain and unshaken. {24}

Therefore I suppose that everything I see is false. I believe that none of what my deceitful memory represents ever existed. I have no senses whatever. Body, shape, extension, movement, and place are all chimeras. What then will be true? Perhaps just the single fact that nothing is certain.

But how do I know there is not something else, over and above all those things that I have just reviewed, concerning which there is not even the slightest occasion for doubt? Is there not some God, or by whatever name I might call him, who instills these very thoughts in me? But why would I think that, since I myself could perhaps be the author of these thoughts? Am I not then at least something? But I have already denied that I have any senses and any body. Still I hesitate; for what follows from this? Am I so tied to a body and to the senses that I cannot exist without them? But I have persuaded myself that there is absolutely nothing in the world: no sky, no earth, no minds, no bodies. Is it then the case that I too do not exist? But doubtless I did exist, if I persuaded myself of something. But there is some deceiver or other who is supremely powerful and supremely sly and who is always deliberately deceiving me. Then too there is no doubt that I exist, if he is deceiving me. And let him do his best at deception, he will never bring it about that I am nothing so long as I shall think that I am something. Thus, after everything has been most carefully weighed, it must finally be established that this pronouncement "I am, I exist" is necessarily true every time I utter it or conceive it in my mind. {25}

But I do not yet understand sufficiently what I am—I, who now necessarily exist. And so from this point on, I must be careful lest I unwittingly mistake something else for myself, and thus err in that very item of knowledge that I claim to be the most certain and evident of all. Thus, I will meditate once more on what I once believed myself to be, prior to embarking upon these thoughts. For this reason, then, I will set aside whatever can be weakened even to the slightest degree by the arguments brought forward, so that eventually all that remains is precisely nothing but what is certain and unshaken.

What then did I formerly think I was? A man, of course. But what is a man? Might I not say a "rational animal"? No, because then I would have to inquire what "animal" and "rational" mean. And thus from one question I would slide into many more difficult ones. Nor do I now have enough free time that I want to waste it on subtleties of this sort. Instead, permit me here
26   to focus here on what came spontaneously and naturally into my thinking whenever I pondered what I was. Now it occurred to me first that I had a face, hands, arms, and this entire mechanism of bodily members: the very same as are discerned in a corpse, and which I referred to by the name "body." It next occurred to me that I took in food, that I walked about, and that I sensed and thought various things; these actions I used to attribute to the soul. But as to what this soul might be, I either did not think about it or else I imagined it a rarefied I-know-not-what, like a wind, or a fire, or ether, which had been infused into my coarser parts. But as to the body I was not in any doubt. On the contrary, I was under the impression that I knew its nature distinctly. Were I perhaps tempted to describe this nature such as I conceived it in my mind, I would have described it thus: by "body," I understand all that is capable of being bounded by some shape, of being enclosed in a place, and of filling up a space in such a way as to exclude any other body from it; of being perceived by touch, sight, hearing, taste, or smell; of being moved in several ways, not, of course, by itself, but by whatever else impinges upon it. For it was my view that the power of self-motion, and likewise of sensing or of thinking, in no way belonged to the nature of the body. Indeed I used rather to marvel that such faculties were to be found in certain bodies.

But now what am I, when I suppose that there is some supremely powerful and, if I may be permitted to say so, malicious deceiver who deliberately tries to fool me in any way he can? Can I not affirm that I possess at least a
27   small measure of all those things which I have already said belong to the nature of the body? I focus my attention on them, I think about them, I review them again, but nothing comes to mind. I am tired of repeating this to no purpose. But what about those things I ascribed to the soul? What about being nourished or moving about? Since I now do not have a body, these are surely nothing but fictions. What about sensing? Surely this too does not take place without a body; and I seemed to have sensed in my dreams many things that I later realized I did not sense. What about thinking? Here

I make my discovery: thought exists; it alone cannot be separated from me. I am; I exist—this is certain. But for how long? For as long as I am thinking; for perhaps it could also come to pass that if I were to cease all thinking I would then utterly cease to exist. At this time I admit nothing that is not necessarily true. I am therefore precisely nothing but a thinking thing; that is, a mind, or intellect, or understanding, or reason—words of whose meanings I was previously ignorant. Yet I am a true thing and am truly existing; but what kind of thing? I have said it already: a thinking thing.

What else am I? I will set my imagination in motion. I am not that concatenation of members we call the human body. Neither am I even some subtle air infused into these members, nor a wind, nor a fire, nor a vapor, nor a breath, nor anything I devise for myself. For I have supposed these things to be nothing. The assumption still stands; yet nevertheless I am something. But is it perhaps the case that these very things which I take to be nothing, because they are unknown to me, nevertheless are in fact no different from that me that I know? This I do not know, and I will not quarrel about it now. I can make a judgment only about things that are known to me. I know that I exist; I ask now who is this "I" whom I know? Most certainly, in the strict sense the knowledge of this "I" does not depend upon things whose existence I do not yet know. Therefore it is not dependent 28 upon any of those things that I simulate in my imagination. But this word "simulate" warns me of my error. For I would indeed be simulating were I to "imagine" that I was something, because imagining is merely the contemplating of the shape or image of a corporeal thing. But I now know with certainty that I am and also that all these images—and, generally, everything belonging to the nature of the body—could turn out to be nothing but dreams. Once I have realized this, I would seem to be speaking no less foolishly were I to say: "I will use my imagination in order to recognize more distinctly who I am," than were I to say: "Now I surely am awake, and I see something true; but since I do not yet see it clearly enough, I will deliberately fall asleep so that my dreams might represent it to me more truly and more clearly." Thus I realize that none of what I can grasp by means of the imagination pertains to this knowledge that I have of myself. Moreover, I realize that I must be most diligent about withdrawing my mind from these things so that it can perceive its nature as distinctly as possible.

But what then am I? A thing that thinks. What is that? A thing that doubts, understands, affirms, denies, wills, refuses, and that also imagines and senses.

Indeed it is no small matter if all of these things belong to me. But why should they not belong to me? Is it not the very same "I" who now doubts almost everything, who nevertheless understands something, who affirms that this one thing is true, who denies other things, who desires to know more, who wishes not to be deceived, who imagines many things even against

my will, who also notices many things which appear to come from the senses?
29   What is there in all of this that is not every bit as true as the fact that I
exist—even if I am always asleep or even if my creator makes every effort
to mislead me? Which of these things is distinct from my thought? Which
of them can be said to be separate from myself? For it is so obvious that it
is I who doubt, I who understand, and I who will, that there is nothing by
which it could be explained more clearly. But indeed it is also the same "I"
who imagines; for although perhaps, as I supposed before, absolutely nothing
that I imagined is true, still the very power of imagining really does exist,
and constitutes a part of my thought. Finally, it is this same "I" who senses
or who is cognizant of bodily things as if through the senses. For example,
I now see a light, I hear a noise, I feel heat. These things are false, since I am
asleep. Yet I certainly do seem to see, hear, and feel warmth. This cannot be
false. Properly speaking, this is what in me is called "sensing." But this, precisely so taken, is nothing other than thinking.

From these considerations I am beginning to know a little better what I
am. But it still seems (and I cannot resist believing) that corporeal things—
whose images are formed by thought, and which the senses themselves
examine—are much more distinctly known than this mysterious "I" which
does not fall within the imagination. And yet it would be strange indeed
were I to grasp the very things I consider to be doubtful, unknown, and foreign to me more distinctly than what is true, what is known—than, in short,
myself. But I see what is happening: my mind loves to wander and does not
30   yet permit itself to be restricted within the confines of truth. So be it then;
let us just this once allow it completely free rein, so that, a little while later,
when the time has come to pull in the reins, the mind may more readily
permit itself to be controlled.

Let us consider those things which are commonly believed to be the most
distinctly grasped of all: namely the bodies we touch and see. Not bodies
in general, mind you, for these general perceptions are apt to be somewhat
more confused, but one body in particular. Let us take, for instance, this
piece of wax. It has been taken quite recently from the honeycomb; it has
not yet lost all the honey flavor. It retains some of the scent of the flowers
from which it was collected. Its color, shape, and size are manifest. It is hard
and cold; it is easy to touch. If you rap on it with your knuckle it will emit
a sound. In short, everything is present in it that appears needed to enable a
body to be known as distinctly as possible. But notice that, as I am speaking,
I am bringing it close to the fire. The remaining traces of the honey flavor
are disappearing; the scent is vanishing; the color is changing; the original
shape is disappearing. Its size is increasing; it is becoming liquid and hot;
you can hardly touch it. And now, when you rap on it, it no longer emits
any sound. Does the same wax still remain? I must confess that it does; no
one denies it; no one thinks otherwise. So what was there in the wax that was

so distinctly grasped? Certainly none of the aspects that I reached by means of the senses. For whatever came under the senses of taste, smell, sight, touch, or hearing has now changed; and yet the wax remains.

Perhaps the wax was what I now think it is: namely, that the wax itself never really was the sweetness of the honey, nor the fragrance of the flowers, nor the whiteness, nor the shape, nor the sound, but instead was a body that a short time ago manifested itself to me in these ways, and now does so in other ways. But just what precisely is this thing that I thus imagine? Let us focus our attention on this and see what remains after we have removed everything that does not belong to the wax: only that it is something 31 extended, flexible, and mutable. But what is it to be flexible and mutable? Is it what my imagination shows it to be: namely, that this piece of wax can change from a round to a square shape, or from the latter to a triangular shape? Not at all; for I grasp that the wax is capable of innumerable changes of this sort, even though I am incapable of running through these innumerable changes by using my imagination. Therefore this insight is not achieved by the faculty of imagination. What is it to be extended? Is this thing's extension also unknown? For it becomes greater in wax that is beginning to melt, greater in boiling wax, and greater still as the heat is increased. And I would not judge correctly what the wax is if I did not believe that it takes on an even greater variety of dimensions than I could ever grasp with the imagination. It remains then for me to concede that I do not grasp what this wax is through the imagination; rather, I perceive it through the mind alone. The point I am making refers to this particular piece of wax, for the case of wax in general is clearer still. But what is this piece of wax which is perceived only by the mind? Surely it is the same piece of wax that I see, touch, and imagine; in short it is the same piece of wax I took it to be from the very beginning. But I need to realize that the perception of the wax is neither a seeing, nor a touching, nor an imagining. Nor has it ever been, even though it previously seemed so; rather it is an inspection on the part of the mind alone. This inspection can be imperfect and confused, as it was before, or clear and distinct, as it is now, depending on how closely I pay attention to the things in which the piece of wax consists.

But meanwhile I marvel at how prone my mind is to errors. For although I am considering these things within myself silently and without words, 32 nevertheless I seize upon words themselves and I am nearly deceived by the ways in which people commonly speak. For we say that we see the wax itself, if it is present, and not that we judge it to be present from its color or shape. Whence I might conclude straightaway that I know the wax through the vision had by the eye, and not through an inspection on the part of the mind alone. But then were I perchance to look out my window and observe men crossing the square, I would ordinarily say I see the men themselves just as I say I see the wax. But what do I see aside from hats and clothes, which could conceal automata? Yet I judge them to be men. Thus what I thought I had seen with my eyes, I actually grasped solely with the faculty of judgment, which is in my mind.

But a person who seeks to know more than the common crowd ought to be ashamed of himself for looking for doubt in common ways of speaking. Let us then go forward, inquiring on when it was that I perceived more perfectly and evidently what the piece of wax was. Was it when I first saw it and believed I knew it by the external sense, or at least by the so-called "common" sense, that is, the power of imagination? Or do I have more perfect knowledge now, when I have diligently examined both what the wax is and how it is known? Surely it is absurd to be in doubt about this matter. For what was there in my initial perception that was distinct? What was there that any animal seemed incapable of possessing? But indeed when I distinguish the wax from its external forms, as if stripping it of its clothing, and look at the wax in its nakedness, then, even though there can be still an error in my judgment, nevertheless I cannot perceive it thus without a human mind.

33   But what am I to say about this mind, that is, about myself? For as yet I admit nothing else to be in me over and above the mind. What, I ask, am I who seem to perceive this wax so distinctly? Do I not know myself not only much more truly and with greater certainty, but also much more distinctly and evidently? For if I judge that the wax exists from the fact that I see it, certainly from this same fact that I see the wax it follows much more evidently that I myself exist. For it could happen that what I see is not truly wax. It could happen that I have no eyes with which to see anything. But it is utterly impossible that, while I see or think I see (I do not now distinguish these two), I who think am not something. Likewise, if I judge that the wax exists from the fact that I touch it, the same outcome will again obtain, namely that I exist. If I judge that the wax exists from the fact that I imagine it, or for any other reason, plainly the same thing follows. But what I note regarding the wax applies to everything else that is external to me. Furthermore, if my perception of the wax seemed more distinct after it became known to me not only on account of sight or touch, but on account of many reasons, one has to admit how much more distinctly I am now known to myself. For there is not a single consideration that can aid in my perception of the wax or of any other body that fails to make even more manifest the nature of my mind. But there are still so many other things in the mind itself on the basis of which my knowledge of it can be rendered more distinct that it hardly seems worth enumerating those things which emanate to it from the body.

34   But lo and behold, I have returned on my own to where I wanted to be. For since I now know that even bodies are not, properly speaking, perceived by the senses or by the faculty of imagination, but by the intellect alone, and

that they are not perceived through their being touched or seen, but only through their being understood, I manifestly know that nothing can be perceived more easily and more evidently than my own mind. But since the tendency to hang on to long-held beliefs cannot be put aside so quickly, I want to stop here, so that by the length of my meditation this new knowledge may be more deeply impressed upon my memory.

MEDITATION THREE: Concerning God, That He Exists

I will now shut my eyes, stop up my ears, and withdraw all my senses. I will also blot out from my thoughts all images of corporeal things, or rather, since the latter is hardly possible, I will regard these images as empty, false, and worthless. And as I converse with myself alone and look more deeply into myself, I will attempt to render myself gradually better known and more familiar to myself. I am a thing that thinks, that is to say, a thing that doubts, affirms, denies, understands a few things, is ignorant of many things, wills, refrains from willing, and also imagines and senses. For as I observed earlier, even though these things that I sense or imagine may perhaps be nothing at all outside me, nevertheless I am certain that these modes of thinking, which are cases of what I call sensing and imagining, insofar as they are merely modes of thinking, do exist within me.   35

In these few words, I have reviewed everything I truly know, or at least what so far I have noticed that I know. Now I will ponder more carefully to see whether perhaps there may be other things belonging to me that up until now I have failed to notice. I am certain that I am a thinking thing. But do I not therefore also know what is required for me to be certain of anything? Surely in this first instance of knowledge, there is nothing but a certain clear and distinct perception of what I affirm. Yet this would hardly be enough to render me certain of the truth of a thing, if it could ever happen that something that I perceived so clearly and distinctly were false. And thus I now seem able to posit as a general rule that everything I very clearly and distinctly perceive is true.

Be that as it may, I have previously admitted many things as wholly certain and evident that nevertheless I later discovered to be doubtful. What sort of things were these? Why, the earth, the sky, the stars, and all the other things I perceived by means of the senses. But what was it about these things that I clearly perceived? Surely the fact that the ideas or thoughts of these things were hovering before my mind. But even now I do not deny that these ideas are in me. Yet there was something else I used to affirm, which, owing to my habitual tendency to believe it, I used to think was something I clearly perceived, even though I actually did not perceive it all: namely, that certain things existed outside me, things from which those ideas proceeded and which those ideas completely resembled. But on this point I was mistaken; or, rather if my judgment was a true one, it was not the result of the force of my perception.

36   But what about when I considered something very simple and easy in the areas of arithmetic or geometry, for example that 2 plus 3 make 5, and the like? Did I not intuit them at least clearly enough so as to affirm them as true? To be sure, I did decide later on that I must doubt these things, but that was only because it occurred to me that some God could perhaps have given me a nature such that I might be deceived even about matters that seemed most evident. But whenever this preconceived opinion about the supreme power of God occurs to me, I cannot help admitting that, were he to wish it, it would be easy for him to cause me to err even in those matters that I think I intuit as clearly as possible with the eyes of the mind. On the other hand, whenever I turn my attention to those very things that I think I perceive with such great clarity, I am so completely persuaded by them that I spontaneously blurt out these words: "let him who can deceive me; so long as I think that I am something, he will never bring it about that I am nothing. Nor will he one day make it true that I never existed, for it is true now that I do exist. Nor will he even bring it about that perhaps 2 plus 3 might equal more or less than 5, or similar items in which I recognize an obvious contradiction." And certainly, because I have no reason for thinking that there is a God who is a deceiver (and of course I do not yet sufficiently know whether there even is a God), the basis for doubting, depending as it does merely on the above hypothesis, is very tenuous and, so to speak, metaphysical. But in order to remove even this basis for doubt, I should at the first opportunity inquire whether there is a God, and, if there is, whether or not he can be a deceiver. For if I am ignorant of this, it appears I am never capable of being completely certain about anything else.

37   However, at this stage good order seems to demand that I first group all my thoughts into certain classes, and ask in which of them truth or falsity properly resides. Some of these thoughts are like images of things; to these alone does the word "idea" properly apply, as when I think of a man, or a chimera, or the sky, or an angel, or God. Again there are other thoughts that take different forms: for example, when I will, or fear, or affirm, or deny, there is always some thing that I grasp as the subject of my thought, yet I embrace in my thought something more than the likeness of that thing. Some of these thoughts are called volitions or affects, while others are called judgments.

Now as far as ideas are concerned, if they are considered alone and in their own right, without being referred to something else, they cannot, properly speaking, be false. For whether it is a she-goat or a chimera that I am imagining, it is no less true that I imagine the one than the other. Moreover, we need not fear that there is falsity in the will itself or in the affects, for although I can choose evil things or even things that are utterly nonexistent, I cannot conclude from this that it is untrue that I do choose these things. Thus there remain only judgments in which I must take care not to be mistaken. Now the principal and most frequent error to be found in judgments consists in the fact that I judge that the ideas which are in me are similar to or in conformity with certain things outside me. Obviously, if I were to consider these ideas merely as certain modes of my thought, and were not to refer them to anything else, they could hardly give me any subject matter for error.

Among these ideas, some appear to me to be innate, some adventitious, and some produced by me. For I understand what a thing is, what truth is, what thought is, and I appear to have derived this exclusively from my very own nature. But say I am now hearing a noise, or looking at the sun, or feeling the fire; up until now I judged that these things proceeded from certain things outside me, and finally, that sirens, hippogriffs, and the like are made by me. Or perhaps I can even think of all these ideas as being adventitious, or as being innate, or as fabrications, for I have not yet clearly ascertained their true origin.

But here I must inquire particularly into those ideas that I believe to be derived from things existing outside me. Just what reason do I have for believing that these ideas resemble those things? Well, I do seem to have been so taught by nature. Moreover, I do know from experience that these ideas do not depend upon my will, nor consequently upon myself, for I often notice them even against my will. Now, for example, whether or not I will it, I feel heat. It is for this reason that I believe this feeling or idea of heat comes to me from something other than myself, namely from heat of the fire by which I am sitting. Nothing is more obvious than the judgment that this thing is sending its likeness rather than something else into me.

I will now see whether these reasons are powerful enough. When I say here "I have been so taught by nature," all I have in mind is that I am driven by a spontaneous impulse to believe this, and not that some light of nature is showing me that it is true. These are two very different things. For whatever is shown me by this light of nature, for example, that from the fact that I doubt, it follows that I am, and the like, cannot in any way be doubtful. This is owing to the fact that there can be no other faculty that I can trust as much as this light and which could teach that these things are not true. But as far as natural impulses are concerned, in the past I have often judged myself to have been driven by them to make the poorer choice when it was a question of choosing a good; and I fail to see why I should place any greater faith in them in other matters.

Again, although these ideas do not depend upon my will, it does not follow that they necessarily proceed from things existing outside me. For just as these impulses about which I spoke just now seem to be different from my will, even though they are in me, so too perhaps there is also in me some other faculty, one not yet sufficiently known to me, which produces these ideas, just as it has always seemed up to now that ideas are formed in me without any help from external things when I am asleep.

And finally, even if these ideas did proceed from things other than myself, it does not therefore follow that they must resemble those things. Indeed it seems I have frequently no̶ ̶ed a vast difference in many respects. For example, I find within myself distinct ideas of the sun. One idea is drawn, as it were, from the senses. Now it is this idea which, of all those that I take to be derived from outside me, is most in need of examination. By means of this idea the sun appears to me to be quite small. But there is another idea, one derived from astronomical reasoning, that is, it is elicited from certain notions that are innate in me, or else is fashioned by me in some other way. Through this idea the sun is shown to be several times larger than the earth. Both ideas surely cannot resemble the same sun existing outside me; and reason convinces me that the idea that seems to have emanated from the sun itself from so close is the very one that least resembles the sun.

40   All these points demonstrate sufficiently that up to this point it was not a well-founded judgment, but only a blind impulse that formed the basis of my belief that things existing outside me send ideas or images of themselves to me through the sense organs or by some other means.

But still another way occurs to me for inquiring whether some of the things of which there are ideas in me do exist outside me: insofar as these ideas are merely modes of thought, I see no inequality among them; they all seem to proceed from me in the same manner. But insofar as one idea represents one thing and another idea another thing, it is obvious that they do differ very greatly from one another. Unquestionably, those ideas that display substances to me are something more and, if I may say so, contain within themselves more objective reality than those which represent only modes or accidents. Again, the idea that enables me to understand a supreme deity, eternal, infinite, omniscient, omnipotent, and creator of all things other than himself, clearly has more objective reality within it than do those ideas through which finite substances are displayed.

Now it is indeed evident by the light of nature that there must be at least as much [reality] in the efficient and total cause as there is in the effect of that same cause. For whence, I ask, could an effect get its reality, if not from its cause? And how could the cause give that reality to the effect, unless it also possessed that reality? Hence it follows that something cannot come into being out of nothing, and also that what is more perfect (that is, what con-
41   tains in itself more reality) cannot come into being from what is less perfect. But this is manifestly true not merely for those effects whose reality is actual or formal, but also for ideas in which only objective reality is considered. For example, not only can a stone which did not exist previously not now

begin to exist unless it is produced by something in which there is, either formally or eminently, everything that is in the stone; nor heat be introduced into a subject which was not already hot unless it is done by something that is of at least as perfect an order as heat—and the same for the rest—but it is also true that there can be in me no idea of heat, or of a stone, unless it is placed in me by some cause that has at least as much reality as I conceive to be in the heat or in the stone. For although this cause conveys none of its actual or formal reality to my idea, it should not be thought for that reason that it must be less real. Rather, the very nature of an idea is such that of itself it needs no formal reality other than what it borrows from my thought, of which it is a mode. But that a particular idea contains this as opposed to that objective reality is surely owing to some cause in which there is at least as much formal reality as there is objective reality contained in the idea. For if we assume that something is found in the idea that was not in its cause, then the idea gets that something from nothing. Yet as imperfect a mode of being as this is by which a thing exists in the intellect objectively through an idea, nevertheless it is plainly not nothing; hence it cannot get its being from nothing.

Moreover, even though the reality that I am considering in my ideas is merely objective reality, I ought not on that account to suspect that there is no need for the same reality to be formally in the causes of these ideas, but that it suffices for it to be in them objectively. For just as the objective mode of being belongs to ideas by their very nature, so the formal mode of being belongs to the causes of ideas, at least to the first and preeminent ones, by their very nature. And although one idea can perhaps issue from another, nevertheless no infinite regress is permitted here; eventually some first idea must be reached whose cause is a sort of archetype that contains formally all the reality that is in the idea merely objectively. Thus it is clear to me by the light of nature that the ideas that are in me are like images that can easily fail to match the perfection of the things from which they have been drawn, but which can contain nothing greater or more perfect.

And the longer and more attentively I examine all these points, the more clearly and distinctly I know they are true. But what am I ultimately to conclude? If the objective reality of any of my ideas is found to be so great that I am certain that the same reality was not in me, either formally or eminently, and that therefore I myself cannot be the cause of the idea, then it necessarily follows that I am not alone in the world, but that something else, which is the cause of this idea, also exists. But if no such idea is found in me, I will have no argument whatsoever to make me certain of the existence of anything other than myself, for I have conscientiously reviewed all these arguments, and so far I have been unable to find any other.

Among my ideas, in addition to the one that displays me to myself (about

42

43   which there can be no difficulty at this point), are others that represent God,
corporeal and inanimate things, angels, animals, and finally other men like
myself.

As to the ideas that display other men, or animals, or angels, I easily understand that they could be fashioned from the ideas that I have of myself, of
corporeal things, and of God—even if no men (except myself), no animals,
and no angels existed in the world.

As to the ideas of corporeal things, there is nothing in them that is so
great that it seems incapable of having originated from me. For if I inves-
tigate them thoroughly and examine each one individually in the way I
examined the idea of wax yesterday, I notice that there are only a very few
things in them that I perceive clearly and distinctly: namely, size, or extension in length, breadth, and depth; shape, which arises from the limits of this
extension; position, which various things possessing shape have in relation
to one another; and motion, or alteration in position. To these can be added
substance, duration, and number. But as for the remaining items, such as light
and colors, sounds, odors, tastes, heat and cold, and other tactile qualities, I
think of these only in a very confused and obscure manner, to the extent
that I do not even know whether they are true or false, that is, whether the
ideas I have of them are ideas of things or ideas of non-things. For although
a short time ago I noted that falsity properly so called (or "formal" falsity) is
to be found only in judgments, nevertheless there is another kind of falsity
(called "material" falsity) which is found in ideas whenever they represent a
non-thing as if it were a thing. For example, the ideas I have of heat and
44   cold fall so far short of being clear and distinct that I cannot tell from them
whether cold is merely the privation of heat or whether heat is the privation of cold, or whether both are real qualities, or whether neither is. And
because ideas can only be, as it were, of things, if it is true that cold is merely
the absence of heat, then an idea that represents cold to me as something
real and positive, will not inappropriately be called false. The same holds for
other similar ideas.

Assuredly I need not assign to these ideas an author distinct from myself.
For if they were false, that is, if they were to represent non-things, I know
by the light of nature that they proceed from nothing; that is, they are in me
for no other reason than that something is lacking in my nature, and that my
nature is not entirely perfect. If, on the other hand, these ideas are true, then
because they exhibit so little reality to me that I cannot distinguish it from
a non-thing, I see no reason why they cannot get their being from me.

As for what is clear and distinct in the ideas of corporeal things, it appears
I could have borrowed some of these from the idea of myself: namely, substance, duration, number, and whatever else there may be of this type. For
instance, I think that a stone is a substance, that is to say, a thing that is suitable for existing in itself; and likewise I think that I too am a substance.

Despite the fact that I conceive myself to be a thinking thing and not an extended thing, whereas I conceive of a stone as an extended thing and not a thinking thing, and hence there is the greatest diversity between these two concepts, nevertheless they seem to agree with one another when considered under the rubric of substance. Furthermore, I perceive that I now exist and recall that I have previously existed for some time. And I have various thoughts and know how many of them there are. It is in doing these things   *45* that I acquire the ideas of duration and number, which I can then apply to other things. However, none of the other components out of which the ideas of corporeal things are fashioned (namely extension, shape, position, and motion) are contained in me formally, since I am merely a thinking thing. But since these are only certain modes of a substance, whereas I am a substance, it seems possible that they are contained in me eminently.

Thus there remains only the idea of God. I must consider whether there is anything in this idea that could not have originated from me. I understand by the name "God" a certain substance that is infinite, independent, supremely intelligent and supremely powerful, and that created me along with everything else that exists—if anything else exists. Indeed all these are such that, the more carefully I focus my attention on them, the less possible it seems they could have arisen from myself alone. Thus, from what has been said, I must conclude that God necessarily exists.

For although the idea of substance is in me by virtue of the fact that I am a substance, that fact is not sufficient to explain my having the idea of an infinite substance, since I am finite, unless this idea proceeded from some substance which really was infinite.

Nor should I think that I do not perceive the infinite by means of a true idea, but only through a negation of the finite, just as I perceive rest and darkness by means of a negation of motion and light. On the contrary, I clearly understand that there is more reality in an infinite substance than there is in a finite one. Thus the perception of the infinite is somehow prior in me to the perception of the finite, that is, my perception of God is prior to my perception of myself. For how would I understand that I doubt and   *46* that I desire, that is, that I lack something and that I am not wholly perfect, unless there were some idea in me of a more perfect being, by comparison with which I might recognize my defects?

Nor can it be said that this idea of God is perhaps materially false and thus can originate from nothing, as I remarked just now about the ideas of heat and cold, and the like. On the contrary, because it is the most clear and distinct and because it contains more objective reality than any other idea, no idea is in and of itself truer and has less of a basis for being suspected of falsehood. I maintain that this idea of a being that is supremely perfect and infinite is true in the highest degree. For although I could perhaps pretend that such a being does not exist, nevertheless I could not pretend that the idea of such a being discloses to me nothing real, as was the case with the idea of cold which I referred to earlier. It is indeed an idea that is utterly clear and distinct; for whatever I clearly and distinctly perceive to be real and true and to involve some perfection is wholly contained in that idea. It is no objection that I do not comprehend the infinite or that there are countless other things in God that I can in no way either comprehend or perhaps even touch with my thought. For the nature of the infinite is such that it is not comprehended by a being such as I, who am finite. And it is sufficient that I understand this very point and judge that all those things that I clearly perceive and that I know to contain some perfection—and perhaps even countless other things of which I am ignorant—are in God either formally or eminently. The result is that, of all the ideas that are in me, the idea that I have of God is the most true, the most clear and distinct.

But perhaps I am something greater than I myself understand. Perhaps all these perfections that I am attributing to God are somehow in me poten-

47   tially, although they do no yet assert themselves and are not yet actualized. For I now observe that my knowledge is gradually being increased, and I see nothing standing in the way of its being increased more and more to infinity. Moreover, I see no reason why, with my knowledge thus increased, I could not acquire all the remaining perfections of God. And, finally, if the potential for these perfections is in me already, I see no reason why this potential would not suffice to produce the idea of these perfections.

Yet none of these things can be the case. First, while it is true that my knowledge is gradually being increased and that there are many things in me potentially that are not yet actual, nevertheless, none of these pertains to the idea of God, in which there is nothing whatever that is potential. Indeed this gradual increase is itself a most certain proof of imperfection. Moreover, although my knowledge may always increase more and more, nevertheless I understand that this knowledge will never by this means be actually infinite, because it will never reach a point where it is incapable of greater increase. On the contrary, I judge God to be actually infinite, so that nothing can be added to his perfection. Finally, I perceive that the objective being of an idea cannot be produced by a merely potential being (which, strictly speaking, is nothing), but only by an actual or formal being.

Indeed, there is nothing in all these things that is not manifest by the light of nature to one who is conscientious and attentive. But when I am less attentive, and the images of sensible things blind the mind's eye, I do not so easily recall why the idea of a being more perfect than me necessarily pro-

48   ceeds from a being that really is more perfect. This being the case, it is appropriate to ask further whether I myself who have this idea could exist, if such a being did not exist.

From what source, then, do I derive my existence? Why, from myself, or from my parents, or from whatever other things there are that are less perfect than God. For nothing more perfect than God, or even as perfect as God, can be thought or imagined.

But if I got my being from myself, I would not doubt, nor would I desire, nor would I lack anything at all. For I would have given myself all the perfections of which I have some idea; in so doing, I myself would be God! I must not think that the things I lack could perhaps be more difficult to acquire than the ones I have now. On the contrary, it is obvious that it would have been much more difficult for me (that is, a thing or substance that thinks) to emerge out of nothing than it would be to acquire the knowledge of many things about which I am ignorant (these items of knowledge being merely accidents of that substance). Certainly, if I got this greater thing from myself, I would not have denied myself at least those things that can be had more easily. Nor would I have denied myself any of those other things that I perceive to be contained in the idea of God, for surely none of them seem to me more difficult to bring about. But if any of them were more difficult to bring about, they would certainly also seem more difficult to me, even if the remaining ones that I possess I got from myself, since it would be on account of them that I would experience that my power is limited.

Nor am I avoiding the force of these arguments, if I suppose that perhaps I have always existed as I do now, as if it then followed that no author of my existence need be sought. For because the entire span of one's life can be divided into countless parts, each one wholly independent of the rest, it does not follow from the fact that I existed a short time ago that I must exist now, unless some cause, as it were, creates me all over again at this moment, that is to say, which preserves me. For it is obvious to one who pays close attention to the nature of time that plainly the same force and action are needed to preserve anything at each individual moment that it lasts as would be required to create that same thing anew, were it not yet in existence. Thus conservation differs from creation solely by virtue of a distinction of reason; this too is one of those things that are manifest by the light of nature.

Therefore I must now ask myself whether I possess some power by which I can bring it about that I myself, who now exist, will also exist a little later on. For since I am nothing but a thinking thing—or at least since I am now dealing simply and precisely with that part of me which is a thinking thing— if such a power were in me, then I would certainly be aware of it. But I observe that there is no such power; and from this very fact I know most clearly that I depend upon some being other than myself.

But perhaps this being is not God, and I have been produced either by my parents or by some other causes less perfect than God. On the contrary, as I said before, it is obvious that there must be at least as much in the cause as there is in the effect. Thus, regardless of what it is that eventually is assigned as my cause, because I am a thinking thing and have within me a certain idea of God, it must be granted that what caused me is also a thinking thing and it too has an idea of all the perfections which I attribute to God. And I can again inquire of this cause whether it got its existence from itself or from another cause. For if it got its existence from itself, it is evident from what has been said that it is itself God, because, having the power of existing in and of itself, it unquestionably also has the power of actually possessing all the perfections of which it has in itself an idea—that is, all the perfections that I conceive to be in God. However, if it got its existence from another cause, I will once again inquire in similar fashion about this other cause: whether it got its existence from itself or from another cause, until finally I arrive at the ultimate cause, which will be God. For it is apparent enough that there can be no infinite regress here, especially since I am not dealing here merely with the cause that once produced me, but also and most especially with the cause that preserves me at the present time.

Nor can one fancy that perhaps several partial causes have concurred in bringing me into being, and that I have taken the ideas of the various perfections I attribute to God from a variety of causes, so that all of these perfections are found somewhere in the universe, but not all joined together in a single being—God. On the contrary, the unity, the simplicity, that is, the inseparability of all those features that are in God is one of the chief perfections that I understand to be in him. Certainly the idea of the unity of all his perfections could not have been placed in me by any cause from which I did not also get the ideas of the other perfections; for neither could some cause have made me understand them joined together and inseparable from one another, unless it also caused me to recognize what they were.

Finally, as to my parents, even if everything that I ever believed about them were true, still it is certainly not they who preserve me; nor is it they who in any way brought me into being, insofar as I am a thinking thing. Rather, they merely placed certain dispositions in the matter which I judged to contain me, that is, a mind, which now is the only thing I take myself to be. And thus there can be no difficulty here concerning my parents. Indeed I have no choice but to conclude that the mere fact of my existing and of there being in me an idea of a most perfect being, that is, God, demonstrates most evidently that God too exists.

All that remains for me is to ask how I received this idea from God. For I did not draw it from the senses; it never came upon me unexpectedly, as is usually the case with the ideas of sensible things when these things present themselves (or seem to present themselves) to the external sense organs. Nor was it made by me, for I plainly can neither subtract anything from it nor add anything to it. Thus the only option remaining is that this idea is innate in me, just as the idea of myself is innate in me.

To be sure, it is not astonishing that in creating me, God should have endowed me with this idea, so that it would be like the mark of the craftsman impressed upon his work, although this mark need not be something distinct from the work itself. But the mere fact that God created me makes it highly plausible that I have somehow been made in his image and likeness, and that I perceive this likeness, in which the idea of God is contained, by means of the same faculty by which I perceive myself. That is, when I turn the mind's eye toward myself, I understand not only that I am something incomplete and dependent upon another, something aspiring indefinitely for greater and greater or better things, but also that the being on whom I depend has in himself all those greater things—not merely indefinitely and potentially, but infinitely and actually, and thus that he is God. The whole force of the argument rests on the fact that I recognize that it would be impossible for me to exist, being of such a nature as I am (namely, having in me the idea of God), unless God did in fact exist. God, I say, that same being the idea of whom is in me: a being having all those perfections that I cannot comprehend, but can somehow touch with my thought, and a being subject to no defects whatever. From these considerations it is quite obvious that he cannot be a deceiver, for it is manifest by the light of nature that all fraud and deception depend on some defect. 52

But before examining this idea more closely and at the same time inquiring into other truths that can be gathered from it, at this point I want to spend some time contemplating this God, to ponder his attributes and, so far as the eye of my darkened mind can take me, to gaze upon, to admire, and to adore the beauty of this immense light. For just as we believe by faith that the greatest felicity of the next life consists solely in this contemplation of the divine majesty, so too we now experience that from the same contemplation, although it is much less perfect, the greatest pleasure of which we are capable in this life can be perceived.

MEDITATION FOUR: Concerning the True and the False

Lately I have become accustomed to withdrawing my mind from the senses, and I have carefully taken note of the fact that very few things are truly perceived regarding corporeal things, although a great many more things are known regarding the human mind, and still many more things regarding God. The upshot is that I now have no difficulty directing my thought away from things that can be imagined to things that can be grasped only by the understanding and are wholly separate from matter. In fact the idea I clearly have of the human mind—insofar as it is a thinking thing, not extended in length, breadth, or depth, and having nothing else from the body—is far more distinct than the idea of any corporeal thing. And when I take note of the fact that I doubt, or that I am a thing that is incomplete and dependent, there comes to mind a clear and distinct idea of a being that is independent and complete, that is, an idea of God. And from the mere fact that such an 53 idea is in me, or that I who have this idea exist, I draw the obvious conclusion that God also exists, and that my existence depends entirely upon him at each and every moment. This conclusion is so obvious that I am confident that the human mind can know nothing more evident or more certain. And now I seem to see a way by which I might progress from this contemplation of the true God, in whom, namely, are hidden all the treasures of the sciences and wisdom, to the knowledge of other things.

To begin with, I acknowledge that it is impossible for God ever to deceive me, for trickery or deception are always indicative of some imperfection. And although the ability to deceive seems to be an indication of cleverness or power, the will to deceive undoubtedly attests to maliciousness or weakness. Accord-ingly, deception is incompatible with God.

Next I experience that there is in me a certain faculty of judgment, which, like everything else that is in me, I undoubtedly received from God. And since he does not wish to deceive me, he assuredly has not given me the sort of faculty with which I could ever make a mistake, when I use it properly.

No doubt regarding this matter would remain, but for the fact that it seems to follow from this that I am never capable of making a mistake. For if everything that is in me I got from God, and he gave me no faculty for making mistakes, it seems I am incapable of ever erring. And thus, so long as I think exclusively about God and focus my attention exclusively on him, I discern no cause of error or falsity. But once I turn my attention back on myself, I nevertheless experience that I am subject to countless errors. As I seek a cause of these errors, I notice that passing before me is not only a real and positive idea of God (that is, of a supremely perfect being), but also, as it were, a certain negative idea of nothingness (that is, of what is at the greatest possible distance from any perfection), and that I have been so constituted as a kind of middle ground between God and nothingness, or between the supreme being and non-being. Thus insofar as I have been created by the supreme being, there is nothing in me by means of which I might be deceived or be led into error; but insofar as I participate in nothingness or non-being, that is, insofar as I am not the supreme being and lack a great many things, it is not surprising that I make mistakes. Thus I certainly understand that error as such is not something real that depends upon God, but rather is merely a defect. And thus there is no need to account for my errors by positing a faculty given to me by God for the purpose. Rather, it just so happens that I make mistakes because the faculty of judging the truth, which I got from God, is not, in my case, infinite.

Still this is not yet altogether satisfactory; for error is not a pure negation, but rather a privation or a lack of some knowledge that somehow ought to be in me. And when I attend to the nature of God, it seems impossible that he would have placed in me a faculty that is not perfect in its kind or that is lacking some perfection it ought to have. For if it is true that the more expert the craftsman, the more perfect the works he produces, what can that supreme creator of all things make that is not perfect in all respects? No doubt God could have created me such that I never erred. No doubt, again, God always wills what is best. Is it then better that I should be in error rather than not?

As I mull these things over more carefully, it occurs to me first that there is no reason to marvel at the fact that God should bring about certain things the reasons for which I do not understand. Nor is his existence therefore to be doubted because I happen to experience other things of which I fail to grasp why and how he made them. For since I know now that my nature is very weak and limited, whereas the nature of God is immense, incomprehensible, and infinite, this is sufficient for me also to know that he can make innumerable things whose causes escape me. For this reason alone the entire class of causes which people customarily derive from a thing's "end," I judge to be utterly useless in physics. It is not without rashness that I think myself capable of inquiring into the ends of God.

It also occurs to me that whenever we ask whether the works of God are perfect, we should keep in view not simply some one creature in isolation from the rest, but the universe as a whole. For perhaps something might rightfully appear very imperfect if it were all by itself, and yet be most perfect, to the extent that it has the status of a part in the universe. And although subsequent to having decided to doubt everything, I have come to know with certainty only that I and God exist, nevertheless, after having taken note of the immense power of God, I cannot deny that many other things have been made by him, or at least could have been made by him. Thus I may have the status of a part in the universal scheme of things.

Next, as I focus more closely on myself and inquire into the nature of my errors (the only things that are indicative of some imperfection in me), I note that these errors depend on the simultaneous concurrence of two causes: the faculty of knowing that is in me and the faculty of choosing, that is, the free choice of the will, in other words, simultaneously on the intellect and will. Through the intellect alone I merely perceive ideas, about which I can render a judgment. Strictly speaking, no error is to be found in the intellect when properly viewed in this manner. For although perhaps there may exist countless things about which I have no idea, nevertheless it must not be said that, strictly speaking, I am deprived of these ideas but only that I lack them in a negative sense. This is because I cannot adduce an argument to prove that God ought to have given me a greater faculty of knowing than he did. No matter how expert a craftsman I understand him to be, still I do not for that reason believe he ought to have bestowed on each one of his works all the perfections that he can put into some. Nor, on the other hand, can I complain that the will or free choice I have received from God is insufficiently ample or perfect, since I experience that it is limited by no boundaries whatever. In fact, it seems to be especially worth noting that no other things in

57   me are so perfect or so great but that I understand that they can be still more
perfect or greater. If, for example, I consider the faculty of understanding, I
immediately recognize that in my case it is very small and quite limited,
and at the very same time I form an idea of another much greater faculty of
understanding—in fact, an understanding which is consummately great and
infinite; and from the fact that I can form an idea of this faculty, I perceive
that it pertains to the nature of God. Similarly, were I to examine the faculties of memory or imagination, or any of the other faculties, I would understand that in my case each of these is without exception feeble and limited,
whereas in the case of God I understand each faculty to be boundless. It is
only the will or free choice that I experience to be so great in me that I
cannot grasp the idea of any greater faculty. This is so much the case that the
will is the chief basis for my understanding that I bear a certain image and
likeness of God. For although the faculty of willing is incomparably greater
in God than it is in me, both by virtue of the knowledge and power that are
joined to it and that render it more resolute and efficacious and by virtue
of its object inasmuch as the divine will stretches over a greater number of
things, nevertheless, when viewed in itself formally and precisely, God's faculty of willing does not appear to be any greater. This is owing to the fact
that willing is merely a matter of being able to do or not do the same thing,
that is, of being able to affirm or deny, to pursue or to shun; or better still,
the will consists solely in the fact that when something is proposed to us by
our intellect either to affirm or deny, to pursue or to shun, we are moved in
such a way that we sense that we are determined to it by no external force.
In order to be free I need not be capable of being moved in each direction;
on the contrary, the more I am inclined toward one direction—either because
58   I clearly understand that there is in it an aspect of the good and the true, or
because God has thus disposed the inner recesses of my thought—the more
freely do I choose that direction. Nor indeed does divine grace or natural
knowledge ever diminish one's freedom; rather, they increase and strengthen
it. However, the indifference that I experience when there is no reason moving me more in one direction than in another is the lowest grade of freedom;
it is indicative not of any perfection in freedom, but rather of a defect, that
is, a certain negation in knowledge. Were I always to see clearly what is true
and good, I would never deliberate about what is to be judged or chosen. In
that event, although I would be entirely free, I could never be indifferent.

But from these considerations I perceive that the power of willing, which
I got from God, is not, taken by itself, the cause of my errors, for it is most
ample as well as perfect in its kind. Nor is my power of understanding the
cause of my errors. For since I got my power of understanding from God,
whatever I understand I doubtless understand rightly, and it is impossible for
me to be deceived in this. What then is the source of my errors? They are
owing simply to the fact that, since the will extends further than the intellect,

I do not contain the will within the same boundaries; rather, I also extend it to things I do not understand. Because the will is indifferent in regard to such matters, it easily turns away from the true and the good; and in this way I am deceived and I sin.

For example, during these last few days I was examining whether anything in the world exists, and I noticed that, from the very fact that I was making this examination, it obviously followed that I exist. Nevertheless, I could not help judging that what I understood so clearly was true; not that I was coerced into making this judgment because of some external force, but because a great light in my intellect gave way to a great inclination in my will, and the less indifferent I was, the more spontaneously and freely did I believe it. But now, in addition to my knowing that I exist, insofar as I am a certain thinking thing, I also observe a certain idea of corporeal nature. It happens that I am in doubt as to whether the thinking nature which is in me, or rather which I am, is something different from this corporeal nature, or whether both natures are one and the same thing. And I assume that as yet no consideration has occurred to my intellect to convince me of the one alternative rather than the other. Certainly in virtue of this very fact I am indifferent about whether to affirm or to deny either alternative, or even whether to make no judgment at all in the matter.

Moreover, this indifference extends not merely to things about which the intellect knows absolutely nothing, but extends generally to everything of which the intellect does not have a clear enough knowledge at the very time when the will is deliberating on them. For although probable guesses may pull me in one direction, the mere knowledge that they are merely guesses and not certain and indubitable proofs is all it takes to push my assent in the opposite direction. These last few days have provided me with ample experience on this point. For all the beliefs that I had once held to be most true I have supposed to be utterly false, and for the sole reason that I determined that I could somehow raise doubts about them.

But if I hold off from making a judgment when I do not perceive what is true with sufficient clarity and distinctness, it is clear that I am acting properly and am not committing an error. But if instead I were to make an assertion or a denial, then I am not using my freedom properly. Were I to select the alternative that is false, then obviously I will be in error. But were I to embrace the other alternative, it will be by sheer luck that I happen upon the truth; but I will still not be without fault, for it is manifest by the light of nature that a perception on the part of the intellect must always precede a determination on the part of the will. Inherent in this incorrect use of free will is the privation that constitutes the very essence of error: the privation, I say, present in this operation insofar as the operation proceeds from me, but not in the faculty given to me by God, nor even in its operation insofar as it depends upon him.

Indeed, I have no cause for complaint on the grounds that God has not given me a greater power of understanding or a greater light of nature than he has, for it is of the essence of a finite intellect not to understand many things, and it is of the essence of a created intellect to be finite. Actually, instead of thinking that he has withheld from me or deprived me of those things that he has not given me, I ought to thank God, who never owed me anything, for what he has bestowed upon me.

Again, I have no cause for complaint on the grounds that God has given me a will that has a wider scope than my intellect. For since the will consists of merely one thing, something indivisible, as it were, it does not seem that its nature could withstand anything being removed from it. Indeed, the more ample the will is, the more I ought to thank the one who gave it to me.

Finally, I should not complain because God concurs with me in eliciting those acts of the will, that is those judgments, in which I am mistaken. For insofar as those acts depend on God, they are absolutely true and good; and in a certain sense, there is greater perfection in me in being able to elicit those acts than in not being able to do so. But privation, in which alone the

61 defining characteristic of falsehood and wrongdoing is to be found, has no need whatever for God's concurrence, since a privation is not a thing, nor, when it is related to God as its cause, is it to be called a privation, but simply a negation. For it is surely no imperfection in God that he has given me the freedom to give or withhold my assent in those instances where he has not placed a clear and distinct perception in my intellect. But surely it is an imperfection in me that I do not use my freedom well and that I make judgments about things I do not properly understand. Nevertheless, I see that God could easily have brought it about that, while still being free and having finite knowledge, I should nonetheless never make a mistake. This result could have been achieved either by his endowing my intellect with a clear and distinct perception of everything about which I would ever deliberate, or by simply impressing the following rule so firmly upon my memory that I could never forget it: I should never judge anything that I do not clearly and distinctly understand. I readily understand that, considered as a totality, I would have been more perfect than I am now, had God made me that way. But I cannot therefore deny that it may somehow be a greater perfection in the universe as a whole that some of its parts are not immune to error, while others are, than if all of them were exactly alike. And I have no right to complain that the part God has wished me to play is not the principal and most perfect one of all.

Furthermore, even if I cannot abstain from errors in the first way mentioned above, which depends upon a clear perception of everything about which I must deliberate, nevertheless I can avoid error in the other way, which

62 depends solely on my remembering to abstain from making judgments whenever the truth of a given matter is not apparent. For although I experience

a certain infirmity in myself, namely, that I am unable to keep my attention constantly focused on one and the same item of knowledge, nevertheless, by attentive and often repeated meditation, I can bring it about that I call this rule to mind whenever the situation calls for it, and thus I would acquire a certain habit of not erring.

Since herein lies the greatest and chief perfection of man, I think today's meditation, in which I investigated the cause of error and falsity, was quite profitable. Nor can this cause be anything other than the one I have described; for as often as I restrain my will when I make judgments, so that it extends only to those matters that the intellect clearly and distinctly discloses to it, it plainly cannot happen that I err. For every clear and distinct perception is surely something, and hence it cannot come from nothing. On the contrary, it must necessarily have God for its author: God, I say, that supremely perfect being to whom it is repugnant to be a deceiver. Therefore the perception is most assuredly true. Today I have learned not merely what I must avoid so as never to make a mistake, but at the same time what I must do to attain truth. For I will indeed attain it, if only I pay enough attention to all the things that I perfectly understand, and separate them off from the rest, which I apprehend more confusedly and more obscurely. I will be conscientious about this in the future.

MEDITATION FIVE: Concerning the Essence of Material Things, and Again Concerning God, That He Exists

63

Several matters remain for me to examine concerning the attributes of God and myself, that is, concerning the nature of my mind. But perhaps I will take these up at some other time. For now, since I have noted what to avoid and what to do in order to attain the truth, nothing seems more pressing than that I try to free myself from the doubts into which I fell a few days ago, and that I see whether anything certain is to be had concerning material things.

Yet, before inquiring whether any such things exist outside me, I surely ought to consider the ideas of these things, insofar as they exist in my thought, and see which ones are distinct and which ones are confused.

I do indeed distinctly imagine the quantity that philosophers commonly call "continuous," that is, the extension of this quantity, or rather of the thing quantified in length, breadth, and depth. I enumerate the various parts in it. I ascribe to these parts any sizes, shapes, positions, and local movements whatever; to these movements I ascribe any durations whatever.

Not only are these things manifestly known and transparent to me, viewed thus in a general way, but also, when I focus my attention on them, I perceive countless particulars concerning shapes, number, movement, and the like. Their truth is so open and so much in accord with my nature that,

64

when I first discover them, it seems I am not so much learning something new as recalling something I knew beforehand. In other words, it seems as though I am noticing things for the first time that were in fact in me for a long while, although I had not previously directed a mental gaze upon them.

What I believe must be considered above all here is the fact that I find within me countless ideas of certain things, that, even if perhaps they do not exist anywhere outside me, still cannot be said to be nothing. And although, in a sense, I think them at will, nevertheless they are not something I have fabricated; rather they have their own true and immutable natures. For example, when I imagine a triangle, even if perhaps no such figure exists outside my thought anywhere in the world and never has, the triangle still has a certain determinate nature, essence, or form which is unchangeable and eternal, which I did not fabricate, and which does not depend on my mind. This is evident from the fact that various properties can be demonstrated regarding this triangle: namely, that its three angles are equal to two right angles, that its longest side is opposite its largest angle, and so on. These are properties I now clearly acknowledge, whether I want to or not, even if I previously had given them no thought whatever when I imagined the triangle. For this reason, then, they were not fabricated by me.

It is irrelevant for me to say that perhaps the idea of a triangle came to me from external things through the sense organs because of course I have on occasion seen triangle-shaped bodies. For I can think of countless other figures, concerning which there can be no suspicion of their ever having entered *65* me through the senses, and yet I can demonstrate various properties of these figures, no less than I can those of the triangle. All these properties are patently true because I know them clearly, and thus they are something and not merely nothing. For it is obvious that whatever is true is something, and I have already demonstrated at some length that all that I know clearly is true. And even if I had not demonstrated this, certainly the nature of my mind is such that nevertheless I cannot refrain from assenting to these things, at least while I perceive them clearly. And I recall that even before now, when I used to keep my attention glued to the objects of the senses, I always took the truths I clearly recognized regarding figures, numbers, or other things pertaining to arithmetic, geometry, or, in general, to pure and abstract mathematics to be the most certain of all.

But if, from the mere fact that I can bring forth from my thought the idea of something, it follows that all that I clearly and distinctly perceive to belong to that thing really does belong to it, then cannot this too be a basis for an argument proving the existence of God? Clearly the idea of God, that is, the idea of a supremely perfect being, is one I discover to be no less within me than the idea of any figure or number. And that it belongs to God's nature that he always exists is something I understand no less clearly and distinctly than is the case when I demonstrate in regard to some figure or number that something also belongs to the nature of that figure or number. Thus, even if not everything that I have meditated upon during these last few days were true, still the existence of God ought to have for me at least the same degree of certainty that truths of mathematics had until now.

66

However, this point is not wholly obvious at first glance, but has a certain look of a sophism about it. Since in all other matters I have become accustomed to distinguishing existence from essence, I easily convince myself that it can even be separated from God's essence and, hence, that God can be thought of as not existing. But nevertheless, it is obvious to anyone who pays close attention that existence can no more be separated from God's essence than its having three angles equal to two right angles can be separated from the essence of a triangle, or than the idea of a valley can be separated from the idea of a mountain. Thus it is no less[4] contradictory to think of God (that is, a supremely perfect being) lacking existence (that is, lacking some perfection), than it is to think of a mountain without a valley.

But granted I can no more think of God as not existing than I can think of a mountain without a valley, nevertheless it surely does not follow from the fact that I think of a mountain with a valley that a mountain exists in the world. Likewise, from the fact that I think of God as existing, it does not seem to follow that God exists, for my thought imposes no necessity on things. And just as one may imagine a winged horse without there being a horse that has wings, in the same way perhaps I can attach existence to God, even though no God exists.

But there is a sophism lurking here. From the fact that I am unable to think of a mountain without a valley, it does not follow that a mountain or a valley exists anywhere, but only that, whether they exist or not, a mountain and a valley are inseparable from one another. But from the fact that I cannot think of God except as existing, it follows that existence is inseparable from God and that for this reason he really exists. Not that my thought brings this about or imposes any necessity on anything; but rather the necessity of the thing itself, namely, of the existence of God, forces me to think this. For I am not free to think of God without existence, that is, a supremely perfect being without a supreme perfection, as I am to imagine a horse with or without wings.

67

Further, it should not be said here that even though I surely need to assent to the existence of God once I have asserted that God has all perfections and that existence is one of these perfections, nevertheless that earlier assertion need not have been made. Likewise, I need not believe that all four-sided figures can be inscribed in a circle; but given that I posit this, it would then be necessary for me to admit that a rhombus can be inscribed

4. A literal translation of the Latin text (*non magis*) is "no more." This is obviously a misstatement on Descartes' part, since it contradicts his own clearly stated views.

in a circle. Yet this is obviously false. For although it is not necessary that I should ever happen upon any thought of God, nevertheless whenever I am of a mind to think of a being that is first and supreme, and bring forth the idea of God as it were from the storehouse of my mind, I must of necessity ascribe all perfections to him, even if I do not at that time enumerate them all or take notice of each one individually. This necessity plainly suffices so that afterwards, when I realize that existence is a perfection, I rightly conclude that a first and supreme being exists. In the same way, there is no necessity for me ever to imagine a triangle, but whenever I do wish to consider a rectilinear figure having but three angles, I must ascribe to it those

68   properties on the basis of which one rightly infers that the three angles of this figure are no greater than two right angles, even though I do not take note of this at the time. But when I inquire as to the figures that may be inscribed in a circle, there is absolutely no need whatever for my thinking that all four-sided figures are of this sort; for that matter, I cannot even fabricate such a thing, so long as I am of a mind to admit only what I clearly and distinctly understand. Consequently, there is a great difference between false assumptions of this sort and the true ideas that are inborn in me, the first and chief of which is the idea of God. For there are a great many ways in which I understand that this idea is not an invention that is dependent upon my thought, but is an image of a true and immutable nature. First, I cannot think of anything aside from God alone to whose essence existence belongs. Next, I cannot understand how there could be two or more Gods of this kind. Again, once I have asserted that one God now exists, I plainly see that it is necessary that he has existed from eternity and will endure for eternity. Finally, I perceive many other features in God, none of which I can remove or change.

But, whatever type of argument I use, it always comes down to the fact that the only things that fully convince me are those that I clearly and distinctly perceive. And although some of these things I thus perceive are obvious to everyone, while others are discovered only by those who look more closely and inquire carefully, nevertheless, once they have been discovered, they are considered no less certain than the others. For example, in the case

69   of a right triangle, although it is not so readily apparent that the square of the hypotenuse is equal to the sum of the squares of the other two sides as it is that the hypotenuse is opposite the largest angle, nevertheless, once the former has been ascertained, it is no less believed. However, as far as God is concerned, if I were not overwhelmed by prejudices and if the images of sensible things were not besieging my thought from all directions, I would certainly acknowledge nothing sooner or more easily than him. For what, in and of itself, is more manifest than that a supreme being exists, that is, that God, to whose essence alone existence belongs, exists?

And although I needed to pay close attention in order to perceive this, nevertheless I now am just as certain about this as I am about everything else that seems most certain. Moreover, I observe also that certitude about other things is so dependent on this, that without it nothing can ever be perfectly known.

For I am indeed of such a nature that, while I perceive something very clearly and distinctly, I cannot help believing it to be true. Nevertheless, my nature is also such that I cannot focus my mental gaze always on the same thing, so as to perceive it clearly. Often the memory of a previously made judgment may return when I am no longer attending to the arguments on account of which I made such a judgment. Thus, other arguments can be brought forward that would easily make me change my opinion, were I ignorant of God. And thus I would never have true and certain knowledge about anything, but merely fickle and changeable opinions. Thus, for example, when I consider the nature of a triangle, it appears most evident to me, steeped as I am in the principles of geometry, that its three angles are equal to two right angles. And so long as I attend to its demonstration I cannot help believing this to be true. But no sooner do I turn the mind's eye away from the demonstration, than, however much I still recall that I had observed it most clearly, nevertheless, it can easily happen that I entertain doubts about whether it is true, were I ignorant of God. For I can convince myself that I have been so constituted by nature that I might occasionally be mistaken about those things I believe I perceive most evidently, especially when I recall that I have often taken many things to be true and certain, which other arguments have subsequently led me to judge to be false. 70

But once I perceived that there is a God, and also understood at the same time that everything else depends on him and that he is not a deceiver, I then concluded that everything that I clearly and distinctly perceive is necessarily true. Hence even if I no longer attend to the reasons leading me to judge this to be true, so long as I merely recall that I did clearly and distinctly observe it, no counterargument can be brought forward that might force me to doubt it. On the contrary, I have a true and certain knowledge of it. And not just of this one fact, but of everything else that I recall once having demonstrated, as in geometry, and so on. For what objections can now be raised against me? That I have been made such that I am often mistaken? But I now know that I cannot be mistaken in matters I plainly understand. That I have taken many things to be true and certain which subsequently I recognized to be false? But none of these were things I clearly and distinctly perceived. But I was ignorant of this rule for determining the truth, and I believed these things perhaps for other reasons, which I later discovered were less firm. What then remains to be said? That perhaps I am dreaming, as I recently objected against myself, in other words, that everything I am now

thinking of is no truer than what occurs to someone who is asleep? Be that
as it may, this changes nothing; for certainly, even if I were dreaming, if any-
71   thing is evident to my intellect, then it is entirely true.

And thus I see plainly that the certainty and truth of every science depends
exclusively upon the knowledge of the true God, to the extent that, prior
to my becoming aware of him, I was incapable of achieving perfect knowledge about anything else. But now it is possible for me to achieve full and
certain knowledge about countless things, both about God and other intellectual matters, as well as about the entirety of that corporeal nature which
is the object of pure mathematics.

MEDITATION SIX: Concerning the Existence of Material Things, and the Real Distinction between Mind and Body

It remains for me to examine whether material things exist. Indeed I now
know that they can exist, at least insofar as they are the object of pure mathematics, since I clearly and distinctly perceive them. For no doubt God is
capable of bringing about everything that I am capable of perceiving in this
way. And I have never judged that God was incapable of something, except
when it was incompatible with my perceiving it distinctly. Moreover, from
the faculty of imagination, which I notice I use while dealing with material
things, it seems to follow that they exist. For to anyone paying very close
72   attention to what imagination is, it appears to be simply a certain application
of the knowing faculty to a body intimately present to it, and which therefore exists.

To make this clear, I first examine the difference between imagination
and pure intellection. So, for example, when I imagine a triangle, I not only
understand that it is a figure bounded by three lines, but at the same time I
also envisage with the mind's eye those lines as if they were present; and this
is what I call "imagining." On the other hand, if I want to think about a
chiliagon, I certainly understand that it is a figure consisting of a thousand
sides, just as well as I understand that a triangle is a figure consisting of three
sides, yet I do not imagine those thousand sides in the same way, or envisage them as if they were present. And although in that case, because of force
of habit I always imagine something whenever I think about a corporeal
thing, I may perchance represent to myself some figure in a confused fashion,
nevertheless this figure is obviously not a chiliagon. For this figure is really
no different from the figure I would represent to myself, were I thinking of
a myriagon or any other figure with a large number of sides. Nor is this
figure of any help in knowing the properties that differentiate a chiliagon
from other polygons. But if the figure in question is a pentagon, I surely can
understand its figure, just as was the case with the chiliagon, without the help

of my imagination. But I can also imagine a pentagon by turning the mind's eye both to its five sides and at the same time to the area bounded by those sides. At this point I am manifestly aware that I am in need of a peculiar sort of effort on the part of the mind in order to imagine, one that I do not   73 employ in order to understand. This new effort on the part of the mind clearly shows the difference between imagination and pure intellection.

Moreover, I consider that this power of imagining that is in me, insofar as it differs from the power of understanding, is not required for my own essence, that is, the essence of my mind. For were I to be lacking this power, I would nevertheless undoubtedly remain the same entity I am now. Thus it seems to follow that the power of imagining depends upon something distinct from me. And I readily understand that, were a body to exist to which a mind is so joined that it may apply itself in order, as it were, to look at it any time it wishes, it could happen that it is by means of this very body that I imagine corporeal things. As a result, this mode of thinking may differ from pure intellection only in the sense that the mind, when it understands, in a sense turns toward itself and looks at one of the ideas that are in it; whereas when it imagines, it turns toward the body and intuits in the body something that conforms to an idea either understood by the mind or perceived by sense. To be sure, I easily understand that the imagination can be actualized in this way, provided a body does exist. And since I can think of no other way of explaining imagination that is equally appropriate, I make a probable conjecture from this that a body exists. But this is only a probability. And even though I may examine everything carefully, nevertheless I do not yet see how the distinct idea of corporeal nature that I find in my imagination can enable me to develop an argument which necessarily concludes that some body exists.

But I am in the habit of imagining many other things over and above that   74 corporeal nature which is the object of pure mathematics, such as colors, sounds, tastes, pain, and the like, though not so distinctly. And I perceive these things better by means of the senses, from which, with the aid of the memory, they seem to have arrived at the imagination. Thus I should pay the same degree of attention to the senses, so that I might deal with them more appropriately. I must see whether I can obtain any reliable argument for the existence of corporeal things from those things that are perceived by the mode of thinking that I call "sense."

First of all, to be sure, I will review here all the things I previously believed to be true because I had perceived them by means of the senses and the causes I had for thinking this. Next I will assess the causes why I later called them into doubt. Finally, I will consider what I must now believe about these things.

So first, I sensed that I had a head, hands, feet, and other members that comprised this body which I viewed as part of me, or perhaps even as the whole of me. I sensed that this body was found among many other bodies, by which my body can be affected in various beneficial or harmful ways. I gauged what was opportune by means of a certain sensation of pleasure, and what was inopportune by a sensation of pain. In addition to pain and pleasure, I also sensed within me hunger, thirst, and other such appetites, as well as certain bodily tendencies toward mirth, sadness, anger, and other such affects. And externally, besides the extension, shapes, and motions of bodies, I also sensed their hardness, heat, and other tactile qualities. I also sensed light, colors, odors, tastes, and sounds, on the basis of whose variety I distinguished the sky, the earth, the seas, and the other bodies, one from the other. Now given the ideas of all these qualities that presented themselves to my thought, and which were all that I properly and immediately sensed, still it was surely not without reason that I thought I sensed things that were manifestly different from my thought, namely, the bodies from which these ideas proceeded. For I knew by experience that these ideas came upon me utterly without my consent, to the extent that, wish as I may, I could not sense any object unless it was present to a sense organ. Nor could I fail to sense it when it was present. And since the ideas perceived by sense were much more vivid and explicit and even, in their own way, more distinct than any of those that I deliberately and knowingly formed through meditation or that I found impressed on my memory, it seemed impossible that they came from myself. Thus the remaining alternative was that they came from other things. Since I had no knowledge of such things except from those same ideas themselves, I could not help entertaining the thought that they were similar to those ideas. Moreover, I also recalled that the use of the senses antedated the use of reason. And since I saw that the ideas that I myself fashioned were not as explicit as those that I perceived through the faculty of sense and were for the most part composed of parts of the latter, I easily convinced myself that I had absolutely no idea in the intellect that I did not have beforehand in the sense faculty. Not without reason did I judge that this body, which by a certain special right I called "mine," belongs more to me than did any other. For I could never be separated from it in the same way I could be from other bodies. I sensed all appetites and feelings in and on behalf of it. Finally, I noticed pain and pleasurable excitement in its parts, but not in other bodies external to it. But why should a certain sadness of spirit arise from some sensation or other of pain, and why should a certain elation arise from a sensation of excitement, or why should that peculiar twitching in the stomach, which I call hunger, warn me to have something to eat, or why should dryness in the throat warn me to take something to drink, and so on? I plainly had no explanation other than that I had been taught this way by nature. For there is no affinity whatsoever, at least none I am aware of, between this twitching in the stomach and the will to have something to eat, or between the sensation of something causing pain and the thought of sadness arising from this sensation. But nature also seems to have taught me everything else as well that I judged concerning the objects of the senses, for I had already convinced myself that this was how things were, prior to my assessing any of the arguments that might prove it.

Afterwards, however, many experiences gradually weakened any faith that I had in the senses. Towers that had seemed round from afar occasionally appeared square at close quarters. Very large statues mounted on their pedestals did not seem large to someone looking at them from ground level. And in countless other such instances I determined that judgments in matters of the external senses were in error. And not just the external senses, but the inter- 77
nal senses as well. For what can be more intimate than pain? But I had some-
times heard it said by people whose leg or arm had been amputated that it seemed to them that they still occasionally sensed pain in the very limb they had lost. Thus, even in my own case it did not seem to be entirely certain that some bodily member was causing me pain, even though I did sense pain in it. To these causes for doubt I recently added two quite general ones. The first was that everything I ever thought I sensed while awake I could believe I also sometimes sensed while asleep, and since I do not believe that what I seem to sense in my dreams comes to me from things external to me, I saw no reason why I should hold this belief about those things I seem to be sensing while awake. The second was that, since I was still ignorant of the author of my origin (or at least pretended to be ignorant of it), I saw nothing to prevent my having been so constituted by nature that I should be mistaken even about what seemed to me most true. As to the arguments that used to convince me of the truth of sensible things, I found no difficulty responding to them. For since I seemed driven by nature toward many things about which reason tried to dissuade me, I did not think that what I was taught by nature deserved much credence. And even though the perceptions of the senses did not depend on my will, I did not think that we must therefore conclude that they came from things distinct from me, since perhaps there is some faculty in me, as yet unknown to me, that produces these perceptions.

But now, having begun to have a better knowledge of myself and the author of my origin, I am of the opinion that I must not rashly admit everything that I seem to derive from the senses; but neither, for that matter, 78
should I call everything into doubt.

First, I know that all the things that I clearly and distinctly understand can be made by God such as I understand them. For this reason, my ability clearly and distinctly to understand one thing without another suffices to make me certain that the one thing is different from the other, since they can be separated from each other, at least by God. The question as to the sort of power that might effect such a separation is not relevant to their being thought to be different. For this reason, from the fact that I know that I exist and that at the same time I judge that obviously nothing else belongs to my nature or essence except that I am a thinking thing, I rightly conclude that my essence consists entirely in my being a thinking thing. And although perhaps (or rather, as I shall soon say, assuredly) I have a body that is very closely joined to me, nevertheless, because on the one hand I have a clear and distinct idea of myself, insofar as I am merely a thinking thing and not an extended thing, and because on the other hand I have a distinct idea of a body, insofar as it is merely an extended thing and not a thinking thing, it is certain that I am really distinct from my body and can exist without it.

Moreover, I find in myself faculties for certain special modes of thinking, namely, the faculties of imagining and sensing. I can clearly and distinctly understand myself in my entirety without these faculties, but not vice versa: I cannot understand them clearly and distinctly without me, that is, without a substance endowed with understanding in which they inhere, for they include an act of understanding in their formal concept. Thus I perceive them to be distinguished from me as modes from a thing. I also acknowledge that there are certain other faculties, such as those of moving from one place to another, of taking on various shapes, and so on, that, like sensing or imag-
79 ining, cannot be understood apart from some substance in which they inhere, and hence without which they cannot exist. But it is clear that these faculties, if in fact they exist, must be in a corporeal or extended substance, not in a substance endowed with understanding. For some extension is contained in a clear and distinct concept of them, though certainly not any understanding. Now there clearly is in me a passive faculty of sensing, that is, a faculty for receiving and knowing the ideas of sensible things; but I could not use it unless there also existed, either in me or in something else, a certain active faculty of producing or bringing about these ideas. But this faculty surely cannot be in me, since it clearly presupposes no act of understanding, and these ideas are produced without my cooperation and often even against my will. Therefore the only alternative is that it is in some substance different from me, containing either formally or eminently all the reality that exists objectively in the ideas produced by that faculty, as I have just noted above. Hence this substance is either a body, that is, a corporeal nature, which contains formally all that is contained objectively in the ideas, or else it is God, or some other creature more noble than a body, which contains eminently all that is contained objectively in the ideas. But since God is not a deceiver, it is patently obvious that he does not send me these ideas either immediately by himself, or even through the mediation of some creature that contains the objective reality of these ideas not formally but only eminently. For since God has given me no faculty whatsoever for
80 making this determination, but instead has given me a great inclination to believe that these ideas issue from corporeal things, I fail to see how God could be understood not to be a deceiver, if these ideas were to issue from

a source other than corporeal things. And, consequently, corporeal things exist. Nevertheless, perhaps not all bodies exist exactly as I grasp them by sense, since this sensory grasp is in many cases very obscure and confused. But at least they do contain everything I clearly and distinctly understand— that is, everything, considered in a general sense, that is encompassed in the object of pure mathematics.

As far as the remaining matters are concerned, which are either merely particular (for example, that the sun is of such and such a size or shape, and so on) or less clearly understood (for example, light, sound, pain, and the like), even though these matters are very doubtful and uncertain, nevertheless the fact that God is no deceiver (and thus no falsity can be found in my opinions, unless there is also in me a faculty given me by God for the purpose of rectifying this falsity) offers me a definite hope of reaching the truth even in these matters. And surely there is no doubt that all that I am taught by nature has some truth to it; for by "nature," taken generally, I understand nothing other than God himself or the ordered network of created things which was instituted by God. By my own particular nature I understand nothing other than the combination of all the things bestowed upon me by God.

There is nothing that this nature teaches me more explicitly than that I have a body that is ill disposed when I feel pain, that needs food and drink when I suffer hunger or thirst, and the like. Therefore, I should not doubt that there is some truth in this.

By means of these sensations of pain, hunger, thirst, and so on, nature also teaches that I am present in my body not merely in the way a sailor is present in a ship, but that I am most tightly joined and, so to speak, commingled with it, so much so that I and the body constitute one single thing. For if this were not the case, then I, who am only a thinking thing, would not sense pain when the body is injured; rather, I would perceive the wound by means of the pure intellect, just as a sailor perceives by sight whether anything in his ship is broken. And when the body is in need of food or drink, I should understand this explicitly, instead of having confused sensations of hunger and thirst. For clearly these sensations of thirst, hunger, pain, and so on are nothing but certain confused modes of thinking arising from the union and, as it were, the commingling of the mind with the body.

Moreover, I am also taught by nature that various other bodies exist around my body, some of which are to be pursued, while others are to be avoided. And to be sure, from the fact that I sense a wide variety of colors, sounds, odors, tastes, levels of heat, and grades of roughness, and the like, I rightly conclude that in the bodies from which these different perceptions of the senses proceed there are differences corresponding to the different perceptions—though perhaps the latter do not resemble the former. And from the fact that some of these perceptions are pleasant while others are unpleasant,

81

it is plainly certain that my body, or rather my whole self, insofar as I am comprised of a body and a mind, can be affected by various beneficial and harmful bodies in the vicinity.

82   Granted, there are many other things that I seem to have been taught by nature; nevertheless it was not really nature that taught them to me but a certain habit of making reckless judgments. And thus it could easily happen that these judgments are false: for example, that any space where there is absolutely nothing happening to move my senses is empty; or that there is something in a hot body that bears an exact likeness to the idea of heat that is in me; or that in a white or green body there is the same whiteness or greenness that I sense; or that in a bitter or sweet body there is the same taste, and so on; or that stars and towers and any other distant bodies have the same size and shape that they present to my senses, and other things of this sort. But to ensure that my perceptions in this matter are sufficiently distinct, I ought to define more precisely what exactly I mean when I say that I am "taught something by nature." For I am taking "nature" here more narrowly than the combination of everything bestowed on me by God. For this combination embraces many things that belong exclusively to my mind, such as my perceiving that what has been done cannot be undone, and everything else that is known by the light of nature. That is not what I am talking about here. There are also many things that belong exclusively to the body, such as that it tends to move downward, and so on. I am not dealing with these either, but only with what God has bestowed on me insofar as I am composed of mind and body. Accordingly, it is this nature that teaches me to avoid things that produce a sensation of pain and to pursue things that produce a sensation of pleasure, and the like. But it does not appear that nature teaches us to conclude anything, besides these things, from these sense perceptions unless the intellect has first conducted its own inquiry regard-

83   ing things external to us. For it seems to belong exclusively to the mind, and not to the composite of mind and body, to know the truth in these matters. Thus, although a star affects my eye no more than does the flame from a small torch, still there is no real or positive tendency in my eye toward believing that the star is no larger than the flame. Yet, ever since my youth, I have made this judgment without any reason for doing so. And although I feel heat as I draw closer to the fire, and I also feel pain upon drawing too close to it, there is not a single argument that persuades me that there is something in the fire similar to that heat, any more than to that pain. On the contrary, I am convinced only that there is something in the fire that, regardless of what it finally turns out to be, causes in us those sensations of heat or pain. And although there may be nothing in a given space that moves the senses, it does not therefore follow that there is no body in it. But I see that in these any many other instances I have been in the habit of subverting the order of nature. For admittedly I use the perceptions of the senses (which are

properly given by nature only for signifying to the mind what things are useful or harmful to the composite of which it is a part, and to that extent they are clear and distinct enough), as reliable rules for immediately discerning what is the essence of bodies located outside us. Yet they signify nothing about that except quite obscurely and confusedly.

I have already examined in sufficient detail how it could happen that my judgments are false, despite the goodness of God. But a new difficulty now arises regarding those very things that nature shows me are either to be sought out or avoided, as well as the internal sensations where I seem to have detected errors, as for example, when someone is deluded by a food's pleasant taste to eat the poison hidden inside it. In this case, however, he is   *84* driven by nature only toward desiring the thing in which the pleasurable taste is found, but not toward the poison, of which he obviously is unaware. I can only conclude that this nature is not omniscient. This is not remarkable, since man is a limited thing, and thus only what is of limited perfection befits him.

But we not infrequently err even in those things to which nature impels us. Take, for example, the case of those who are ill and who desire food or drink that will soon afterwards be injurious to them. Perhaps it could be said here that they erred because their nature was corrupt. However, this does not remove our difficulty, for a sick man is no less a creature of God than a healthy one, and thus it seems no less inconsistent that the sick man got a deception-prone nature from God. And a clock made of wheels and counterweights follows all the laws of nature no less closely when it has been badly constructed and does not tell time accurately than it does when it completely satisfies the wish of its maker. Likewise, I might regard a man's body as a kind of mechanism that is outfitted with and composed of bones, nerves, muscles, veins, blood, and skin in such a way that, even if no mind existed in it, the man's body would still exhibit all the same motions that are in it now except for those motions that proceed either from a command of the will or, consequently, from the mind. I easily recognize that it would be natural for this body, were it, say, suffering from dropsy and experiencing dryness in the throat (which typically produces a thirst sensation in the mind), and also so disposed by its nerves and other parts to take something to drink, the result of which would be to exacerbate the illness. This is as natural as for a body without any such illness to be moved by the same dryness   *85* in the throat to take something to drink that is useful to it. And given the intended purpose of the clock, I could say that it deviates from its nature when it fails to tell the right time. And similarly, considering the mechanism of the human body in terms of its being equipped for the motions that typically occur in it, I may think that it too is deviating from its nature, if its throat were dry when having something to drink is not beneficial to its conservation. Nevertheless, I am well aware that this last use of "nature" differs greatly from the other. For this latter "nature" is merely a designation dependent on my thought, since it compares a man in poor health and a poorly constructed clock with the ideas of a healthy man and of a well-made clock, a designation extrinsic to the things to which it is applied. But by "nature" taken in the former sense, I understand something that is really in things and thus is not without some truth.

When we say, then, in the case of the body suffering from dropsy, that its "nature" is corrupt, given the fact that it has a parched throat and yet does not need something to drink, "nature" obviously is merely an extrinsic designation. Nevertheless, in the case of the composite, that is, of a mind joined to such a body, it is not a mere designation, but a true error of nature that this body should be thirsty when having something to drink would be harmful to it. It therefore remains to inquire here how the goodness of God does not prevent "nature," thus considered, from being deceptive.

Now my first observation here is that there is a great difference between a mind and a body, in that a body, by its very nature, is always divisible. On 86 the other hand, the mind is utterly indivisible. For when I consider the mind, that is, myself insofar as I am only a thinking thing, I cannot distinguish any parts within me; rather, I understand myself to be manifestly one complete thing. Although the entire mind seems to be united to the entire body, nevertheless, were a foot or an arm or any other bodily part to be amputated, I know that nothing has been taken away from the mind on that account. Nor can the faculties of willing, sensing, understanding, and so on be called "parts" of the mind, since it is one and the same mind that wills, senses, and understands. On the other hand, there is no corporeal or extended thing I can think of that I may not in my thought easily divide into parts; and in this way I understand that it is divisible. This consideration alone would suffice to teach me that the mind is wholly diverse from the body, had I not yet known it well enough in any other way.

My second observation is that my mind is not immediately affected by all the parts of the body but only by the brain or, perhaps, even by just one small part of the brain, namely, by that part where the "common" sense is said to reside. Whenever this part of the brain is disposed in the same manner, it presents the same thing to the mind, even if the other parts of the body are able meanwhile to be related in diverse ways. Countless experiments show this, none of which need be reviewed here.

My next observation is that the nature of the body is such that whenever any of its parts can be moved by another part some distance away, it can also be moved in the same manner by any of the parts that lie between them, 87 even if this more distant part is doing nothing. For example, in the cord ABCD, if the final part D is pulled, the first part A would be moved in exactly the same manner as it could be if one of the intermediate parts B or C were pulled while the end part D remained immobile. Likewise, when I feel a pain in my foot, physics teaches me that this sensation took place by means of nerves distributed throughout the foot, like stretched cords extending from the foot all the way to the brain. When these nerves are pulled in the foot, they also pull on the inner parts of the brain to which they extend, and produce a certain motion in them. This motion has been constituted by nature so as to affect the mind with a sensation of pain, as if it occurred in the foot. But because these nerves need to pass through the shin, thigh, loins, back, and neck to get from the foot to the brain, it can happen that even if it is not the part in the foot, but merely one of the intermediate parts that is being struck, the very same movement will occur in the brain that would occur were the foot badly injured. The inevitable result will be that the mind feels the same pain. The same opinion should hold for any other sensation.

My final observation is that, since any given motion occurring in that part of the brain immediately affecting the mind produces but one sensation in it, I can think of no better arrangement than that it produces the one sensation that, of all the ones it is able to produce, is most especially and most often conducive to the maintenance of a healthy man. Moreover, experience shows that all the sensations bestowed on us by nature are like this. Hence there is absolutely nothing to be found in them that does not bear witness to God's power and goodness. Thus, for example, when the nerves in the foot are agitated in a violent and unusual manner, this motion of theirs extends through the marrow of the spine to the inner reaches of the brain, where it gives the mind the sign to sense something, namely, the pain as if it is occurring in the foot. This provokes the mind to do its utmost to move away from the cause of the pain, since it is seen as harmful to the foot. But the nature of man could have been so constituted by God that this same motion in the brain might have indicated something else to the mind: for example, either the motion itself as it occurs in the brain, or in the foot, or in some place in between, or something else entirely different. But nothing else would have served so well the maintenance of the body. Similarly, when we need something to drink, a certain dryness arises in the throat that moves the nerves in the throat, and, by means of them, the inner parts of the brain. And this motion affects the mind with a sensation of thirst, because in this entire affair nothing is more useful for us to know than that we need something to drink in order to maintain our health; the same holds in the other cases.

From these considerations it is utterly apparent that, notwithstanding the immense goodness of God, the nature of man, insofar as it is composed of mind and body, cannot help being sometimes mistaken. For if some cause, not in the foot but in some other part through which the nerves extend from the foot to the brain, or perhaps even in the brain itself, were to produce the same motion that would normally be produced by a badly injured foot, the pain will be felt as if it were in the foot, and the senses will naturally be deceived. For since an identical motion in the brain can only bring about an identical sensation in the mind, and it is more frequently the case that this motion is wont to arise on account of a cause that harms the foot than on account of some other thing existing elsewhere, it is reasonable that the motion should always show pain to the mind as something belonging to the foot rather than to some other part. And if dryness in the throat does not arise, as is normal, from drink's contributing to bodily health, but from a contrary cause, as happens in the case of someone with dropsy, then it is far better that it should deceive on that occasion than that it should always be deceptive when the body is in good health. The same holds for the other cases.

This consideration is most helpful, not only for my noticing all the errors to which my nature is liable but also for enabling me to correct or avoid them without difficulty. To be sure, I know that all the senses set forth what is true more frequently than what is false regarding what concerns the welfare of the body. Moreover, I can nearly always make use of several of them in order to examine the same thing. Furthermore, I can use my memory, which connects current happenings with past ones, and my intellect, which now has examined all the causes of error. Hence I should no longer fear that those things that are daily shown me by the senses are false. On the contrary, the hyperbolic doubts of the last few days ought to be rejected as ludicrous. This goes especially for the chief reason for doubting, which dealt with my failure to distinguish being asleep from being awake. For I now notice that there is a considerable difference between these two; dreams are never joined by the memory with all the other actions of life, as is the case with those actions that occur when one is awake. For surely, if, while I am awake, someone were suddenly to appear to me and then immediately disappear, as occurs in dreams, so that I see neither where he came from nor where he went, it is not without reason that I would judge him to be a ghost or a phantom conjured up in my brain, rather than a true man. But when these things happen, and I notice distinctly where they come from, where they are now, and when they come to me, and when I connect my perception of them without interruption with the whole rest of my life, I am clearly certain that these perceptions have happened to me not while I was dreaming but while I was awake. Nor ought I have even the least doubt regarding the truth of these things, if, having mustered all the senses, in addition to my memory and my intellect, in order to examine them, nothing is passed on to me by one of these sources that conflicts with the others. For from the fact that God is no deceiver, it follows that I am in no way mistaken in these matters. But because the need to get things done does not always permit us the leisure for such a careful inquiry, we must confess that the life of man is apt to commit errors regarding particular things, and we must acknowledge the infirmity of our nature.

OBJECTIONS BY SOME LEARNED MEN TO THE PRECEDING MEDITATIONS, WITH REPLIES BY THE AUTHOR

First Set of Objections

Gentlemen:[1]

When I[2] realized that you were absolutely resolved that I should examine more deeply the writings of M. Descartes, I could not help complying in this matter with men who have been so particularly friendly to me. I am complying with this request both so that you may see how great is my esteem for you and so that it may be apparent how much my powers and acumen fall short, with the result that you might both give me greater support in the future, if I need it, and hold me less accountable, if I am not up to the task.

As I see it, M. Descartes is clearly a man whose intelligence is without match and whose moderation is unrivaled—traits that even Momus[3] would cherish, were he alive today. I think, says M. Descartes, therefore I exist. In fact, I am that very thought or mind. So be it. Moreover, in thinking, I have the ideas of things within me, and, above all, an idea of a most perfect and infinite being. I will grant this as well. But I, who do not equal the objective reality of this idea, am not the cause of this idea. Therefore the cause of this idea is something more perfect than me. Hence there exists something other than myself. There exists something more perfect than me. There exists someone who is a being not in some restricted fashion or other, but who embraces in himself all being equally and without qualification or limitation, and is, as it were, an anticipatory cause, as Dionysius[4] declares in his *On Divine Names,* Chapter Eight.

Selections on pp. 51–153 and 162–80 translated by Donald Cress.

1. This set of objections is addressed to two friends of Descartes, Ban (Bannius in Latin) and Bloemaert. Both of these individuals were canons of the chapter of Harlem. More information on the objectors, with analyses of their objections and Descartes' replies, can be found in the various essays collected in Ariew and Grene.

2. Johan de Kater (1590–1655), whose latinized name was Johannes Caterus, was a Catholic priest and theologian at Alkmaar, Holland. Bannius and Bloemaert had forwarded to Caterus prepublication copies of Descartes' *Meditations on First Philosophy* together with the request that he provide comments and objections, which Descartes would publish along with his replies.

3. Greek god of censure and mockery.

4. A late neo-Platonic writer whose works were for a long time mistakenly thought to be those of the Dionysius the Areopagite mentioned in Acts 17:34; hence this writer is often referred to as (the) Pseudo-Dionysius.

But I am compelled to stop here for a short while, lest I become utterly exhausted. For, just like the billowing Euripus,[5] my mind is in a whirl. I affirm, I deny, I approve, and again I disapprove. I do not want to disagree with the man, yet I cannot agree with him. Indeed, I ask, what cause does an idea require? Or what, pray, is an idea? It is the very thing thought insofar as it exists objectively in the intellect. But what is it to exist objectively in the intellect? I was once taught that to exist objectively is to terminate the act of the intellect after the manner of an object. This characterization is surely an extrinsic denomination and it has no bearing on the thing itself. For just as being seen is simply an act of seeing terminating in me, so, being thought or existing objectively in the intellect is an act of thinking on the part of the mind stopping at and terminating in itself. This process can occur whether the thing be motionless or unchanged, nay even nonexistent. Why, therefore, do I seek the cause of what is not actual, of what is a mere denomination, of what is nothing?

Nevertheless, this great genius declares "that this idea contains this as opposed to that objective reality is surely owing to some cause. . ."[6] In point of fact, it gets it from no cause at all, for objective reality is just a pure denomination and is nothing actual, whereas a cause imparts a real and actual influence. What is not actual does not receive anything and thus does not undergo the actual influence of a cause, nor does it need to. Thus I grant that I have ideas but not that ideas have a cause, let alone a cause that is greater than me and infinite.

But if you do not grant that ideas have a cause, then at least state some reason why this idea has this objective reality rather than that objective reality. A point well taken, for I am not in the habit of being tightfisted with friends; on the contrary, I am quite openhanded. I declare universally with respect to all ideas what M. Descartes has said elsewhere regarding the triangle: ". . . even if perhaps," he says, "no such figure exists outside my thought anywhere in the world and never has, the triangle still has a certain determinate nature, essence, or form which is immutable and eternal. . ." It is, to be sure, an eternal truth, which requires no cause. A boat is a boat and not something else; Davus is Davus and not Oedipus.[7] If, however, you insist on a reason, it is the imperfection of our intellect, which is not infinite. For since our intellect does not comprehend the entire universe all at once in a single grasp, the intellect divides and separates every good; and thus, what

93

---

5. A narrow strait in the Aegean Sea between the island of Euboea and the Greek mainland. Its strong tidal currents change directions several times a day.

6. When a passage is cited verbatim or nearly verbatim, quotation marks are used. Quotation marks are not used when a passage is merely paraphrased.

7. Caterus gilds the lily somewhat in alluding to Terence, *Andria,* Act I, Scene ii, line 194. In this passage the slave Davus, vexed by a somewhat enigmatic question, declares in frustration that "I am Davus, not Oedipus"—his point being that he is neither a mind reader nor a guesser of riddles.

it cannot bring forth whole it conceives by degrees, or, as they also say, "inadequately."

The gentleman continues further: "Yet as imperfect a mode of being as this is by which a thing exists in the intellect objectively through an idea, nevertheless it is plainly not nothing; hence it cannot get its being from nothing." There is an equivocation here. For if "nothing" means the same thing as a being that is not actual, then it is absolutely nothing, because it is not actual and thus is from nothing, that is, it is not derived from some cause. But if "nothing" means something conjured up in the mind (that is, something traditionally called a "being of reason"), then it is not nothing, but something real that is distinctly conceived. Nevertheless, though it can indeed be conceived, it can hardly be caused, since it is merely conceived and is not actual.

But ". . . it is appropriate to ask further whether I myself who have this idea could exist, if such a being did not exist, namely the source from which proceeds the idea of a being more perfect than myself," as he states just prior to this. "From what source, then," he says, "do I derive my existence? Why, from myself, or from my parents, or from whatever other things . . . But if I got my being from myself, I would not doubt, I would not hope, nor would I lack anything at all. For I would have given myself all the perfections of which I have some idea; in so doing, I would myself be God!" But if I am derived from something else, I would eventually arrive at something that is derived from itself. Now precisely the same line of reasoning applies to it as applies to me. This is precisely the very same way that St. Thomas[8] follows and which he calls his way "from the causality of the efficient cause."[9] He picked this up from the Philosopher;[10] however, neither of them is concerned with the causes of ideas. And perhaps there was no need for such concern. After all, should I not advance by a straight and narrow way? I think, therefore I am—to the extent that I am a mind and an act of thinking. However, this mind, this act of thinking, is derived either from itself or from something else. If the latter, from what further source is that something else derived? If it is derived from itself, then it is God, for what is derived from itself would easily confer all things upon itself.

I implore and entreat the gentleman not to hide himself from a reader who is eager and is perhaps of inferior intellect. "From itself" is understood in two senses. The first is the positive sense, namely "from itself as from a

94

95

8. St. Thomas Aquinas (1225?–74), sometimes referred to as the "Doctor Angelicus" for his writings on the theology of angels, was a Dominican theologian and philosopher who is one of the principal figures in medieval thought. Even during his lifetime, no little controversy arose in response to Aquinas' extensive use of newly translated writings of Aristotle to help explicate Christian beliefs.

9. *Summa Theologiae* I, Q. 2, a. 3, corpus.

10. Aristotle.

cause." Thus what is derived from itself would give its own existence to itself. If by a prior choice it should give itself whatever it wanted, then it undoubtedly would give itself everything, and would thus be God. In the second sense, "from itself" is taken negatively; it means the same thing as "by itself" or "not from another." And, as I recall, everyone understands "from itself" in this latter sense.

But if something is derived from itself (that is to say, not from something else), how am I to prove that it encompasses all things and that it is infinite? For I do not follow you now when you say: if it is derived from itself, it would easily have given itself all things. For neither is it derived from itself as from a cause, nor did it exist prior to itself in such a way that it would chose beforehand what it would later be. I know I once heard Suárez[11] declare that every limitation is derived from a cause. Thus a thing is limited and finite because its cause either could not or would not give anything greater and more perfect. If, therefore, something is derived from itself and not from a cause, it is truly unlimited and infinite.

But I am not really in total agreement with this. For what if the limitation were derived from intrinsic constitutive principles, that is to say, from the very form and essence—which you nevertheless have not yet proved to be infinite, even if the thing is derived from itself, that is to say, not from something else? Clearly something hot (if you suppose that there is something hot) will be hot—and not cold—by virtue of intrinsic constitutive principles, even if you were to imagine that the very object itself which exists is derived from nothing. I have every confidence that M. Descartes is not without arguments to support what others perhaps have not established with sufficient clarity.

At last there is agreement between myself and the gentleman. He declares the following as a general rule: whatever I clearly and distinctly know is obviously a true being.[12] Indeed, whatever I think is true. For almost from our youth we banned all chimeras and any being of reason. For no power can deviate from its proper object: if the will is moved, it tends toward the good. Nor indeed do the senses themselves err, for sight sees what it sees and the ear hears what it hears. If you see brass, you see rightly; but you are mistaken when in your judgment you decide that what you see is gold. Thus M. Descartes most appropriately attributes every error to judgment and to the will.

---

11. Francisco Suárez (1548–1617). Spanish Jesuit theologian of the Counter-Reformation who was perhaps best known for his treatises in political philosophy. In addition to lengthy commentaries on Aquinas' *Summa Theologiae*, Suárez also wrote the *Metaphysical Disputations*. The manner of exposition employed in this latter work marked a substantial innovation in philosophical style. A selection from the *Disputations* of particular relevance to Descartes, can be found in Ariew, Cottingham, and Sorell, pp. 29–50.

12. The text cited actually says: "everything I very clearly and distinctly perceive is true."

But I now gather from this rule what you had in mind. I clearly and distinctly know an infinite being; therefore it is a true being and is something. But someone will ask: do you clearly and distinctly know an infinite being? What then does he make of the traditional commonplace that "the infinite qua infinite is unknown"? For if, when I think about a chiliagon and confusedly represent to myself some figure, I do not distinctly imagine or know a chiliagon, because I do not distinctly intuit its thousand sides, surely that same person will ask: how is it that he thinks distinctly and not merely confusedly of the infinite as such, if he cannot see clearly the infinite perfections that constitute it, as if it were before his very eyes?

Perhaps this is what St. Thomas had in mind, for when he denied that the proposition "God exists" is self-evident, he brought to bear against himself a text from St. John Damascene:[13] "the knowledge that God exists has been naturally implanted in everyone; therefore it is self-evident that God exists."[14] And to this St. Thomas replies: "it is naturally implanted in us to know that God exists in some general sense and in a certain confused manner, that is to say, insofar as God is man's beatitude. . . . But this," he says, "is not to know without qualification that God exists; just as knowing that someone is approaching is not the same thing as knowing that it is Peter, even though it is Peter who is approaching . . ."[15] St. Thomas seems to be saying that God is known under a general rubric—either as ultimate end or as first and most perfect being—or ultimately under the rubric of something that embraces all things in a confused and common manner, but not under the precise rubric of his being, for God is infinite and unknown to us. I know that M. Descartes will respond with ease to anyone who asks such a question. Nevertheless, I believe that because of these matters, which I bring up simply for the sake of argument, he will call to mind the dictum of Boethius:[16] "There are certain common conceptions in the mind which are self-evident only to the wise. . . ."[17] Hence there is no cause for wonder if those who are desirous of understanding more ask a lot of questions and if they dwell for a long time upon those matters which they know have been laid down as the primary foundation for the whole enterprise, and which they still do not understand without a great deal of investigation.

97

13. St. John Damascene or St. John of Damascus (c. 675–749), a Greek theologian perhaps most famous for his polemical writings against the iconoclasts.

14. *Summa Theologiae* I, Q. 2, a. 1, obj. 1. Aquinas is citing John Damascene's *De Fide Orthodoxa* I.1.

15. Caterus' citation of Aquinas contains a slight transposition.

16. Anicius Manlius Severimus Boethius (c. 470–524), Roman scholar and Christian theologian and philosopher, perhaps best known for his *On the Consolation of Philosophy,* a somewhat neo-Platonic treatise in which the search for wisdom and the love of God are judged to be the keys to human happiness. Boethius is sometimes referred to as the last of the Romans and the first of the Scholastics.

17. *Summa Theologiae* I, Q. 2, a. 1, corpus. Aquinas is paraphrasing Boethius' *De Hebdomadibus (Quomodo Substantiae Bonae Sint),* principle 1.

Let us then grant that someone has a clear and distinct idea of a supreme
and most perfect being. Where do you go from there? Namely to the conclusion that this infinite being exists; and this conclusion is so certain that
"I ought to be at least as certain of the existence of God as I have hitherto
been about the truths of mathematics," so "it is no less contradictory[18] to
think of God (that is, a supremely perfect being) lacking existence (that is,
lacking some perfection), than it is to think of a mountain without a valley."
The whole argument hinges on this; whoever makes a concession at this
point must admit defeat. Because I am dealing with someone stronger than
98   myself, I would like to skirmish for a short while, so that, since I must eventually be defeated, I might nevertheless delay what I cannot avoid.

First, although we are proceeding not merely on the basis of authority
but rather on the basis of reason alone, still, lest I seem arbitrarily to resist
such a great mind, let us listen instead to St. Thomas himself. He urges the
following objection against himself: "once one understands what is signified
by the word 'God,' one immediately grasps the fact that God exists; for we
signify by the word 'God' something than which a greater cannot be signified. But what exists in reality and in the intellect is greater than what exists
in the intellect alone. Thus it follows that God also exists in reality, because,
upon understanding the word 'God,' God exists in the intellect."[19] I put
this argument in proper logical form thus: God is something than which a
greater cannot be signified. But something than which a greater cannot
be signified includes existence. Therefore existence is included in the very
word "God" or in the concept of God. Thus God can neither be nor be
conceived without existence. Now please tell me, is this not the argument
of M. Descartes? St. Thomas defines God thus: that than which a greater
cannot be signified. M. Descartes calls God a being who is supremely perfect. Clearly nothing greater than this being can be signified. St. Thomas
states the following minor premise: that than which a greater cannot be signified includes existence, otherwise something greater than it can be signified, namely, that which is also signified as including existence. But does
not M. Descartes seem to state the same minor premise? God, he says, is a
supremely perfect being; but a supremely perfect being includes existence,
otherwise it would not be supremely perfect. St. Thomas concludes: therefore, since the word "God" is immediately in the intellect once it is understood, it follows that God also exists in reality. In other words, from the very
fact that existence is involved in the essential concept of a being than which
a greater cannot be signified, it follows that this very being exists. M. Descartes
99   draws the same conclusion: "But," he says, "from the fact that I cannot think

18. A literal translation of the Latin text (*non magis*) is "no more." This is obviously a misstatement
on Descartes' part, since it contradicts his own clearly stated views.
19. *Summa Theologiae* I, Q. 2, a. 1, obj. 2.

of God except as existing, it follows that existence is inseparable from God; and thus he truly exists."[20] But then let St. Thomas reply to himself and to M. Descartes: "Granted," he says, "everyone understands that what is signified . . . by this word 'God' is what it is said to signify, namely something than which a greater cannot be thought. Still it does not follow on account of this that one understands that what is signified by the word exists in reality, but only that it exists in the apprehension of the intellect. Nor can one argue that it exists in reality, unless one grants that there exists in reality something than which a greater cannot be thought—a point not granted by those who claim that God does not exist."[21] On the basis of this argument, my reply is surely a brief one: even if it be granted that a "supremely perfect being" entails existence in its very defining formula, still it does not follow that that existence is something actual and real, but only that the concept of existence is inseparably joined to the concept of a supreme being. From this it follows that you do not infer that the existence of God is something actual, unless you presuppose that this supreme being actually exists, for then it will actually include all perfections, and surely the perfection of real existence.

Forgive me, gentlemen, for I am weary and will engage in a slight bit of frivolity. The compound "existing lion" includes both lion and the mode of existence, and it surely includes them essentially. For if you remove either of the two elements, it will not be this very same compound. But then, has not God throughout all eternity known this compound clearly and distinctly? And does not the idea of this compound, precisely as a compound, essentially involve each part of it? That is to say, is it not the case that existence is of the very essence of this compound "existing lion"? And yet a distinct knowledge on the part of God—a distinct knowledge, I say, on the part of God throughout all eternity—does not necessarily require that either of the parts of this compound exists, unless one supposes that the compound itself exists, for then it involves all its essential perfections, and thus it also involves actual existence. Consequently, even if I distinctly know a supreme being, and although a being that is supremely perfect may include existence in its essential concept, nevertheless it does not follow that its existence is anything actual, unless you presume that this supreme being exists; for then, since it includes all its perfections, it will also include this actual existence. But then we must prove by some other means that this supremely perfect being exists.

100

I shall say a little bit about the essence of the soul and about the distinction between the soul and the body. For I confess that this great genius has already so tired me out that I can scarcely go on any further. He seems to

---

20. Caterus' citation of Descartes is nearly but not quite verbatim.
21. *Summa Theologiae* I, Q. 2, a. 1, ad 2.

prove the distinction (if that is what it is) between the soul and the body by the fact that they can be conceived distinctly and separately. Here I leave the very learned gentleman with Duns Scotus,[22] who declares that for one thing to be conceived distinctly and separately from another, it suffices that there be a distinction which he calls "formal and objective," which he claims to be midway between a real distinction and a distinction of reason.[23] And thus Scotus distinguishes between God's justice and his mercy; "for," he says, "before every operation of the intellect these attributes have formally diverse meanings, so that even then the one is not the other. Nevertheless, it does not follow, from the fact that God's justice can be conceived separately from his mercy, that God's justice therefore exists separately."[24]

101 But I see that I have totally exceeded the conventions of a letter. These are the points regarding the matter before us that I observed to be in need of discussion. But you, gentlemen, must select what you judge to be of superior quality. If you support me, we will easily overcome M. Descartes with friendship, lest in the future he have any bad feelings toward me, were I to have contradicted him a little. If you support him, I surrender, I am conquered; and I readily admit as much, lest I be vanquished yet again. I send you my greetings.

Reply by the Author to the First Set of Objections

Gentlemen:[25]

You have certainly stirred up against me a mighty adversary, whose wit and learning could have given me a great deal of trouble were it not for the fact that, being a theologian who is both pious and thoroughly civilized, he preferred championing the cause of God and any of its defenders to making a serious attack upon it. But though this minor trickery is a very fine trait in him, nonetheless, such collusion on my part would not warrant praise. And so I prefer here to expose his ruse for aiding me rather than to respond to him as if he were an adversary.

First of all, he has brought together in a few words my chief argument for proving the existence of God, so that it might better remain in the reader's

22. John Duns Scotus (1266?–1308), sometimes referred to as "Doctor Subtilis," was a major figure in the Franciscan school of philosophy.

23. For accounts of Scotus' doctrine of formal distinctions, see Maurice J. Grajewski, *The Formal Distinction of Duns Scotus: A Study in Metaphysics* (Washington, DC: Catholic University of America, Ph.D. thesis, 1944) and Michael J. Jordan, *Duns Scotus on the Formal Distinction* (New Brunswick, NJ: Rutgers University, Ph.D. thesis, 1984).

24. *Ordinatio* I, Dist. 8, part 1, q. 4. The topic of q. 4 is the simplicity of God.

25. Again Descartes is addressing Bannius and Bloemaert.

memory. And, having briefly indicated his assent to what he judged to be demonstrated with sufficient clarity and having thus strengthened them with his own authority, he inquired into that single matter upon which the main difficulty rests, namely, what we are to understand here by the word "idea" and what cause an idea requires. *102*

I have written that "an idea is the very thing thought, insofar as it exists objectively in the intellect," but he pretends to understand these words in a sense quite different from that in which I meant them, so that he can provide me an opportunity to explain them more clearly. ". . . to exist objectively in the intellect," he says, "is to terminate the act of the intellect after the manner of an object. This characterization is surely an extrinsic denomination and it has no bearing on the thing itself." Note that he is referring to the thing itself insofar as it exists outside the intellect. Seen in this light, it certainly is an extrinsic denomination for the thing to exist objectively in the intellect. But I was talking about an idea which is never outside the intellect, and thus "objective existence" merely means that the thing exists in the intellect in just the way that objects normally exist in the intellect. Thus, for example, were a person to ask what happens to the sun as a result of its existing objectively in my intellect, the best answer would be that nothing happens to it except an extrinsic denomination, to wit, that the sun terminates the operation of the intellect after the manner of an object. But were one to ask what the idea of the sun is and were the answer that it is the very thing thought insofar as it exists objectively in the intellect, no one would take it to be the very sun itself insofar as that extrinsic denomination is in it. Nor will "objective existence in the intellect" signify that it terminates the operation of the intellect after the manner of an object, but rather that it is in the intellect in the manner in which its objects normally exist in it—surely not formally, as it is in the heavens, but objectively, that is, in *103* the way in which objects normally exist in the intellect. Clearly this mode of existence is definitely far less perfect than that mode of existence by which things exist outside the intellect; but it is not for that reason simply nothing, as I have already written.

And when this most learned theologian declares that there is an "equivocation" in these words, he seems to have wanted to warn me about what I have just now noted, lest perhaps I not be mindful of it. For he says first that a thing existing thus in the intellect through an idea is not an "actual being," that is, it is not something existing outside the intellect. This is true. Then he also says that objective being is not something conjured up in the mind or a being or reason, but something real which is distinctly conceived. With these words he admits all that I have assumed. But he still makes the further point that "since it is merely conceived and is not actual" (that is, because it is merely an idea and not something existing outside the intellect), "though it can indeed be conceived, it can hardly be caused" (that is, it does not need a cause in order to exist outside the intellect). I grant this; but it clearly does need a cause in order to be conceived, and the point at issue is with respect to this cause alone. Thus, were one to have in one's intellect an idea of a machine devised with the greatest of skill, one indeed could with justification ask what the cause is of that idea. Now it will not suffice for one to declare that the idea is nothing outside of the mind and thus cannot be caused but only conceived; for all that is asked for here is what the cause is in virtue of which it is conceived. Nor again will it suffice to say that the intellect is itself the cause, insofar as it is the cause of its operation. For regarding this cause there can be no doubt, but only regarding the cause of the "objective skill" which is in the idea. For it ought to be the result of

104   some cause that this idea of a machine contains this "objective skill" rather than some other, and the "objective skill" of this idea of the machine is in the same relationship to the idea of the machine as the objective reality of the idea of God is to the idea of God. And surely various things could be reckoned to be the cause of this skill: either some such real machine has been seen beforehand, in accordance with whose likeness the idea has been formed, or a great knowledge of mechanics, which is in this intellect, or perhaps a great subtlety of mind by which one might even invent the machine without any previous knowledge. Note that all the skill that exists merely objectively in this idea ought necessarily to exist either formally or eminently in its cause, whatever that cause finally turns out to be—be it a formal cause or an eminent cause. And the same thing is to be reckoned even with respect to the objective reality which is in the idea of God. But in what will such a reality thus exist, except in a God who really exists? But the insightful gentleman has seen all these things quite well and therefore admits that one can ask ". . . why a given idea has this objective reality rather than that one." To this question he responds first that what I wrote regarding the triangle holds for all ideas, namely that, even if perhaps the triangle exists nowhere in the world, still its determinate nature, essence, or form is immutable and eternal. Indeed he declares that this requires no cause. But this reply does not seem satisfactory; for although the nature of the triangle is immutable and eternal, nevertheless it is not therefore any less incumbent upon us to ask why the idea of a triangle is in us. Thus he added by way of a postscript that if I insist upon a reason, it is the imperfection of our intellect, and so on. By this answer he seems to have wanted to show merely that those who wished to disagree with me in this matter offer no answer that has

105   any semblance of truth about it. For it is certainly no more probable that the reason why there exists in us an idea of God is the imperfection of our intellect, than that the lack of experience in mechanics is the cause of our imagining some very skillfully made machine rather than some other less perfect machine. On the contrary, were one to have an idea of a machine in which every conceivable skill is contained, the most appropriate inference

is that this idea issued from some cause in which every conceivable skill really existed, even though in the idea it existed only objectively. And for the same reason, since we have in us an idea of God in which every conceivable perfection is contained, it can then most manifestly be concluded that this idea depends upon some cause in which there is also all this perfection, namely in a God who really exists. Nor does there seem more difficulty in the one case than in the other: just as not all are experts in mechanics and thus cannot have ideas of very skillfully produced machines, so too not all have the same power of conceiving the idea of God. However, since this idea has been implanted in the minds of all in the same way and since we never observe that it comes to us from anywhere but ourselves, we assume that it pertains to the nature of our intellect. Surely none of this is incorrect, but we are leaving out something else that is especially in need of consideration, something on which the whole force and lucidity of this argument depend, namely, that this power of having within oneself the idea of God could not be in our intellect, were this intellect merely a finite being (as in fact it is) *106* and did it not have God as its cause. And thus I inquired further whether I could exist if God did not exist—not so much to offer a proof different from the preceding one, but rather to explain the very same proof more fully.

But here the gentleman, by being excessively obliging, has placed me in an awkward position, for he compares my argument with another one drawn from St. Thomas and Aristotle, with the result that he seems to demand a reason, when I set out on the same path as these two, why I did not follow it in all respects. But I beg him to allow me to give an account of those things which I myself have written and to be silent about what others have written.

And so, first of all, I have not based my argument on my having observed a certain order or succession of efficient causes in the realm of sensible things. For one thing, I thought it much more evident that God exists than that any sensible things exist; for another thing, the only conclusion I seemed able to arrive at was that I ought to acknowledge the imperfection of my intellect, given that admittedly I could not comprehend how an infinite number of such causes succeeded one another in such a way that none of them was first. For certainly from the fact that I could not comprehend this it does not follow that one of them ought to be a first cause, any more than it follows from the fact that I cannot also comprehend the infinite divisions in a finite quantity that there is a final division, such that it cannot be divided further. All that follows is that my intellect, which is finite, does not grasp the infinite. *107* Thus I preferred to use my own existence as the foundation of my argument, since my existence depends on no series of causes and is so well known to me that nothing else could be more well known. And, in order to free myself from the whole problem of the succession of causes, I asked concerning myself not so much what the cause was by which I was at one time produced, as the cause by which I am being conserved at the present time.

Next, I inquired about the cause of myself, not insofar as I am composed of mind and body but only and precisely insofar as I am a thing that thinks. I believe that this is quite relevant to the matter at hand; for in so doing I have been able to free myself much more effectively from prejudices, to attend to the light of nature, to question myself, and to affirm as certain that there cannot be anything within me of which I am not somehow aware. This approach is clearly different from seeing that I was begotten by my father and concluding from this that he in turn was begotten by my grandfather, and from putting an end to my search by declaring that some cause is first, because in seeking the parents of parents I could not go on to infinity.

Moreover, I inquired about the cause of myself, not merely insofar as I am a thing that thinks, but, most especially and primarily, insofar as I observe that, among my other thoughts, there is within me the idea of a supremely perfect being. On this one point hangs the entire force of my demonstration. First, because in this idea is contained what God is, at least insofar as he can be understood by me; and, according to the rules of the true logic, one should never ask whether something exists unless one first understands what it is. Second, because it is this very idea which gives me the opportunity to examine whether I am derived from myself or from something else, as well as to acknowledge my defects. And lastly, because this idea is what teaches not only that something is the cause of me but also that in this cause are contained all perfections, and hence that this cause is God.

Finally, I did not say that it is impossible for something to be the efficient cause of itself. For although this obviously is the case when the term "efficient cause" is restricted to those causes which are temporally prior to their effects or are different from them, still it does not seem that such a restriction is appropriate in this inquiry. First, the inquiry would be pointless (for who does not know that the same thing can neither exist prior to itself nor be different from itself?). Second, the light of nature does not stipulate that the nature of an efficient cause requires that it be temporally prior to its effect. On the contrary, a thing does not bear the trademark of a cause except during the time it is producing an effect, and thus it is not prior to the effect. However, the light of nature does surely stipulate that there exists nothing about which it is inappropriate to ask why it exists or to inquire into its efficient cause, or, if it has none, to demand to know why it does not need one. Thus, if I believed that nothing could in any respect stand in relation to itself the way an efficient cause stands to its effect, it is utterly out of the question that I should then conclude that something is the first cause. On the contrary, I should again ask for the cause of what was called the "first cause," and thus I would never arrive at anything that was the first cause of all things. But I do readily admit that there could exist something in which there is such a great and inexhaustible power that it never needs the help of anything in order to exist. Nor again does it now need a cause in order to be conserved. Thus, in a manner of speaking, it is the cause of itself. And I understand God to be such a cause. For even if I had existed from all eternity and thus nothing existed prior to me, nevertheless, considering the fact that the parts of time can be separated one from another (and thus from the fact that I now exist it does not follow that I will exist in the future unless some cause were, so to speak, to remake me over and over at each individual moment in time), I would not hesitate to call that cause which conserves me an "efficient cause." Thus, even though there has never been a time when God did not exist, nevertheless, because it is he who truly conserves himself, it does not seem wholly inappropriate to call God the cause of himself. Still, we should note here that by "conservation" we do not mean the sort of conservation that takes place through any positive influence on the part of an efficient cause, but only that the very essence of God is such that God must always exist.

On the basis of these considerations it will be easy for me to reply to the distinction drawn with respect to the expression "derived from itself," an expression, the very learned theologian warns me, that requires an explanation. For some people, attending only to the strict and literal meaning of "efficient cause," think it impossible for something to be the efficient cause of itself, and do not discern here a place for any other type of cause analogous to an efficient cause. When these people say that something is "derived from itself," they are in the habit of understanding only that it has no cause. Nevertheless, if these very same people were of a mind to pay more attention to the facts than to words, they would easily observe that the negative rendering of the expression "derived from itself" proceeds merely from the imperfection of the human intellect and has no foundation in reality. But there is another rendering, a positive one, which has been sought from the truth of things and from which alone my argument proceeds. For were one to believe, for example, that some body were derived from itself, one may simply mean that it has no cause. Now it is not the case that one affirms this on the basis of some positive consideration, but only negatively, in the sense that one fails to recognize the cause of the body. But this is a certain imperfection in oneself, as one will easily come to find out for oneself later when one considers that the parts of time do not depend one upon another. Thus, the fact that this body is presumed up until the present time to have been derived from itself (that is, it has no cause) does not suffice to make it also exist in the future, unless there is in it some power which, as it were, continuously "remakes" it. For then, seeing that no such power is contained in the idea of a body, one immediately gathers from this that this body is not derived from itself, taking the expression, "derived from itself," in a positive sense. In like manner, when we say that God is derived from himself, we

110

surely can also understand this negatively, that is, such that the entire meaning of the expression is that he has no cause. But if we have previously asked
why God exists or why he continues to exist, and, on noting the immense
and incomprehensible power which is contained in the idea of God, we
acknowledged that this power is so overwhelming that it is clearly the cause
of God's continuing to exist and that nothing but this can be the cause, then
we are saying that God is derived from himself—this no longer in a negative sense but in a thoroughly positive sense. For although we need not say
111   that God is the efficient cause of himself (lest perhaps we be arguing about
words), still, because we perceive that his being derived from himself or his
having no cause different from himself is itself derived not from nothing
but from a real immensity of power, it is wholly fitting for us to think that
God stands in the same relationship to himself as an efficient cause does to
its effect, and thus that God is derived from himself positively. And it is also
fitting for each person to ask himself whether he is derived from himself
in the same sense. On finding in himself no power sufficient to conserve
him through even a moment of time, he rightly concludes that he is derived
from another, and this is surely derived from something else which is derived
from itself, because this inquiry cannot go on to infinity, since it is a question
here of the present and not of the past or the future. In fact, I will also add
here something I have not put in writing before, namely, that it is not even
a secondary cause at which one arrives, but certainly that cause in which
there is enough power to conserve something existing outside it and a fortiori conserves itself by its own power and thus is derived from itself.

However, when it is said that "every limitation is derived from a cause,"
I believe something true is being understood, but it is not expressed in very
appropriate terms and the difficulty is not resolved. For, strictly speaking,
limitation is merely the negation of a further perfection; and this negation
is not derived from a cause but is the very thing being limited. However,
even if it were true that everything is limited by a cause, still it is not self-
evident but must be proved some other way, for, as the subtle theologian very
112   well replies, anything can be thought to be limited either in the way just
mentioned or in virtue of the fact that it pertains to its nature, just as it is of
the nature of the triangle that it is composed of no more than three lines.
However, what does seem self-evident to me is that everything that exists is
derived either from a cause or from itself as from a cause. For since we understand not only existence but also the negation of existence, we cannot pretend that anything is derived from itself without there being some reason
why it should exist rather than not. In other words, we should not interpret
the expression "derived from itself" so as to mean "as from a cause," in view
of the overwhelming fullness of power which can easily be demonstrated to
be in God alone.

What the gentleman does finally grant me is something that hardly allows of any doubt, but which commonly is hardly ever given serious consideration. It is of such importance for plucking the whole of philosophy from out of the shadows, that he helps me greatly in my project by confirming it with his authority.

But here he judiciously asks whether I know the infinite clearly and distinctly. For although I have tried to anticipate this objection, still it occurs so spontaneously to everyone that it is worth responding to it at some length. And so, to begin with, I will declare here that the infinite qua infinite is in no way comprehended; nonetheless it is still understood, insofar as understanding clearly and distinctly that a thing is such that plainly no limits can be found in it is tantamount to understanding clearly that it is infinite.

And indeed I do distinguish here between "indefinite" and "infinite"; strictly speaking, I designate only that thing to be "infinite" in which no limits of any kind are found. In this sense God alone is infinite. However, there are things in which I discern no limit, but only in a certain respect (such as the extension of imaginary space, a series of numbers, the divisibility of the parts of a quantity, and the like). These I call "indefinite" but not "infinite," since such things do not lack a limit in every respect.

Moreover, I distinguish between the formal meaning of "infinite," or "infinity," and the thing that is infinite. For as far as infinity is concerned, even if we understand that it is positive in the highest degree, nevertheless we understand it only in a certain negative fashion, because it depends on our not noticing any limitation in the thing. But as to the thing itself which is infinite, although our understanding of the thing is surely positive, still it is not adequate, that is, we do not comprehend all that is capable of being understood in it. But were we to turn our eyes toward the sea, even though we neither grasp the whole thing in our sight nor traverse its great vastness, nevertheless we are said to "see" it. And were we to view the sea from a distance, so as to take it in all at once, as it were, with our eyes, we see it only in a confused fashion, just as we have a confused image of a chiliagon when we take in all of its sides at the same time. But were we to direct our gaze at close quarters toward some portion of the sea, such a sight can be very clear and distinct, just as would be the case with imagining a chiliagon, were our vision restricted to merely one or other of the chiliagon's sides. By a similar line of reasoning, I grant, as do all the theologians, that God cannot be grasped by the human intellect, and that he cannot be distinctly known by those who gaze upon him, as it were, from afar and try mentally to grasp him whole and all at once. This is the sense in which St. Thomas declared in the text cited that the knowledge of God is present in us merely "in a certain confused manner." But those who try to take notice of each of God's perfections one by one and try not so much to grasp them as to be grasped

113

114

by them, and to engage all the powers of their intellect in contemplating them, will surely find that God is a much fuller and easier subject matter for clear and distinct knowledge than are any created things.

Nor in that text did St. Thomas deny this, as is obvious from his affirming in the following article that the existence of God can be demonstrated. However, wherever I claimed that God could be clearly and distinctly known, I had in mind only the aforementioned knowledge, which is finite and proportionate to the humble modality of our mind. Besides, it was not necessary to have a different understanding of the matter in order to establish the truth of what I have claimed, as will be readily apparent if one takes note of the fact that I said this in just two places. The first place was where there was a question of whether there is contained in the idea that we form of God anything real or just the negation of something real, just as perhaps is the case in the idea of cold where there is nothing more than the negation of heat—a matter about which there can be no doubt. The second place was where I claimed that existence belongs no less to the nature of a being that is supremely perfect than having three sides belongs to the nature

115 of a triangle—a fact that can also be understood without an adequate knowledge of God.

Here again he compares one of my arguments with another from St. Thomas, in order to compel me, as it were, to specify just what greater force is to be found in the one argument rather than in the other. Now I seem able to do this without any great degree of vexatiousness, since St. Thomas did not use this argument as his own, nor did he draw the same conclusion as I do; consequently, I am not at variance here on any point with the Angelic Doctor. For his question was whether the proposition "God exists" is self-evident to us, that is, whether it is obvious to everyone. He denies that it is, and rightly so. But the argument he puts to himself can be stated thus: when we understand what is signified by the word "God," we understand it to signify "that than which a greater cannot be signified." But to exist in reality as well as in the intellect is greater than to exist merely in the intellect. Therefore, when we understand what is signified by the word "God," we understand that what is being signified is that God exists in reality as well as in the intellect. There is an obvious flaw in the form of this argument, for the only conclusion he should have drawn is: therefore, when we understand what the word "God" signifies, we understand that God exists in reality as well as in the intellect. But merely being signified by a word does not automatically make what is signified to be true. But my argument went as follows: what we clearly and distinctly understand to belong to the true and

116 immutable nature, or essence, or form of a thing, can truly be affirmed of that thing. But after having investigated with sufficient care what God is, we clearly and distinctly understand that it belongs to his true and immutable nature that he exists. Thus we can at that point rightfully affirm of God that

he exists. At least we now have a validly drawn conclusion. Moreover, we cannot deny the major premise, since we have already granted that everything we clearly and distinctly understand is true. We are left with only the minor premise, and here I confess there is no little difficulty. One reason for this is that we are so accustomed to distinguishing existence from essence in the case of all other things, that we do not sufficiently take notice of the extent to which existence belongs more to the essence of God than to the essences of other things. Second, by failing to distinguish what belongs to the true and immutable essence of a thing from what is ascribed to it merely by a construction on the part of the intellect, even if we take sufficient notice of the fact that existence belongs to the essence of God, we do not then conclude that God exists, because we do not know whether God's essence is immutable and true or whether it is merely an artifact of our own making.

But in order to remove the first part of this difficulty, we must distinguish between possible and necessary existence. We must also take note of the fact that possible existence is contained in the concept or idea of everything that is clearly and distinctly understood, but in no instance is necessary existence so contained, except in the case of the idea of God. For those who pay close attention to the difference between the idea of God and all other ideas will no doubt perceive that even though we surely understand other things only   *117* as existing, it still does not follow from this that they do exist but only that they can exist, because we do not understand it to be necessary that actual existence be joined with the other properties of these things. But, from the fact that we understand that actual existence is necessarily and always joined with God's other attributes, it readily follows that God exists.

Next, in order to remove the remaining part of this difficulty, we must take notice of the fact that those ideas which do not contain true and immutable natures, but natures that are mere constructions devised by the intellect, can be divided by the very same intellect, not merely by an act of abstraction but by a clear and distinct operation. As a consequence, what cannot be divided thus by the intellect surely was not devised by the intellect. For example, when I think of a winged horse or an actually existing lion or a triangle inscribed in a square, I easily understand that I could just as well think of a horse without wings or a nonexistent lion or a triangle apart from a square, and so on. As a consequence, these things do not have true and immutable natures. But if I think of a triangle or a square (I leave the lion and the horse out of the discussion here because their natures are not plainly evident to us), then certainly whatever I discern as being contained in the idea of a triangle, such as that its three angles are equal to two right angles, and so on, I will rightfully affirm of the triangle. The same holds for the square with regard to whatever I find in the idea of a square. For although I could understand a triangle while abstracting from the fact that its three

118   angles are equal to two right angles, still I cannot deny this of the triangle
by a clear and distinct operation, that is, while correctly understanding what
I am saying. Moreover, if I consider a triangle inscribed in a square, not with
the purpose of attributing to the square what pertains solely to the triangle
or to the triangle what belongs solely to the square, but with the purpose
of examining only what arises out of the conjunction of the two together,
the nature of this conjunction will be no less true and immutable than that
of the square alone or the triangle alone. And thus it will be appropriate to
affirm that the area of the square is not less than double the area of the triangle inscribed in it, and to affirm other similar properties that pertain to the
nature of this composite figure.

But if I were to think that existence is contained in the idea of a body
that is supremely perfect because it is a greater perfection to exist in reality
as well as in the intellect than to exist in the intellect alone, I cannot for that
reason conclude that this supremely perfect body exists, but only that it can
exist. For I am sufficiently cognizant both of the fact that this idea had been
devised by my own intellect, which has joined together all bodily perfections,
as well as of the fact that existence does not arise from the other bodily perfections, since existence can just as easily be denied or affirmed of them. In
fact, in examining the idea of a body, I perceive that there is no power existing in it by means of which a body produces or conserves itself. From this
I rightly conclude that necessary existence (which alone is in question here)
no more belongs to the nature of a body, supremely perfect though it may
be, than it belongs to the nature of a mountain not to have a valley, or to
the nature of a triangle to have angles whose sum is greater than two right
angles. However, if we now ask not about a body but about a thing that has
all the perfections that can exist together and without any regard for the sort
119   of thing it may finally turn out to be, and if we inquire whether existence
is to be counted among these perfections, on first blush we surely will be in
some doubt. The reason for this is that since our mind, which is finite, is
accustomed to ponder these perfections only one by one, it perhaps does
not immediately notice how necessary is the conjunction between them.
However, were we to examine carefully whether existence belongs to a being
which is supremely powerful and what kind of existence it is, we will be
able to perceive clearly and distinctly first that at least possible existence
belongs to such a being, just as it belongs to all other things of which there
is a distinct idea in us, even to those things which are devised through a construction on the part of the intellect. Next, since we cannot think the existence of this being to be possible unless at the same time, taking note of its
immense power, we acknowledge that this being can exist by its own power,
we here conclude that this being truly exists and has existed from all eternity, for it is very obvious by the light of nature that what can exist by its
very own power always exists. And thus we will understand that necessary

existence is contained in the idea of a supremely powerful being, not by virtue of a construction on the part of the intellect, but because it belongs to the true and immutable nature of such a being that it exists. And thus, we shall easily perceive that this being, which is supremely perfect, must have in itself all the other perfections that are contained in the idea of God, such that, by their very nature and without any construction on the part of the intellect, they are all joined together and exist in God.

All of these points are readily apparent to one who pays careful attention, and they differ from what I have previously written only in the manner of their explanation, which I have deliberately altered so that I might suit a wide variety of minds. Nor will I here deny that this argument is such that those who do not recall all of what constitutes its proof will easily take it to be a sophism. Thus at the outset I did have considerable doubts about whether I ought to use it, lest perhaps I should provide those who might not grasp the argument with an occasion for disavowing the remaining arguments as well. However, because there are but two ways by which one can prove that God exists (namely, the one through effects and the other through God's essence or nature); and because I explained the former as best I could in the Third Meditation, I did not believe that the latter argument ought to be overlooked later on.

120

As far as the formal distinction is concerned, which the very learned theologian draws from Duns Scotus, I declare briefly[26] that a formal distinction does not differ from a modal distinction, and that it applies only to incomplete beings, which I have carefully distinguished from complete beings. Moreover, it surely suffices for a formal distinction that one thing be conceived distinctly and separately from another by an act of abstraction on the part of the intellect inadequately conceiving the thing, yet not so distinctly and separately that we understand each one as something existing in its own right and different from every other thing; for this to be the case a real distinction is absolutely required. Thus, for example, the distinction between the motion and the shape of the same body is a formal one. I can understand perfectly well the motion apart from the shape and the shape apart from the motion and either in abstraction from the body. Nevertheless, I still cannot completely understand the motion apart from the thing in which the motion takes place, or even the shape apart from the thing which has the shape. Moreover, I cannot imagine motion existing in a thing in which there can be no shape, nor a shape existing in a thing which cannot move. In the same way, I cannot understand justice apart from someone who is just, or mercy apart from someone who is merciful. Nor can I imagine that that very same person who is just is incapable of being merciful. But I completely understand what a body is when I think that it merely has extension

---

26. Descartes has a lengthier discussion of the various types of distinctions in *Principles* I, arts. 60–2.

and shape, is capable of moving, and so on; and I deny that there is anything whatsoever in it that belongs to the nature of the mind. Conversely, I understand that the mind is a complete thing which doubts, understands, wills, and so on, even though I deny that there is anything in it that is contained in the idea of a body. This would be utterly impossible, were there not a real distinction between mind and body.

These, dear gentlemen, are the answers that I have made to the very helpful and intelligent observations of your friend. If I have not yet satisfied him in regard to these observations, I ask that he put me on notice as to what is either lacking or in error. If I might seek this from him through you, I will hold it a great kindness.

Second Set of Objections[27]

Sir, so successful have been your efforts at defending the cause of the author of all things against a new cadre of "giants," and at demonstrating his exis-
122 tence, that henceforth men of honor can hope that no one who does a close reading of your *Meditations* will fail to acknowledge that there is an eternal power on which each individual thing depends. For this reason, we wanted to bring to your attention certain passages noted below and to put questions to you, so that you might shed such light on these passages, and thus nothing would remain in your work which is not clearly demonstrated, insofar as such demonstration is possible. However, you have for many years exercised your mind by such continual meditation that matters that seemed doubtful and quite obscure to others are to you most certain. Moreover, you perceive them by a very clear intuition of the mind as if they were first and preeminent lights of nature. Hence we here draw your attention solely to those things that you should take the trouble to explain and demonstrate more clearly and more fully. This accomplished, there will be hardly anyone who could deny that your arguments, which you entered into for the greater glory of God and for the immense benefit of all mortal men, have the force of demonstrations.

First of all, you will recall that it surely was not actually and truly but merely by a contrivance of the mind that you rejected as best you could the images [*phantasmata*] of all bodies, so that you might conclude that you were merely a thinking thing, lest perhaps you believe later on that you could conclude that you are really nothing but a mind, or a thought, or a thinking thing. We draw your attention to this only in connection with the first two Meditations, in which you clearly show that it is certain that at least you,

---

27. This set of objections was gathered and edited by Marin Mersenne, who is also believed to be the author of many of these objections.

who are thinking, exist. But let us pause here for a little while. Up until now you acknowledge that you are a thinking thing, but you do not know what this thing is that thinks. But what if it were a body that by its various movements and encounters produces what we call thought? For although you think you have rejected every body, you could have been mistaken in this, since you hardly rejected yourself, who may be a body. For how do you demonstrate that a body cannot think? Or that corporeal motions are not thought itself? But the entire system of your body, which you believe you   123 have rejected, or some part of it (for example, those parts which make up the brain), can come together to form those motions which we call thoughts. I am, you say, a thinking thing; but are you a thing that knows if you are a corporeal motion or a body that is being moved?

Second, from the idea of a supreme being, an idea you contend could hardly have been produced by you, you make bold to infer the necessity of the existence of a supreme being from which alone it would be possible to derive this idea that your mind observes. But in truth we find within ourselves a sufficient basis for forming this idea; and, relying on it alone, we can form the above mentioned idea, even if a supreme being did not exist or we did not know that it exists and did not even give a thought to its existence. For do I not see that I, as a thinking thing, have a certain degree of perfection? And thus others besides myself have a similar degree perfection, whence I have a basis for thinking of some or other number and thus for building one degree of perfection upon another to infinity. In the same way, were there to exist just a single degree of light or heat, I can always add and imagine further degrees to infinity. Why, by a similar line of reasoning, could I not add another degree to some specific degree of being that I perceive in myself and form an idea of a perfect being out of all the degrees that can be added on? But, you say, an effect cannot have any degree of perfection or reality that did not exist beforehand in its cause. We observe that flies and other animals and even plants are produced by the sun, rain, and soil—things in which there is no life. Yet life is more noble than any mere corporeal degree of perfection. Whence it follows that an effect gets from its cause a certain reality that nevertheless is not in the cause. Yet despite this observation, this idea is merely a being of reason [*ens rationis*],[28] which is no more noble than your mind that thinks it. Moreover, how do you know that this   124 idea would still be present to you, had you not been raised among learned people but had instead spent your entire life alone in a deserted place? The only answer is that you drew this idea from meditations of the mind conceived

---

28. The term "being of reason" was commonly used by scholastic philosophers and theologians to refer to a thing that has merely objective being in the intellect. See, for example, Thomas Aquinas, *Commentary on Aristotle's Metaphysics,* Book IV, lect. 4, sec. 574.

previously, from books, from conversations with friends, and so on, but not from your own mind alone or from a supreme being that exists. And thus you need to prove more clearly that this idea could not be present to you if a supreme being did not exist. But when you do show us this proof, we shall all surrender. But that this idea comes from previously conceived notions seems to be established by the fact that indigenous people of Canada—Hurons and other primitive men—entertain no such idea. Moreover, it is an idea you could form from a prior examination of corporeal things, so that your idea refers to nothing beyond this corporeal world, which embraces every manner of perfection you can think of. Thus you would not yet infer anything but a corporeal being that is most perfect, unless you add something else that leads us to something incorporeal or spiritual. Let us add that you can form the idea of an angel just as you can form the idea of a most perfect being; but this idea will not be made in you by an angel, even though you are less perfect than it. But neither do you have an idea of God any more than you have an idea of an infinite number or an infinite line. And if you could have an idea of such a number, it is still an impossible number. Add to this the fact that the idea of the unity and simplicity of one perfection embracing all others arises merely from an operation of the understanding reasoning [*intellectus rationantis*],[29] in the same way as universal unities, which do not exist in reality but only in the understanding, as is shown in the cases of generic unity, transcendental unity, and so on.

Third, since you are not yet certain of the existence of God and are unable to say that you are certain of anything or that you clearly and dis-
125 tinctly know something unless you knew beforehand with certainty and clarity that God exists, it follows that you do not yet clearly and distinctly know that you are a thinking thing, since, according to you, this knowledge depends on a clear knowledge of an existing God, a knowledge that you have not yet proved in those passages where you conclude that you know clearly that you exist.

Consider also the fact that an atheist knows clearly and distinctly that the three angles of a triangle are equal to two right angles, even though it is alien to him to suppose that God exists—something he obviously denies, since, he says, were God to exist, there would be a supreme being and a supreme good, that is, there would be something infinite. But something infinite in every type of perfection excludes everything else whatsoever, namely, every being and every good; nay, every non-being and every evil.

---

29. Scholastic theologians commonly held that divine properties are not distinguished one from the other except by means of a "distinction of reason reasoning," that is, by a distinction made by the mind without a foundation in reality. Thus, for example, we could distinguish divine mercy from divine justice, but such a distinction would have no foundation in reality on account of God's utter simplicity.

Nevertheless, there do in fact exist many beings, many good things, many non-beings and many evil things. We believe you ought to give a satisfactory reply to this objection, lest anything be left to the impious with which to plead their case.

Fourth, you deny that God can lie or deceive, and yet there have been Schoolmen who affirm this. For example, Gabriel Biel,[30] Gregory of Rimini,[31] and others think that, in virtue of his absolute power, God can lie, that is, he can communicate something to men which is contrary to his own mind and contrary to what he has decreed, as when he declared unconditionally to the Ninevites through the prophet: "come forty days and Ninevah shall be destroyed";[32] and when he said many other things that did not take place at all, since he did not wish these words to correspond either to his mind or to his decree. Now if God hardened the heart of Pharaoh and blinded him,[33] and if he instilled a spirit of mendaciousness in his prophets, why do you hold that we cannot be deceived by him? Cannot God deal with men the way a physician deals with the sick and a father deals with his children, where both men often deceive their charges and for a wise and useful purpose? For were God to show us the pure truth, what eye, what power of discernment could endure it? 126

Nevertheless, you need not suppose God to be a deceiver in order to be deceived in those things you think you know clearly and distinctly, since the cause of this deception could be in you, even though you are not thinking of it at all. For why should your nature not be such as to be deceived at all times, or at least more often than not? But on what grounds do you hold it to be certain that you are neither deceived nor capable of being deceived in those things you think you know clearly and distinctly? For how often have we not observed that someone has been deceived in those things that he believed he knew more clearly than the light of day? Hence this principle

30. Gabriel Biel, *Collectorium circa quattuor libros sententiarum, prologus et liber primus,* Dist. 42–3, edited by H. Rückert, M. Elze, and R. Steiger (Tübingen: J. C. B. Mohr [Paul Siebeck], 1973), pp. 736–54. For a brief survey of the life and thought of Gabriel Biel (c. 1425–95), see John L. Farthing, "Gabriel Biel," *Routledge Encyclopedia of Philosophy* (New York: Routledge, 1998), Vol. 1, pp. 769–72. For an extended account of the life and thought of Biel, see Heiko Augustinus Oberman, *The Harvest of Medieval Theology* (Cambridge, MA: Harvard University Press, 1963).

31. Gregory of Rimini, *Super primum et secundum Sententiarum,* Dist 42–4 (Saint Bonaventure: Franciscan Institute, 1955 [reprint of 1522 edition]), 161v–177r. For a brief survey of the life and thought of Gregory of Rimini (c. 1300–58), see Stephen F. Brown, "Gregory of Rimini," *Routledge Encyclopedia of Philosophy* (New York: Routledge, 1998), Vol. 4, pp. 170–2. Two recent surveys of medieval views regarding divine omnipotence are: Lawrence Moonan, *Divine Power: The Medieval Power Distinction up to Its Adoption by Albert, Bonaventure, and Aquinas* (New York: Oxford University Press, 1994); and Olivier Boulnois, *La Puissance et son ombre: de Pierre Lombard à Luther,* textes traduits et présentés par Olivier Boulnois et al. (Paris: Aubier, 1994).

32. Jonah 3:4.

33. Exodus 7:22–14:8 passim.

of clear and distinct knowledge ought to be explained so clearly and distinctly that no one of sound mind could ever be deceived in those things that he believed he knew clearly and distinctly. Otherwise, up to this point we discern no degree of certainty to be possible either to mankind or to you.

Fifth, if the will never goes astray or errs when it follows the mind's clear and distinct knowledge, and if the will lays itself open to danger when it allows a conception of the understanding that is not at all clear and distinct, then take note of the consequences of this. A Turk or anyone else not only does not err in having failed to embrace the Christian religion, but actually would err if he were to embrace it, for indeed he knows the truth of it neither clearly nor distinctly. In fact, if this rule of yours were true, there would be practically nothing that might permissibly be embraced by the will, since we know practically nothing with the sort of clarity and distinctness you require for that kind of certainty which is immune to all doubt. Take care, therefore, in your eagerness to defend the truth, that you do not prove too much and destroy the truth rather than establish it.

Sixth, in your reply to the theologian,[34] you appear to go astray in what you propose as your conclusion: "what we clearly and distinctly understand to belong to the true and unchangeable nature of a thing . . . can truly be affirmed of that thing; but after having investigated with sufficient care what God is, we clearly and distinctly understand that it belongs to his nature to exist."[35] You ought to have concluded: "therefore, after we have investigated with sufficient care what God is, we can truly affirm that it belongs to God's nature to exist." From this it follows not that God really exists, but only that he ought to exist if his nature is something possible or non-contradictory. In other words, the nature or essence of God cannot be conceived apart from existence; thus if this is the case, then God does really exist. Others state the content of this argument in the following way: if "God exists" does not entail a contradiction, then certainly God does exist. But "God exists" does not entail a contradiction. Now there is a problem in the minor premise ("but 'God exists' does not entail a contradiction"), the truth of which opponents either claim to doubt or else deny. Moreover, that little clause in your argument ("after having investigated with sufficient clarity and distinctness what God is") assumes as true what not all accept (and even you admit that you grasp the infinite only in an inadequate fashion!). Obviously the same should be said of every one of God's attributes, for since whatever is in him is utterly infinite, who can grasp with his mind anything about God, unless it be in the most inadequate fashion, as they say, or over a rather long period of time? How then can you say that "you have investigated with sufficient clarity and distinctness what God is"?

34. Johan de Kater (Caterus), author of the *First Set of Objections*.
35. AT VII, 115.

Seventh, you have not the least thing to say about the immortality of the human mind, which nevertheless you really should have proved and demonstrated against those men—themselves unworthy of immortality— who utterly deny it and perhaps hold it in contempt. But neither do you seem to have sufficiently proved the distinction of the mind from all bodies, as we stated in our first point. To this we now add that it does not seem to follow from this distinction from the body that the mind is incorruptible or immortal, for what if its nature were limited to the duration of the body's lifetime, and God gave it only so much power and existence, with the result that it ceased to exist at the same time as the life of the body?

These, sir, are the points on which we desire to be enlightened by you, so that a reading of your most subtle and, we believe, true Meditations may be especially profitable to everyone. Thus it would be useful if, at the end of your explanations, you were to set forth the entire proof in geometrical form (in which you are so well versed), after establishing as premises certain definitions, postulates, and axioms, so that, with a single intuition, the mind of any reader might be satisfied by you and imbued with divine power.

Reply to the Second Set of Objections

I read with great pleasure the observations you made regarding my little work on first philosophy, and I recognize from these observations that your kindness toward me is coupled with piety toward God and a concern for promoting his glory. And I cannot help rejoicing, not only because you have deemed my arguments worthy of your consideration but also because you bring forward nothing in them to which I seem unable to provide an adequate response.

First, you admonish me to recall that it was not actually and truly but merely by a contrivance of the mind that I rejected the images [*phantasmata*] of all bodies, so that I might conclude that I am a thinking thing, lest perhaps I think later on that it follows that I am nothing but a mind.[36] That I have been sufficiently mindful of this is borne out in what I said in the Second Meditation: "But it is perhaps the case that these very things which I take to be nothing, because they are unknown to me, nevertheless are in fact no different from that me that I know. This I do not know, and I will not quarrel about it now," and so on.[37] With these words I expressly intended to warn the reader that at that point I was not yet seeking to know whether the mind is distinct from the body; rather, I was merely examining those of its properties of which I can have certain and evident knowledge. And

128

129

---

36. AT VII, 122.
37. AT VII, 27.

because I did observe many such properties there, I cannot admit without qualification what you added further on: "nevertheless I do not know what a thinking thing is."[38] For although I admit I did not yet know whether this thinking thing is the same thing as the body or is something different from it, I do not therefore admit that I had no knowledge of it. For what man ever knew a thing to such an extent that he knew that there is obviously nothing in it except what he knew to be in it? But the more we perceive about a thing the better we are said to know it. Just so, we know those men with whom we have lived a long time better than those whose faces alone we have seen or whose names we have merely heard, although even they are obviously not said to be unknown to us. In this sense I think I have demonstrated that the mind, considered apart from those properties commonly attributed to the body, is more known than the body when the latter is viewed apart from the mind. And this was all I had in mind there.

But I see what you are getting at, namely, that, since I wrote only six Meditations on First Philosophy, readers will wonder why nothing else but what I just now said is concluded in the first two Meditations, and they will therefore judge them to be meager and unworthy of public attention. To those points I simply answer that I have no fear that those who read with discernment the rest of what I have written would have an occasion to suspect that I came up short. Moreover, it seemed quite reasonable that I should place in separate Meditations those things that required special attention and needed to be treated separately from the rest.

And so, nothing is more conducive to obtaining a firm knowledge of things than that we become accustomed beforehand to doubt all things, especially corporeal things. And although it has been some time since I had seen several books on this subject written by the Academicians and Skeptics,[39] and although it is not without some distaste that I reheat the same old cabbage, nevertheless I had to devote an entire Meditation to this subject. And I would like my readers not just to spend the short amount of time it takes to get through the Meditation but rather to devote a few months or at least a few weeks to the topics requiring consideration before going on to the rest of the work. For in so doing, they no doubt could gain much greater profit from the rest of the work.

Further, because up until now all the ideas we had of what pertains to the mind have been utterly confused and intermingled with the ideas of sen-

---

38. AT VII, 122.

39. Cicero's *Academica* and Sextus Empiricus' *Outlines of Pyrrhonism* and *Against the Dogmatists* are perhaps the most influential ancient skeptical works. For a thorough discussion of the impact of these works on 16th-century European thought, see Richard H. Popkin's *The History of Scepticism from Erasmus to Descartes,* Chapter Two: "The Revival of Greek Scepticism in the 16th Century" (New York: Harper-Row, 1964), pp. 17–43.

sible things, and because this was the first and principal reason why none of what has been said about the soul and God could have been understood clearly enough, I thought I would be doing something worthwhile were I to explain how the properties or qualities of the mind are to be differentiated from the qualities of the body. For although many have already maintained that we must withdraw the mind from the senses in order to understand metaphysical subjects, nevertheless, to my knowledge, no one to date has shown how this can be achieved. However, the true way and, in my judgment, the only way to do this is contained in my Second Meditation, but it is not the sort of thing for which just one examination is sufficient. One must spend a great deal of time on it and repeat it often, so that the lifelong habit of confusing things grasped by the understanding with things that are corporeal would be eradicated by the contrary habit of at least a few days' duration of distinguishing them from one another. This seems to me to have been a most fitting reason for not treating anything else in the Second Meditation.

But in addition to this, you here ask how I can demonstrate that a body cannot think.[40] Please forgive me if I answer that I have not yet provided a place for this question to arise, since I first dealt with it in the Sixth Meditation, where I said: "my ability clearly and distinctly to understand one thing without another suffices to make me certain that the one thing is different from the other," and so on.[41] And a little further: "although I have a body[42] that is very closely joined to me, nevertheless, because on the one hand I have a clear and distinct idea of myself, insofar as I am merely[43] a thinking thing and not an extended thing, and because on the other hand I have a distinct idea of a body, insofar as it is merely[44] an extended thing and not a thinking thing, it is certain that I" (that is, a mind) "am really distinct from my body and can exist without it." To this one readily adds: "whatever is capable of thinking is a mind, or is called a mind; but since mind and body are really distinct from one another, no body is a mind; therefore no body can think."

132

I utterly fail to see what you are able to deny here. Do you deny that a clear understanding of one thing without the other suffices for the recognition of a real distinction between them? If you do, then give us a surer sign of a real distinction, for I confess that none can be given. What will you say? Are those things really distinct if each can exist without the other? But again I ask how you know that one thing can exist without the other. For if it is

40. AT VII, 122.

41. AT VII, 78.

42. This is an abbreviated version of: "although perhaps (or rather, as I shall soon say, assuredly) I have a body" (AT VII 78).

43. This word is added here by Descartes; it does not appear in AT VII 78.

44. This word is added here by Descartes; it does not appear in AT VII 78.

to be a sign of a real distinction, then this ought to be known. Perhaps you will say that this is obtained from the senses, since you see, touch, and so on, the one thing while the other is absent. But the trustworthiness of the senses is less certain than that of the understanding, and there are many ways in which it could happen that one and the same thing appears in several forms, or in several places, or in several different ways, and thus could be taken to be two things. And finally, if you recall what was said regarding the wax at the end of the Second Meditation,[45] you will notice that, properly speaking, not even bodies themselves are perceived by the senses, but by the understanding alone, so that sensing one thing without some other thing is merely a matter of having an idea of one thing and understanding that this idea is not the same as the idea of the other thing. However, the sole basis for such an understanding is that the one thing is perceived without the other thing. Nor can this understanding be certain unless the idea of each thing is clear and distinct. Thus, in order for it to be certain, this sign of a real distinction ought to be reduced to my own.

But if there are those who deny that they have distinct ideas of mind and body, all I can do is ask them to give sufficient attention to what is contained in the Second Meditation and to be cognizant of the fact that the opinion they entertain (if by chance they do entertain it)—namely, that the parts of the brain make a combined effort to form thoughts—arose not from any positive argument but merely from the fact that they have never had the experience of lacking a body, and that not infrequently they have been impeded by the body in their operations. It is just as if a person were to have been shackled in leg irons from infancy: he would think the leg irons were part of his body and that he needs them in order to walk.

Second, when you say that there is to be found within us a sufficient basis for forming the idea of God,[46] you are asserting nothing that differs from my opinion. For I myself expressly stated at the end of the Third Meditation that "this idea is innate in me,"[47] that is, it comes to me from no other source than myself. I also grant that "this idea could be formed even if we were ignorant of the fact that a supreme being exists, but not if he really were non-existent"; for, on the contrary, I have warned that "the whole force of the argument rests on the fact that it is impossible for the faculty of forming this idea to be in me, unless I were created by God."[48]

What you say about flies, plants, and so on does not succeed in proving the thesis that there can be a degree of perfection in the effect that did not exist beforehand in the cause. For it is certain that either in animals lacking

45. AT VII, 30.
46. AT VII, 123.
47. AT VII, 51.
48. AT VII, 51–2.

reason there is no perfection that is not also in inanimate bodies, or else, if there is such a perfection, this perfection would originate from somewhere else, and the sun, rain, and soil would not be the adequate cause of animals. Suppose someone fails to detect any cause which plays a part in the production of a fly and which possesses as many degrees of perfection as the fly. Suppose too that this person is not certain whether or not there is any perfection beyond the ones about which he is cognizant. It would be highly irrational for him to make this an occasion for doubting something that, as I will state in greater detail a bit later, is evident to the natural light itself.

To this I add that what was alleged about flies, having been taken from a consideration of material things, cannot enter the minds of those who follow my Meditations and withdraw their thoughts from sensible things so that they might philosophize in an orderly manner.

Nor does the fact that you call the idea of God, which is in us a "being of reason" [*ens rationis*], press your case any more effectively. For it is not true that the idea of God is a being of reason in the sense that "being of reason" is understood to mean something that does not exist; however, it is true in the sense that every operation of the understanding is a being of reason, that is, a being produced by reason. And even this entire world can be called a being of the divine reason, that is, a being created by a simple act of the divine mind. And now I have sufficiently underscored in various passages the fact that I am dealing only with the objective perfection or reality of the idea, which, no less than the objective craftsmanship that is in the idea of some very cleverly designed machine, demands a cause in which is really contained everything that is contained only objectively in the idea. 135

I utterly fail so see what I could add to make it more clearly apparent that this idea could not be present to me unless there exists a supreme being, except to say what role the reader plays: namely, if he pays careful attention to what I have already written, he might free himself from the prejudices that perhaps overwhelm his natural light and might accustom himself to believe in first notions (than which nothing can be more evident or more true) rather than in false and obscure opinions that have been fixed in his mind by prolonged usage.

The maxim that "there is nothing in the effect that did not exist beforehand in the cause, either in a similar or in a more eminent way" is a first notion, than which none clearer can be had. Now the commonplace "from nothing nothing comes" does not differ from it, for if one grants that something is in the effect that was not in the cause, one must also grant that this something was made by nothing. The only reason why nothing cannot be the cause of a thing is the fact that in such a cause there would not be the same thing as there is in the effect.

It is also a first notion that every reality or perfection that exists only objectively in ideas ought to exist either formally or eminently in their causes.

Upon this foundation alone rest all our beliefs that we have always entertained regarding the existence of things outside our mind. For what would have been the basis for our having suspected that these things exist, if not for the sole reason that the ideas of these things came to our mind through the senses?

But it will become clear to those who will pay sufficient attention and who will meditate for a long time with me on the fact that there is in us an idea of a supremely powerful and perfect being, and also that the objective reality of this idea is found in us neither formally nor eminently. For I cannot force upon a listless person what depends completely on the thought of others.

However, from these considerations the existence of God is most manifestly concluded. But for those whose natural light is so dim that they do not see that it is a first notion that every perfection that exists objectively in an idea ought to exist really in what causes it, I have hitherto demonstrated the conclusion in an even more palpable fashion, namely, from the fact that the mind which has this idea could not be derived from itself. Thus I do not see what else might be desired to win your surrender.

And there is no persuasiveness in the view that perhaps I might have received the idea that represents God to me from preconceived notions of the mind, from books, conversations with friends, and so on, but not from my mind alone.[49] For were I to ask these other people from whom I am said to have received the idea whether they got it from themselves or from someone else, the argument proceeds the same way as it does in my own case. And I will always conclude that the thing from which the idea first proceeded is God.

But what you add here, namely, that this idea could be formed from a prior inspection of corporeal things,[50] seems no more likely to me than if you were to declare that we have no faculty of hearing but that our awareness of sounds derives solely from seeing colors. For I can imagine a greater analogy or parity between colors and sounds than between corporeal things and God. And when you ask that I add something that brings us to an incorporeal or spiritual being, I can do nothing better than to send you back to my Second Meditation, so that you may observe that there is at least some purpose to it. For what could I accomplish here in one or two sentences, if I accomplished nothing there in a lengthy discourse specifically designed to address this point, a passage on which, it seems to me, I have worked as hard as on anything else I have written?

Nor is there an obstacle in the fact that in the Second Meditation I dealt only with the human mind; for I freely and gladly confess that the idea we

49. AT VII, 124.
50. Ibid.

have, for example, of the divine understanding, differs from the idea we have of our own understanding only in the way that the idea of an infinite number differs from the idea of the number four or the number two. And it is the same with the other attributes of God, a vestige of which we recognize in ourselves.

But besides this, we understand that there is in God an absolute immensity, simplicity, and unity which embraces all the other attributes and which has absolutely no copy. Rather it is, as I said before, "like the mark of a craftsman impressed upon his work." For this reason we recognize that none of the properties which, on account of the imperfection of our understanding, we ascribe piecemeal to God just as we perceive them in ourselves, belong univocally to God and to us. And we also discern that many of the indefinite particulars of which we have ideas, such as indefinite (or infinite) knowledge, likewise power, number, length, and so on, are also infinite. Some of these are contained formally in the idea of God (such as knowledge and power), while others are contained merely eminently (such as number and length); but this obviously would not be the case, were that idea nothing more than a figment in us.

Moreover, were this idea of God a mere figment, it would not be conceived in such a consistently similar fashion by everyone, for it is especially worth noting that metaphysicians are all in unanimous agreement about the description of God's attributes (that is, with respect to those that can be known through human reason alone). There is a greater difference of opinion among philosophers about the nature of anything physical and sensible, however straightforward and palpable the idea that we have of it might be.

Indeed, no men could err in conceiving this idea of God correctly, were they willing to attend exclusively to the nature of a supremely perfect being. But there are those who mix in other things at the same time, and in doing so they utter a contradiction. They contrive an imaginary idea of God, and then later on they not surprisingly deny the existence of this God that is represented through such an idea. So here, when you speak of a "most perfect corporeal being,"[51] if you take the expression "most perfect" in an absolute sense (the sense in which a corporeal thing is a being in which all perfections are to be found), then you are uttering a contradiction, because the very nature of a body entails many imperfections, such as that a body is divisible into parts, that each of its parts is not another part, and the like, for it is self-evident that it is a greater perfection not to be divided than to be divided, and so on. But if you understand "most perfect" merely in a qualified sense, as is appropriate to a body, this is not God.

I readily grant what you add regarding the idea of an angel. Even though we are less perfect than this idea, it is unnecessary for the idea to have been

138

139

---

51. AT VII, 124.

produced in us by an angel,[52] since I have already declared in the Third Meditation that this idea can be composed from the ideas we have of God and man.[53] This in no way conflicts with my views.

However, those who deny they have an idea of God, but in place of it form some image [*idolum*], and so on, deny the name but concede the fact. For I certainly do not believe that this idea is of the same nature as the images of material things depicted in the imagination, but rather that it is merely something we perceive by means of acts of simple apprehension, judgment, or reasoning on the part of the understanding. And I contend that from the mere fact that I somehow encounter by means of thought or understanding a perfection which is above me (say, from the mere fact that I notice that when I count I cannot reach the greatest of all numbers, and hence I recognize that there is something in the nature of counting that exceeds my powers), it does not necessarily follow that an infinite number exists or for that matter that the expression "infinite number" entails a contradiction.[54] But it does necessarily follow, as you say, that I have a power of conceiving that there is a number that can be thought of which is greater than any that I could have ever thought of, and that I received this power not from myself but from some being more perfect than me.

Nor is it relevant whether or not this concept of an indefinite number is called an idea. However, in order to understand what this being is that is more perfect than me, that is, whether it is this infinite number itself that really exists, or is instead something else, we must consider all the other properties, over and above the power of giving me this idea, that can exist in the same thing from which the idea originates, and thus it will be found to be God alone.

Finally, when it is said that God "cannot be thought of," this is understood with respect to the sort of thought that adequately comprehends God, but not with respect to the sort of inadequate thought that is in us and that suffices for knowing that God exists. And it is of no importance that the idea of the unity of all God's perfections is said to be formed in the same way as Porphyry's universals,[55] although there certainly is this important difference, namely, that unity designates a certain special and positive perfection in God, whereas generic unity adds nothing real to the natures of single individuals.

Third, when I said that we can know nothing for certain unless we first know that God exists, I declared in express terms that I was speaking only of

---

52. AT VII, 124.

53. AT VII, 43.

54. AT VII, 124.

55. Porphyry, a second-century AD Neoplatonist, proposed a classification of things under genera and species. Thus, "Porphyry's universals" here refers to generic unities, "universal unities which do not exist in reality but only in the intellect," AT VII, 124.

the knowledge of those conclusions that can be recalled without our attending any further to the premises from which we deduced them.[56] For the knowledge [*notitia*] of principles is not customarily called "scientific knowledge" [*scientia*] by dialecticians. However, when we are cognizant of the fact we are thinking things, this is a certain [*quaedam*] first notion which is concluded to from no syllogism. Again, it is not the case when someone says "I think, therefore I am, or I exist," that he is deducing existence from thought by means of a syllogism; rather he is recognizing it as something self-evident by a simple intuition of the mind. This is evident from the fact that were he to deduce it by means of a syllogism, he would have to have known beforehand the major premise ("whatever thinks is or exists"). But surely it is instead the case that he learns this by experiencing for himself that it is impossible for him to be thinking without existing. For such is the nature of our mind that it forms general propositions out of the knowledge of particular ones.   *141*

However, I do not deny that an atheist could know [*cognoscere*] clearly that the three angles of a triangle are equal to two right angles; I am simply affirming that his knowledge [*cognitionem*] is not true scientific knowledge [*scientiam*], since no knowledge [*cognitio*] that can be rendered doubtful seems to deserve to be called scientific knowledge [*scientia*]. And since we are supposing him to be an atheist, this person cannot be certain that he is not being deceived in those very things that seem most evident to him, as has been sufficiently shown. And although perhaps this doubt may not occur to him, nevertheless it can occur to him if he examines the matter or if someone else brings it to his attention. And he will never be safe from it unless he acknowledges God beforehand.

And it is of no importance that perhaps he thinks he has demonstrations to prove that there is no God. For since they are in no way true, their defects can always be pointed out to him. When this happens, he will be dislodged from his opinion.

This will surely not be difficult to accomplish, if all he were to bring to bear on behalf of his arguments is what you append here, namely, that a being which is infinite in every class of perfection excludes any other being, and so on.[57] For first, if we were to ask how he knows that this exclusion of all other beings belongs to the nature of infinity, he will have nothing with which to make a rational response, since the word "infinity" is not normally understood to refer to something that excludes the existence of finite things. And all he can know of the nature of something he believes to be nothing, and thus to have no nature, is what is contained in the mere nominal mean-   *142* ing of the word that he has acquired from others. Next, what would take place by means of the infinite power of this imaginary infinity, were it unable

56. AT VII, 69.
57. AT VII, 125.

ever to create anything? And finally, since we observe in ourselves some power of thinking, we easily conceive that a power of thinking can also be in some other being and that this power is greater than the power that is in ourselves. But even if we suppose this power is increased to infinity, we will have no fear on this score that our own power may be lessened. And the same holds for all the other properties that are attributed to God, even his power (provided we do not suppose there is any power in us except what is subject to the divine will). Thus, he can be understood to be utterly infinite without this in any way excluding created things.

Fourth, when I deny that God lies or is a deceiver, I think I am in agreement with all the metaphysicians and theologians who ever were or ever will be. Nor is what you have alleged to the contrary any more a hindrance than if I were to have denied that God becomes angry or that he is subject to the other agitations of the mind, and you were to have brought forward passages from Scripture where human emotions are attributed to him. For everyone knows the distinction between the ways of speaking about God which are proportioned to the common way of thinking and which surely contain some truth, but a truth geared to men (the kind Sacred Scripture usually employs). The other way of speaking expresses more closely the naked truth, though it is not geared to men, and this way ought to be used by those engaged in philosophy. And it was especially incumbent on me to have used this latter way of speaking in my *Meditations,* since not even there did I as yet suppose other men were known to me; moreover, I did not regard myself as consisting of mind and body, but of mind alone. Whence it is apparent that I was not speaking of the sort of lying that is expressed in words, but only of the internal and formal ill will that is entailed in deception.

Thus, although what is said about the prophet ("come forty days and Nineveh shall be destroyed," and so on) was not even a verbal lie but merely a threat whose fulfillment depended upon the fulfillment of a particular condition. And when it is said that God "hardened the heart of Pharaoh," or words to that effect, we must not take this to mean that he did this in some positive sense. On the contrary, he did this in a negative sense by not bestowing on Pharaoh the grace that would have brought about his change of heart. Still, I did not wish to criticize those who grant that God can utter through his prophets something that is literally a lie (similar to the lies told by physicians who use them to deceive the sick in order to make them well, that is, lying in which there is no malicious intention to deceive).

Nevertheless, and this is the more important point, we really do sometimes seem to be deceived by the natural instinct that God has given us, as when a man with dropsy is thirsty. For then he is positively driven to drink by the nature that has been given him by God for the preservation of his body, yet this nature is deceiving him, since taking a drink will prove harmful to him. But I have explained in the Sixth Meditation why this is not in conflict with God's goodness or veracity.

However, in those cases that cannot be thus explained, namely, in our clearest and most careful judgments, which, if they were false, could not be corrected by any clearer ones or with the aid of any other natural faculty, I straightforwardly affirm that we cannot be deceived. For since God is a supreme being, he must be the supreme good and the supreme truth; it is therefore contradictory for anything to originate from him that positively tends toward what is false. But since there can be nothing real in us that has not been given by him (as was proved at the same time we proved God's existence), and since we do have a real faculty for recognizing what is true and for distinguishing it from what is false (as is evident from the mere fact that ideas of the false and the true are in us), unless this faculty tended to what is true—at least when we use it properly (that is, when we assent to nothing but what is clearly and distinctly perceived), God, who gave us this faculty, would rightly be taken to be a deceiver.

Thus you see that, after we know that God exists, we need to imagine him to be a deceiver if we wish to call into doubt what we clearly and distinctly perceive; and because he cannot be imagined to be a deceiver, these perceptions must be accepted as true and certain.

But since I here observe that you are still mired in the doubts which I proposed in the First Meditation and which I believed I had disposed of with sufficient care in the succeeding Meditations, I will expound again here the foundation on which it seems to me all human certainty can be based.

In the first place, as soon as we think we correctly perceive something, we spontaneously persuade ourselves that it is true. But if this persuasion is so firm that we could never have any reason for doubting what we are thus persuaded of, there is nothing left for us to inquire about: we have all that we could reasonably hope for.

For what is it to us if perhaps someone imagines that something of whose truth we have been persuaded so firmly appears false to God or to an angel and hence it is, absolutely speaking, false? What do we care about this absolute falsity, since we in no way believe in it and do not in the least suspect it? For we presume so firm a conviction that it cannot in any way be removed, and this conviction is thus plainly equivalent to the most perfect certainty.

But one can doubt whether any such certainty, or so firm and unchangeable a conviction, is to be had.

And it is indeed obvious that such certainty is not to be had in regard to those things we perceive with the least bit of obscurity or confusion, for obscurity of any sort is a sufficient reason for our doubting these things. Nor is such certainty to be had in regard to things perceived by sense alone, regardless of how clear the perception might be. For we have often noticed that error can be found in sensation, as when someone with dropsy is thirsty, or when a man with jaundice sees snow as yellow, for he sees it with no less clarity and distinctness than we, when we see the snow as white. Thus it remains that this certainty, if it is to be had at all, is to be had only with respect to what is perceived clearly by the understanding.

However, some of these perceptions are so evident and at the same time so simple that we could never think of them without believing them to be true, as, for example, that while I think, I exist, or that what was once done cannot be undone, and the like—about which things it is obvious that this certainty is to be had. For we cannot doubt these things unless we think of them; but we cannot think about them without at the same time believing them to be true, as has been supposed. Therefore we cannot doubt them without at the same time believing them to be true; in other words, we can never doubt them.

No difficulty is raised by the claim that we have often observed other people having been deceived in what they believed they knew more clearly than the light of day.[58] For we have never observed, nor could anyone ever observe, that this has happened to those who sought the clarity of their perception from the understanding alone; rather, this happens only to those who have drawn their clarity either from the senses or from some false prejudice.

Again, no difficulty is raised were someone to suppose that these things appear false to God or to an angel, for the evidence of our perception does not permit us to listen to someone conjuring up such a scenario.

There are other things that surely are perceived most clearly by our understanding when we pay sufficient attention to the reasons on which the knowledge of these things depends, and thus during that time we cannot doubt them. But because we can forget these reasons and in the meantime recall the conclusions deduced from them, there is a question of whether a firm and unchangeable conviction is also to be had with regard to these conclusions when we recall that they had been deduced from evident principles, for this recollection must be assumed if they are to be called conclusions. And I reply by saying that this certainty is surely possessed by those who have known God in such a way that they understand that it must be the case that the faculty of understanding given them by God tends toward the truth. But this certainty is not had by others. And this has been explained so clearly at the end of the Fifth Meditation that it seems nothing here need be added.[59]

Fifth, I marvel that you deny that the will lays itself open to peril if it follows a concept of the understanding that is not at all clear and distinct.

58. AT VII, 126.
59. AT VII, 70.

For what renders the will certain, if what it follows is not clearly perceived? And who has ever denied—be he philosopher, theologian, or just an ordinary man using his reason—that the more clearly we understand something before assenting to it, the less danger there is of our being involved in error, and that those who make their judgment in ignorance of the basis of their judgment are the ones who are making a mistake? But a concept is said to be obscure or confused only because something unknown is contained in it.

Consequently, what you raise as an objection regarding the faith one should embrace[60] has no more force against me than it does against all other people who have ever cultivated their human reason, and it certainly has no force against them. For although faith is said to be a matter of things obscure, nevertheless the reason why we embrace it is not obscure but is more translucent than any natural light. Surely a distinction needs to be made between the subject matter, or the thing to which we give our assent, and the formal reason [*rationem formalem*] that moves the will to give its assent. For it is only in this formal reason that we require transparency [*perspecui-tatem*]. And as to the subject matter, no one has ever denied that it can be obscure; indeed, it can be obscurity itself. For when I judge that obscurity needs to be removed from our concepts so that we could assent to them without any danger of erring, it is in regard to this very obscurity that I form a clear judgment. In addition, it should be noted that the clarity or transparency by which our will can be moved to give our assent is of two sorts: namely, one derived from the light of nature and the other from divine grace. But now, although faith is commonly said to be a matter of things obscure, nevertheless this is understood only in regard to the thing or the subject matter with which our faith is concerned. One should not draw the conclusion that the formal reason, in virtue of which we assent to matters of faith, is obscure. For on the contrary, this formal reason consists in a certain inner light, and, having been supernaturally illumined by God with this light, we firmly believe [*confidimus*] that what is proposed for our belief has been revealed by God and that it is utterly impossible for God to lie. And this is more certain than any light of nature, and often it is even more evident because of the light of grace.

Surely, when the Turks and other unbelievers do not embrace the Christian religion, their erring [*peccare*] is not owing to the fact that they did not wish to give their assent to obscure matters (for they really are obscure). Rather it is owing to the fact that either they are fighting against the divine grace internally moving within them or else they are rendering themselves unworthy of grace because they erred [*peccando*] in some other undertakings. And if there were an unbeliever who was bereft of all supernatural grace and was completely ignorant of the teachings we Christians believe to have been

60. AT VII,126.

revealed by God, and yet if the unbeliever, led on by certain false reasonings, were to embrace these teachings even though they are obscure to him, I boldly declare that this man would not be a believer but instead would err [*peccaturum*] in not having used his reason rightly. Nor do I believe that any orthodox theologian has ever thought otherwise on the matter. Nor even will those who read my writings be able to believe that I have not acknowledged the supernatural light, since I stated in no uncertain terms in the

149   Fourth Meditation, where I investigated the cause of falsity, that it disposes the innermost parts of our thought to an act of willing and yet does not diminish our liberty.[61]

Moreover, I would like you to recall that in matters that can be embraced by the will I drew a very careful distinction between the conduct of life and the contemplation of truth. For as far as the conduct of life is concerned, so foreign is it to me to think that we should give our assent only to what is clearly observed that, on the contrary, I think that not even probable truths are always to be hoped for. Yet from time to time one thing must be chosen from among a number of things that are completely unknown and, once chosen, it is no less to be held on to than if it had been chosen for very evident reasons, so long as no reason can be entertained to the contrary, as I explained on page 26 of my *Discourse on Method*.[62] But where there is only a question of the contemplation of truth, who has ever denied that assent is to be withheld from matters that are obscure and that are observed with insufficient distinctness? But the fact that the contemplation of truth was the only topic I dealt with in my *Meditations* is borne out both by the entire project and by what I declared in no uncertain terms at the end of the First Meditation, where I said that I could not indulge too much in distrust, since I was bent not on outward accomplishments but only on knowledge.[63]

Sixth, in the place where you criticize the conclusion of a syllogism I constructed,[64] you yourselves seem to have misunderstood the argument. For in order to get the conclusion you want, the major premise should have been worded thus: what we clearly understand to belong to the nature of a thing can truly be affirmed to belong to that thing's nature. But then it would contain nothing but a useless tautology. But my major premise was

150   as follows: what we clearly understand to belong to the nature of a thing can truly be affirmed of that thing. In other words, if it belongs to the nature of man to be an animal, it can be affirmed that man is an animal; if it belongs to the nature of a triangle to have three angles equal to two right angles, it can be affirmed that a triangle has three angles equal to two right angles;

---

61. AT VII, 58.
62. That is, AT VI, 24–5.
63. AT VII, 22.
64. AT VII, 127.

if it belongs to the nature of God to exist, it can be affirmed that God exists, and so on. But my minor premise was: but it pertains to the nature of God to exist. From this the obvious conclusion to be drawn is the one I have drawn: therefore it can truly be affirmed of God that he exists; but not the conclusion you want: therefore we can truly affirm that it belongs to God's nature to exist.

And so, to make use of the criticism you attach,[65] you should have denied the major premise and said: what we clearly understand to belong to the nature of something cannot therefore be affirmed of it unless its nature is possible or non-contradictory. But please observe how little force this criticism has. For if by "possible" you understand, as everyone commonly does, "whatever is not repugnant to human conception," then, according this use of the term, it is obvious that the nature of God, as I have described it, is possible, since I have supposed there is contained in God's nature only what we clearly and distinctly perceive ought to belong to it, and thus it could not conflict with human ways of conceiving things. On the other hand, surely you are imagining some other sort of possibility relating to the object itself. But this latter sort of possibility cannot be known by the human understanding unless this latter possibility parallels the former type of possibility. This latter sort of possibility can never be known by the human understanding, and thus it does not so much cause us to deny the nature or exis- *151* tence of God as to overturn all the rest of what is known by men. No impossibility is to be found in the nature of God as far as our concept is concerned; indeed, all the properties that we embrace in the concept of the divine nature are so interconnected with one another that it seems to us to entail a contradiction to say that one of these properties does not belong to God. Thus, were we to deny the nature of God to be possible, we would be equally entitled to deny that the three angles of a triangle are equal to two right angles, or that he who is actually [*actu*] thinking exists. And a fortiori we will be permitted to deny that anything we get from the senses is true, and thus all human knowledge is destroyed, but for no good reason.

As to the argument you conflate with mine, namely: if the statement "God exists" is not self-contradictory, then it is certain that God exists; but "God exists" is not self-contradictory; therefore, and so on.[66] Surely this is materially true, but formally it is a sophism. For in the major premise the expression "is not self-contradictory" has reference to the concept of a cause in virtue of which God can exist; however, in the minor premise it has reference simply to the concept of the divine existence and nature itself. This is evident from the fact that, were the major premise to be denied, the proof will have to be worded in the following way: if God does not yet exist, then

65. AT VII, 127.
66. AT VII, 151.

"God exists" is self-contradictory, since there cannot be a cause sufficient to produce God. But "God exists" is not self-contradictory, as was supposed. Therefore, and so on. But if the minor premise were denied, the following will have to be said: there is no self-contradiction in a thing in whose formal concept there is nothing involving a self-contradiction. But there is in the formal concept of divine existence or nature nothing that involves a

152   self-contradiction. Therefore, and so on. These two arguments are quite different from one another. For it is possible to understand, regarding a thing, that there is nothing that prevents its being able to exist; meanwhile something may be understood on the part of its cause that prevents its being produced.

However, even if we conceive God only inadequately, or, if you wish, most inadequately,[67] this does not prevent it being certain that his nature is possible or is not self-contradictory. Nor does it prevent our being able to affirm truly that we have examined his nature with sufficient clarity (that is, with as much clarity as is needed to know this and also to know that necessary existence belongs to this same nature of God). For every self-contradiction or impossibility consists in our own conception, which improperly combines ideas that are at odds with one another; nor can it reside in anything outside the understanding, because, by the very fact that there is something outside the understanding, it is obvious that it is not self-contradictory but is possible. However, self-contradiction in our concepts arises solely from the fact that they are obscure and confused; but no self-contradiction can ever be found among clear and distinct concepts. And thus it suffices that we understand clearly and distinctly those few things that we perceive about God, even if in a completely inadequate fashion, and that, among other things, we notice that necessary existence is contained in our concept of God, inadequately as it is, in order to affirm that we have examined his nature with sufficient clarity and that it is not self-contradictory.

153   **Seventh,** I have already stated in the Synopsis of my *Meditations*[68] why I wrote nothing about the immortality of the soul. I have shown above that I sufficiently proved the real distinction of the soul from every body. But I confess I cannot refute your further contention, namely, that the immortality of the soul does not follow from its being really distinct from the body, since it still can be said that it has been made by God to be of such a nature that its duration comes to an end at the same time as the body's life comes to an end.[69] For I do not presume to undertake to determine, by means of the power of human reason, anything with respect to what depends upon the free will of God. Natural knowledge teaches that the mind is different [*esse*

67. AT VII, 127.

68. AT VII, 13–4.

69. AT VII 128.

diversum] from the body, and that it is a substance. But as far as the human body is concerned, the difference between it and other bodies consists solely in the configuration of its members and other such accidents; ultimately the death of the body is completely dependent on some division or change of shape. And we have neither proof nor precedent to convince us that the death or annihilation of a substance such as the mind ought to follow from so slight a cause as a change in shape, which is merely a mode and, then, not a mode of the mind but of the body, which is really distinct from the mind. Moreover, we have neither proof nor precedent to convince us that any substance can perish. This is sufficient to let us conclude that the mind, insofar   *154* as it can be known by natural philosophy, is immortal.

But if one asks regarding the absolute power of God whether perhaps God may have decreed that human souls cease to exist at the same moment when the bodies God has joined to them are destroyed, then it is for God alone to answer. And since God himself has already revealed to us that this will not happen, there obviously is no, or a very slight, occasion for doubting.

It remains for me now to thank you for seeing fit to warn me with such kindness and honesty not only of things you yourselves have noticed but also of things that could be stated by detractors or atheists. For I see nothing in what you have proposed that I have not already either solved or ruled out. (For as to what you brought forward regarding flies produced by the sun, and about the indigenous people of Canada, the Ninevites, the Turks and the like,[70] these things cannot enter the minds of those who have followed the path I have pointed out and who for a time put a distance between themselves and all they receive from the senses, so that they may observe what reason, pure and uncorrupted, teaches them. Thus I thought I had already ruled out such things. But be that as it may, I nevertheless judge that these objections of yours will be especially valuable to my project. For I anticipate that hardly any readers who will attend so carefully to what I have tried to put on paper will remember all of what went before when they reach the end of the work. And those who do not do so will easily run into some doubts which they will later see have been dealt with satisfactorily in my   *155* reply, or else my reply will at least provide the occasion for examining further the truth of the matter.

Finally, as to your suggestion[71] that I should put forward my arguments in geometrical fashion so that the reader could perceive them, as it were, in a single intuition, it is worthwhile to indicate here how much I have already followed this suggestion and how much I think it should be followed in the future. I draw a distinction between two things in the geometrical style of writing, namely the order and the mode [*ratio*] of the demonstration.

70. AT VII, 123–6.
71. Ibid.

Order consists simply in putting forward as first what ought to be known without any help from what comes afterward and then in arranging all the rest in such a way that they are demonstrated solely by means of what preceded them. And I certainly did try to follow this order as carefully as possible in my Meditations. And it was owing to my observance of it that I treated the distinction between the mind and the body not in the Second Meditation but at the end in the Sixth Meditation. And it also explains why I deliberately and knowingly omitted many other things, since they required an explanation of a great many more.

But the mode [*ratio*] of an argument is of two sorts: one that proceeds by way of analysis, the other by way of synthesis.

Analysis shows the true way by which a thing has been discovered methodically, and, as it were, "a priori," so that were the reader willing to follow it and to pay sufficient attention to everything, he will no less perfectly understand a thing and render it his own than had he himself discovered it. However, analysis possesses nothing with which to compel belief in
156   a less attentive or hostile reader, for if he fails to pay attention to the least thing among those that this mode [*ratio*] proposes, the necessity of its conclusions is not apparent; and it often hardly touches at all on many things that nevertheless ought to be carefully noted, since they are obvious to anyone who is sufficiently attentive.

Synthesis, on the other hand, indeed clearly demonstrates its conclusions by an opposite way, where the investigation is conducted, as it were, "a posteriori" (although it is often the case here that this proof is more "a priori" than it is in the analytic mode). And it uses a long series of definitions, postulates, axioms, theorems, and problems, so that if something in what follows is denied, this mode may at once point out that it is contained in what went before. And thus it wrests from the reader his assent, however hostile and obstinate he may be. But this mode is not as satisfactory as the other one nor does it satisfy the minds of those who desire to learn, since it does not teach the way in which the thing was discovered.

It was this mode alone that the ancient geometricians were wont to use in their writings—not that they were utterly ignorant of the other mode, but rather, as I see it, they held it in such high regard that they kept it to themselves alone as a secret.

But in my Meditations I followed analysis exclusively, which is the true and best way to teach. But as to synthesis, which is undoubtedly what you are asking me about here, even though in geometry it is most suitably placed after analysis, nevertheless it cannot be so conveniently applied to these metaphysical matters.

For there is this difference: that the first notions that are presupposed for demonstrating things geometrical are readily admitted by everyone, since they accord with the use of the senses. Thus there is no difficulty there, except

in correctly deducing the consequences, which can be done by all sorts of *157*
people, even the less attentive, provided only that they remember what went
before. And the minute differentiation of propositions was done for the purpose of making them easy to recite and thus can be committed to memory
even by the recalcitrant.

But in these metaphysical matters, on the contrary, nothing is more an
object of intense effort than causing its first notions to be clearly and distinctly perceived. For although they are by their nature no less known or
even more known than those studied by geometricians, nevertheless, because
many of the prejudices of the senses (with which we have been accustomed
since our infancy) are at odds with them, they are perfectly known only by
those who are especially attentive and meditative and who withdraw their
minds from corporeal things as much as possible. And if these first notions
were put forward by themselves, they could easily be denied by those who
are eager to engage in conflict.

This was why I wrote "meditations," rather than "disputations," as the
philosophers do, or theorems and problems, as the geometricians do:
namely, so that by this very fact I might attest that the only dealings I would
have were with those who, along with myself, did not refuse to consider
the matter attentively and to meditate. For the very fact that someone girds
himself to attack the truth renders him less suitable for perceiving it, since
he is withdrawing himself from considering the arguments that attest to the
truth in order to find other arguments that dissuade him of the truth.

But perhaps someone will object here that a person should not seek
arguments for the sake of being contentious when he knows that the truth *158*
is set before him. But so long as this is in doubt, all the arguments on both
sides ought to be assessed in order to know which ones are the more firm.
And it would be unfair of me to want my arguments to be admitted as true
before they had been scrutinized, while at the same time not allowing the
consideration of opposing arguments.

This would certainly be a just criticism, if any of those things which I
desire in an attentive and non-hostile reader were such that they could
withdraw him from considering any other arguments in which there was
the slightest hope of finding more truth than in my arguments. However,
the greatest doubt is contained among the things I am proposing; moreover,
there is nothing I more strongly urge than that each thing be scrutinized
most diligently and that nothing is to be straightforwardly accepted except
what has been so clearly and distinctly examined that we cannot but give
our assent to it. On the other hand, the only matters from which I desire to
divert the minds of my readers are things they have never sufficiently examined and that they derived not on the basis of a firm reason, but from the
senses alone. As a consequence, I do not think anyone can believe that he
will be in greater danger of error were he to consider only those things that

I propose to him than were he to withdraw his mind from them and turn it toward other things—things that are opposed to them in some way and that spread darkness—that is, toward the prejudices of the senses.

And thus I am right in desiring especially close attention on the part of my readers; and I have chosen the one style of writing over all the others with which I thought it can most especially be procured and from which I *159* am convinced that readers will discern a greater profit than they would have thought, since, on the other hand, when the synthetic mode of writing is employed, people are likely to seem to themselves to have learned more than they actually did. But I also think it is fair for me straightforwardly to reject as worthless those criticisms made against me by those who have refused to meditate with me and who cling to their preformed opinions.

But I know how difficult it will be, even for those who pay close attention and earnestly search for the truth, to intuit the entire body of my Meditations and at the same time to discern its individual parts. I think both of these things ought to be done so that the full benefit may be derived from my Meditations. I shall therefore append here a few things in the synthetic style that I hope will prove somewhat helpful to my readers. Nevertheless, I wish they would take note of the fact that I did not intend to cover as much here as is found in my Meditations, otherwise I should then be more loquacious here than in the Meditations themselves; moreover, I will not explain in detail what I do include, partly out of a desire for brevity and partly to prevent anyone who thinks that my remarks here were sufficient from making a very cursory examination of the Meditations themselves, from which I am convinced that much more benefit is to be discerned.

160   ARGUMENTS PROVING THE EXISTENCE OF GOD AND
              THE DISTINCTION OF THE SOUL FROM THE BODY,
                   ARRANGED IN GEOMETRICAL FASHION

Definitions

I. By the word "thought" I include everything that is in us in such a way that we are immediately aware of it. Thus all the operations of the will, understanding, imagination, and senses are thoughts. But I added "immediately" to exclude those things that follow from these operations, such as voluntary motion, which surely has thought as its principle but nevertheless is not itself a thought.

II. By the word "idea" I understand that form of any thought through the immediate perception of which I am aware of that very same thought. Thus I could not express anything in words and understand what I am saying, without this very fact making it certain that there exists in me an idea of what is being signified by those words. And thus it is not the mere images depicted in the corporeal imagination that I call "ideas." In point of fact, I in no way call these images "ideas," insofar as they are in the corporeal imagination, that is, insofar as they have been depicted in some part of the brain, but only insofar as they inform the mind itself that is turned toward that part of the brain.

III. By the "objective reality of an idea" I understand the being of the thing represented by an idea, insofar as it exists in the idea. In the same way one can speak of "objective perfection," "objective skill," and so on. For whatever we perceive to exist in the objects of our ideas exists objectively in these very ideas.

IV. The same things are said to exist "formally" in the objects of our ideas when they exist in these objects in just the way we perceive them, and to exist "eminently" in the objects of our ideas when they indeed are not in these objects in the way we perceive them, but have such an amount of perfection that they could fill the role of things existing formally.

V. Everything in which there immediately inheres, as in a subject, or through which there exists, something we perceive (that is, some property, or quality, or attribute whose real idea is in us) is called a "substance." For we have no other idea of substance itself, taken in the strict sense, except that it is a thing in which whatever we perceive or whatever is objectively in one of our ideas exists either formally or eminently, since it is evident by the light of nature that no real attribute can belong to nothing.

VI. That substance in which thought immediately resides is called "mind." However, I am speaking here of the mind rather than of the soul, since the word "soul" is equivocal and is often used for something corporeal.

VII. That substance which is the immediate subject of local extension and of the accidents that presuppose extension, such as shape, position, movement from place to place, and so on, is called "body." Whether what we call "mind" and what we call "body" are one and the same substance or two different ones, must be examined later on.

VIII. That substance which we understand to be supremely perfect and in which we conceive absolutely nothing that involves any defect or limitation upon its perfection is called "God."

IX. When we say that something is contained in the nature or concept of something, this is the same as saying that it is true of that thing or that it can be affirmed of that thing.

X. Two substances are said to be really distinct from one another when each of them can exist without the other.

Postulates

I ask first that readers take note of how feeble are the reasons why they have up until now put their faith in their senses, and how uncertain are all the judgments that they have constructed upon them; and that they review this within themselves for so long and so often that they finally acquire the habit of no longer placing too much faith in them. For I deem this necessary for perceiving the certainty of things metaphysical.

Second, I ask that readers ponder their own mind and all its attributes. They will discover that they cannot be in doubt about these things, even though they suppose that everything they ever received from the senses is false. And I ask them not to stop pondering this point until they have acquired for themselves the habit of perceiving it clearly and of believing that it is easier to know than anything corporeal.

163   Third, I ask that readers weigh diligently the self-evident propositions that they find within themselves, such as that the same thing cannot be and not be at the same time, that nothingness cannot be the efficient cause of anything, and the like. And thus readers may exercise the astuteness implanted in them by nature, pure and freed from the senses, but which the objects of sense are wont to cloud and obscure as much as possible. For by this means the truth of the axioms that follow will easily be known to them.

Fourth, I ask readers to examine the ideas of those natures that contain a combination of many accidents together, such as the nature of a triangle, the nature of a square, or of some other figure; and likewise the nature of the mind, the nature of the body, and, above all, the nature of God, the supremely perfect being. And I ask them to realize that all that we perceive to be contained in them truly can be affirmed of them. For example, the equality of its three angles to two right angles is contained in the nature of a triangle, and divisibility is contained in the nature of a body, that is, of an extended thing (for we can conceive of no extended thing that is so small that we could not at least divide it in thought). Such being the case, it is true to say of every triangle that its three angles are equal to two right angles, and that every body is divisible.

Fifth, I ask readers to dwell long and earnestly in the contemplation of the nature of the supremely perfect being; and to consider, among other things, that possible existence is indeed contained in the ideas of all other things, whereas the idea of God contains not merely possible existence, but absolutely necessary existence. For from this fact alone and without any discursive reasoning they will know that God exists. And it will be no less self-

164   evident to them than that the number two is even or that the number three is odd, and the like. For there are some things that are self-evident to some and understood by others only through discursive reasoning.

Sixth, I ask the readers to get into the habit of distinguishing things that are clearly known from things that are obscure, by carefully reviewing all the examples of clear and distinct perception, and likewise of obscure and confused perception that I have recounted in my Meditations. For this is something more easily learned from examples than from rules, and I think that therein I have either explained or at least to some extent touched upon all the examples pertaining to this subject.

Seventh, and finally, when readers perceive that they have never discovered any falsity in things they clearly perceived and that, on the other hand, they have never found truth in things they only obscurely grasped, except by chance, I ask them to consider that it is utterly irrational to call into doubt things that are clearly and distinctly perceived by the pure understanding merely on account of prejudices based on the senses or on account of hypotheses in which something unknown is contained. For thus they will easily admit the following axioms as true and indubitable. Nevertheless, many of these axioms could admittedly have been much better explained and ought to have been put forward as theorems rather than as axioms, had I wanted to be more precise.

Axioms, or Common Notions

I. Nothing exists concerning which we could not ask what the cause is of its existence. For this can be asked of God himself, not that he needs any cause in order to exist but because the very immensity of his nature is the cause or the reason why he needs no cause in order to exist.

II. The present time does not depend on the time immediately preceding it, and therefore no less a cause is required to preserve a thing than is initially required to produce it.

III. No thing, and no perfection of a thing actually existing in it, can have nothing, or a non-existing thing, as the cause of its existence.

IV. Whatever reality or perfection there is in a thing is formally or eminently in its first and adequate cause.

V. Whence it also follows that the objective reality of our ideas requires a cause that contains this very same reality, and not merely objectively, but either formally or eminently. And we should note that the acceptance of this axiom is so necessary that the knowledge of all things, sensible as well as insensible, depends on it alone. For example, how is it we know that the sky exists? Because we see it? But this vision does not touch the mind except insofar as it is an idea: an idea, I say, inhering in the mind itself, not an image depicted in the corporeal imagination. And on account of this idea we are able to judge that the sky exists only because every idea must have a really existing cause of its objective reality; and we judge this cause to be the sky itself. The same holds for the rest.

VI. There are several degrees of reality or being; for a substance has more reality than an accident or a mode, and an infinite substance has more reality than a finite substance. Thus there is also more objective reality in the

166   idea of a substance than there is in the idea of an accident, and there is more
objective reality in the idea of an infinite substance than there is in the idea
of a finite substance.

VII. The will of a thinking thing is surely borne voluntarily and freely
(for this is the essence of the will) but nonetheless infallibly toward the good
that it clearly knows, and therefore, if it should know of any perfections that
it lacks, it will immediately give them to itself, if they are within its power.

VIII. Whatever can make what is greater or more difficult can also make
what is less.

IX. It is greater to create or preserve a substance than to create or preserve the attributes or properties of a substance; however, it is not greater to
create something than to preserve it, as has already been said.

X. Existence is contained in the idea or concept of everything, because
we cannot conceive of something except as existing [*sub ratione existentiae*].
Possible or contingent existence is contained in the concept of a limited
thing, whereas necessary and perfect existence is contained in the concept
of a supremely perfect being.

Proposition I: The existence of God is known from the mere consideration of his nature.

Demonstration: To say that something is contained in the nature or
concept of a thing is the same thing as saying that it is true of that thing
167   (Def. IX). But necessary existence is contained in the concept of God (Ax. X).
Therefore it is true to say of God that necessary existence is in him, or that
he exists.

And this is the syllogism I already made use of above in reply to the Sixth
Objection[72]; and its conclusion can be self-evident to those who are free of
prejudices, as was stated in Postulate V. But since it is not easy to arrive at
such astuteness, we will seek the same thing in other ways.

Proposition II: The existence of God is demonstrated a posteriori from
the mere fact that the idea of God is in us.

Demonstration: The objective reality of any of our ideas requires a cause
that contains this same reality not merely objectively but either formally or
eminently (Ax. V). However, we have an idea of God (Defs. II and VII), the
objective reality of which is contained in us neither formally nor eminently
(Ax. VI), nor could it be contained in anything other than God (Def. VIII).
Therefore this idea of God that is in us requires God as its cause, and thus
God exists (Ax. III).

---

72. Descartes' reply to the sixth point raised in the *Second Set of Objections* discusses the criterion of
clarity and distinctness and the proof of the existence of God found in Meditation Five. This reply
may be found in AT VII 149–52.

Proposition III: The existence of God is also demonstrated from the fact   *168*
that we ourselves who have the idea of God exist.

Demonstration: Had I the power to preserve myself, so much the more
would I also have the power to give myself the perfections I lack (Axs. VIII
and IX); for these are merely attributes of a substance, whereas I am a substance. But I do not have the power to give myself these perfections, otherwise I would already have them (Ax. VII). Therefore I do not have the power
to preserve myself.

Next, I cannot exist without my being preserved during the time I exist,
either by myself, if indeed I have this power, or by something else which has
this power (Axs. I and II). But I do exist, and yet I do not have the power to
preserve myself, as has already been proved. Therefore I am being preserved
by something else.

Moreover, he who preserves me has within himself either formally or
eminently all that is in me (Ax. IV). However, there is in me a perception
of many of the perfections I lack, and at the same time there is in me the
perception of the idea of God (Defs. II and VIII). Therefore, the perception
of these same perfections is also in him who preserves me.

Finally, this same being cannot have a perception of any perfections he
lacks or does not have in himself either formally or eminently (Ax. VIII), for
since he has the power to preserve me, as has already been said, so much the
more would he have the power to give himself those perfections were he to
lack them (Axs. VIII and IX). But he has the perception of all the perfec-   *169*
tions I lack and that I conceive to be capable of existing in God alone, as
has just been proved. Therefore he has these perfections within himself
either formally or eminently, and thus he is God.

Corollary: God created the heavens and the earth and all that is in them.
Moreover, he can bring about all that we clearly perceive, precisely as we
perceive it.

Demonstration: All these things clearly follow from the preceding proposition. For in that proposition I proved the existence of God from the fact
that there must exist someone in whom either formally or eminently are all
the perfections of which there is some idea in us. But there is in us an idea
of such great power that the one in whom this power resides, and he alone,
created the heavens and the earth and can also bring about all the other things
that I understand to be possible. Thus, along with the existence of God, all
these things have also been proved about him.

Proposition IV: Mind and body are really distinct.

Demonstration: Whatever we clearly perceive can be brought about by
God in precisely the way we perceive it (by the preceding corollary). But
we clearly perceive the mind, that is, a substance that thinks, apart from the   *170*
body, that is, apart from any extended substance (Post. II); and vice versa, we

clearly perceive the body apart from the mind (as everyone readily admits). Therefore, at least by the divine power, the mind can exist without the body, and the body without the mind.

Now certainly, substances that can exist one without the other are really distinct (Def. X). But the mind and the body are substances (Defs. V, VI, and VII) that can exist one without the other (as has just been proved). Therefore the mind and the body are really distinct.

And we should note here that I used divine power as a means of separating mind and body, not because some extraordinary power is required to achieve this separation, but because I had dealt exclusively with God in what preceded, and thus I had nothing else I could use as a means. Nor is it of any importance what power it is that separates two things in order for us to know that they are really distinct.

171   ### Third Set of Objections, by a famous English philosopher,[73] with the Author's Replies

Against Meditation I: Concerning Those Things That Can Be Called into Doubt

Objection I: It is sufficiently obvious from what has been said in this Meditation that there is no κριτήριον [criterion] by which we may distinguish our dreams from the waking state and from true sensation; and for this reason the phantasms we have while awake and using our senses are not accidents inhering in external objects, nor do they prove that such objects do in fact exist. Therefore, if we follow our senses without any other process of reasoning, we will be justified in doubting whether anything exists. Therefore, we acknowledge the truth of this Meditation. But since Plato and other ancient philosophers have discussed this same uncertainty in sensible things, and since it is commonly observed that there is a difficulty in distinguishing waking from dreams, I would have preferred the author, so very distinguished in the realm of new speculations, not to have published these old things.

Reply: The reasons for doubting, which are accepted here as true by the philosopher, were proposed by me as merely probable; and I made use of them not to peddle them as something new, but partly to prepare the minds
172   of readers for the consideration of matters geared to the understanding and for distinguishing them from corporeal things, goals for which these arguments seem to me wholly necessary; partly to respond to these same arguments in subsequent Meditations; and partly also to show how firm those

---

73. That is, Thomas Hobbes.

truths are that I later propose, given the fact that they cannot be shaken by these metaphysical doubts. And thus I never sought any praise for recounting them again; but I do not think I could have omitted them any more than a medical writer could omit a description of a disease whose method of treatment he is trying to teach.

Against Meditation II: Concerning the Nature of the Human Mind

Objection II: "I am a thing that thinks"; quite true. For from the fact that I think or have a phantasm, whether I am asleep or awake, it can be inferred that I am thinking, for "I think" means the same thing as "I am thinking." From the fact that I am thinking it follows that I am, since that which thinks is not nothing. But when he appends "that is, a mind, or soul, or understanding, or reason," a doubt arises. For it does not seem a valid argument to say: "I am thinking, therefore I am a thought" or "I am understanding, therefore I am an understanding." For in the same way I could just as well say: "I am walking, therefore I am an act of walking." Thus M. Descartes equates the thing that understands with an act of understanding, which is an act of the thing that understands. Or he at least is equating a thing that understands with the faculty of understanding, which is a power of a thing that understands. Nevertheless, all philosophers draw a distinction between a subject and its faculties and acts, that is, between a subject and its properties and essences; for a being itself is one thing and its essence is another. Therefore it is possible for a thing that thinks to be the subject in which the mind, reason or understanding inhere, and therefore this subject may be something corporeal. The opposite is assumed and not proved. Nevertheless, this inference is the basis for the conclusion that M. Descartes seems to want to establish. *173*

In the same passage he says: "I know that I exist; I ask now who is this 'I' whom I know. Most certainly, in the strict sense, the knowledge of this 'I' does not depend upon things of whose existence I do not yet have knowledge."[74]

Certainly the knowledge of the proposition "I exist" depends on the proposition "I think," as he rightly instructed us. But what is the source of the knowledge of the proposition "I think"? Certainly from the mere fact that we cannot conceive any activity without its subject, for example, leaping without one who leaps, knowing without one who knows, or thinking apart from one who thinks.

And from this it seems to follow that a thing that thinks is something corporeal, for the subjects of all acts seem to be understood only in terms of matter [*sub ratione materiae*], as he later points out in the example of the

---

74. AT VII, 27.

piece of wax, which, while its color, hardness, shape, and other acts undergo change, is nevertheless understood always to be the same thing, that is, the same matter undergoing a number of changes. However, it is not to be concluded that I think by means of another thought; for although a person can think that he has been thinking (this sort of thinking being merely a case of remembering), nevertheless, it is utterly impossible to think that one thinks, or to know that one knows. For it would involve an infinite series of questions: how do you know that you know that you know that you know?

Therefore, since the knowledge of the proposition "I exist" depends on the knowledge of the proposition "I think," and the knowledge of this latter proposition depends on the fact that we cannot separate thought from the matter that thinks, it seems we should infer that a thing that thinks is material, rather than immaterial.

174

Reply: Where I said "that is, a mind, or soul, or understanding, or reason," and so on, I did not understand by these terms merely the faculties, but the thing endowed with the faculty of thinking, and this is what everyone ordinarily has in mind with regard to the first two terms, and the second two terms are often understood in this sense. And I explained this so explicitly and in so many places that there does not seem to be any room for doubt.

Nor is there a parity here between walking and thinking, since walking is ordinarily taken to refer only to the action itself; whereas thought is sometimes taken to refer to an action, sometimes to refer to a faculty, and sometimes to refer to the thing that has the faculty.

Moreover, I am not asserting that the thing that understands and the act of understanding are identical, nor indeed that the identity of the thing that understands and the faculty of understanding are identical, if "understanding" is taken to refer to a faculty, but only when it is taken for the thing itself that understands. However, I also freely admit that I have used the most abstract terminology possible to signify the thing or substance, which I wanted to divest of all that did not belong to it, just as, contrariwise, the philosopher uses the most concrete terminology possible (namely, "subject," "matter," and "body") to signify a thing that thinks, in order to prevent its being separated from the body.

But I am not concerned that it may seem to someone that the philosopher's way of joining several things together may be more suitable for finding the truth than mine, wherein I distinguish each single thing as much as possible. But let us put aside verbal disputes and talk about the matter at hand.

175   He says that it is possible for a thing that thinks to be something corporeal, but the contrary is assumed and not proved. I did not at all assume the contrary, nor did I use it in any way as a basis for my argument. Rather, I left it completely undetermined until the Sixth Meditation, where it is proved.

Then he correctly says that we cannot conceive any act without its subject, such as an act of thinking without a thing that thinks, since that which thinks is not nothing. But then he adds, without any reason at all and contrary to the usual manner of speaking and to all logic, that hence it seems to follow that a thing that thinks is something corporeal; for the subjects of all acts are surely understood from the viewpoint of their being a substance [*sub ratione substantiae*] (or even, if you please, from the viewpoint of their being matter [*sub ratione materiae*], i.e., metaphysical matter), but it does not follow from this that it must be understood from the viewpoint of their being bodies [*sub ratione corporum*].

However, logicians and people in general are wont to say that some substances are spiritual while others are corporeal. And the only thing I proved by means of the example of the piece of wax was that color, hardness, and shape do not belong to the essence [*rationem formalem*] of the wax. For in that passage I was treating neither the essence of the mind nor that of the body.

Nor is it relevant for the philosopher to say here that one thought cannot be the subject of another thought. For who, besides him, has ever imagined that it could be? But, to explain the matter briefly, it is certainly the case that an act of thinking cannot exist without a thing that thinks, nor in general any act or accident without a substance in which it inheres. However, since we do not immediately know this substance itself through itself, but only through its being a subject of certain acts, it is quite in keeping with the demands of reason and custom for us to call by different names those substances that we recognize to be subjects of obviously different acts or accidents, and afterwards to inquire whether these different names signify one and the same thing. But there are certain acts which we call "corporeal," such as size, shape, motion, and all the other properties that cannot be thought of apart from their being extended in space; and the substance in which they inhere we call "body." Nor is it possible to imagine that it is one substance that is the subject of shape and another substance that is the subject of movement from place to place, and so on, since all these acts have in common the one feature of being extended. In addition, there are other acts, which we call "cogitative" (such as understanding, willing, imagining, sensing, and so on), all of which have in common the one feature of thought or perception or consciousness; but the substance in which they inhere we say is "a thing that thinks," or a "mind," or any other thing we choose, provided we do not confuse it with corporeal substance, since cogitative acts have no affinity to corporeal acts, and thought, which is the feature they have in common, is utterly different in kind from extension, which is the feature [*ratio*] the others have in common. But after we have formed two distinct concepts of these two substances, it is easy, from what has been said in the Sixth Meditation, to know whether they are one and the same or different.

176

177   Objection III: "Which of these things is distinct from my thought? Which
of them can be said to be separate from myself?"[75]

Perhaps someone will answer this question thus: I myself who think am
distinct from my act of thinking; and, though surely not separated from me,
my act of thinking is nevertheless different from me, just as leaping is different from the one who leaps, as has been said before. But if M. Descartes
were to show that he who understands and his understanding are one and
the same, we shall lapse into the parlance of the Schools: the understanding
understands, the sight sees, the will wills, and by an exact analogy, the act
of walking, or at least the faculty of walking, will walk. All of this is obscure, untoward, and most unworthy of that astuteness which is typical of
M. Descartes.

Reply: I do not deny that I who think am distinct from my act of thinking, as a thing is distinct from a mode. But when I ask, "What then is there
that is distinct from my act of thinking?", I understand this to refer to the
various modes of thinking that are recounted there, and not to my substance.
And when I add, "What can be said to be separate from myself?", I have in
mind simply that all those modes of thinking are within me. I fail to see
what occasion for doubt or obscurity can be imagined here.

Objection IV: "It remains then for me to concede that I do not grasp what
this piece of wax is through the imagination; rather I conceive[76] it through
the mind alone."

178   There is a tremendous difference between imagining (that is, having
some idea) and conceiving with the mind (that is, concluding by a process
of reasoning that something is or exists). But M. Descartes has not explained
to us the basis for their being different. Even the ancient peripatetic philosophers have taught clearly enough that a substance is not perceived by the
senses but is inferred by means of arguments.

But what are we to say now, were reasoning perhaps merely the joining
together and linking of names or designations by means of the word "is"? It
would follow from this that we draw no conclusions whatever by way of
argument [*ratione*] about the nature of things. Rather, it is about the designations of things that we draw any conclusions, that is, whether or not we
in fact join the names of things in accordance with some convention that
we have arbitrarily established regarding the meanings of these terms. If this
is the case, as it may well be, then reasoning will depend upon names, names
upon imagination, and imagination perhaps, as I see it, upon the motions of

75. AT VII, 29.

76. AT VII, 31. Hobbes here misquotes Descartes (Meditation Two; AT VII, 131). The original has
"perceive" [*percipere*], whereas Hobbes has "conceive" [*concipere*].

the corporeal organs. And thus the mind will be nothing but movements in certain parts of an organic body.

Reply: I have explained here the difference between imagination and a concept of the pure mind when in the example of the piece of wax I enumerated those things in the wax that we entertain in our imagination and those that we conceive with the mind alone. But I also explained elsewhere how one and the same thing, say a pentagon, can be understood by us in one way and imagined by us in another. However, in reasoning there is a joining together not of names but of things signified by these names; and I marvel that the contrary could enter anyone's mind. For who doubts that a Frenchman and a German could come to precisely the same conclusions   *179* about the very same things, even though they conceive very different words? And does not the philosopher bring about his own undoing when he speaks of conventions [*pactis*] that we have arbitrarily established regarding the significations of words? For if he admits that something is being signified by these words, why does he not want our reasonings to be about this something that is signified, rather than about mere words? And certainly by the same license with which he concludes that the mind is a motion he could also conclude that the sky is the earth, or whatever else he pleases.

Against Meditation III: Concerning God

Objection V: "Some of these thoughts are like images of things; to these alone does the word "idea" properly apply, as when I think of a man, or a chimera, or the sky, or an angel, or God."[77]

When I think of a man, I recognize an idea or an image made up of shape and color, concerning which I can doubt whether or not it is the likeness of a man, and likewise, when I think of the sky. When I think of a chimera, I recognize an idea or an image, concerning which I can doubt whether or not it is the likeness of some animal that does not exist but that could exist or that may or may not have existed at some other time.

But a person who is thinking of an angel at times observes in his mind the image of a flame, at other times the image of a beautiful little boy with wings. It seems certain to me that this image bears no resemblance to an angel, and thus is not the idea of an angel. But believing that there are crea-   *180* tures who minister unto God, who are invisible and immaterial, we ascribe the name "angel" to this thing that we believe in and suppose to exist. Nevertheless, the idea under which I imagine an angel is composed of the ideas of visible things.

It is the same with the sacred name "God": we have neither an image nor

77. AT VII, 37.

an idea of God. And thus we are forbidden to worship God under the form of an image, lest we seem to conceive him who is inconceivable.

It therefore seems there is no idea in us of God. But just as a person born blind who has often been brought close to a fire, and, feeling himself growing warm, recognizes that there is something that is warming him, and, on hearing that this is called "fire," concludes that fire exists, even though he does not know what shape or color it has, and has absolutely no idea or image of fire appearing before his mind; just so, a man who knows that there ought to be some cause of his images or ideas, and some other cause prior to this cause, and so on, is lead finally to an end of this series, namely to the supposition of some eternal cause that, since it never began to be, cannot have a cause prior to itself, and necessarily concludes that something eternal exists. Nevertheless, he has no idea that he could call the idea of this eternal something; rather he gives a name to this thing he believes in and acknowledges, calling it "God."

Now since it is from this thesis (namely, that we have an idea of God in our soul) that M. Descartes proceeds to prove this theorem (namely, that God—that is, the supremely powerful, wise creator of the world—exists), he ought to have given a better explanation of this idea of God, and he ought thence to have deduced not only the existence of God but also the creation of the world.

181   Reply: Here the philosopher wants the word "idea" to be understood to refer exclusively to images that are of material things and are depicted in the corporeal imagination. Once this thesis has been posited, it is easy for him to prove that there is no proper idea either of an angel or of God. But from time to time throughout the work, and especially in this passage, I point out that I take the word "idea" to refer to whatever is immediately perceived by the mind, so that, when I will or fear something, I number those very acts of willing and fearing among my ideas, since at the same time I perceive that I will and fear. And I used this word because it was common practice for philosophers to use it to signify the forms of perception proper to the divine mind, even though we acknowledge that there is no corporeal imagination in God; moreover, I had no term available to me that was more suitable. However, I think I have given a sufficient explanation of the idea of God to take care of those wishing to pay attention to my meaning; but I could never fully satisfy those preferring to understand my words otherwise than I intend. Finally, what is added here about the creation of the world is utterly irrelevant to the question at hand.

Objection VI: "Again there are other thoughts that take different forms: for example, when I will, or fear, or affirm, or deny, there is always something that I grasp as the subject of my thought, yet I embrace in my thought something more than the likeness of that thing. Some of these thoughts are called volitions or affects, while others are called judgments."[78]

When someone wills or fears, he surely has an image of the thing he fears *182* or the action he wills; but what more it is that a person who wills or fears embraces in his thought is not explained. Although fear is indeed a thought, I fail to see how it can be anything but the thought of the thing that someone fears. For what is the fear of a charging lion if not the idea of a charging lion combined with the effect that such an idea produces in the heart, which induces in a person who is frightened that animal motion we call "flight"? Now this motion of flight is not thought. It remains therefore that there is no thought in fear except the one that consists in the likeness of the thing feared. The same thing could be said of the will.

Moreover, affirmation and negation are not found without language and designations, so that brute animals can neither affirm nor deny, not even in thought, and therefore they cannot make judgments. Nevertheless, a thought can be similar in both man and beast. For when we affirm that a man is running, the thought we have is no different from the one a dog has when it sees its master running. Therefore the only thing affirmation or negation adds to simple thoughts is perhaps the thought that the names of which an affirmation is composed are the names of the same thing in the one who affirms. This is not a matter of grasping in thought something more than the likeness of the thing, but merely the same likeness for a second time.

Reply: It is self-evident that seeing a lion and simultaneously fearing it is different from merely seeing it. Likewise seeing a man running is different from affirming to oneself that one sees him, an act which takes place with- *183* out using language. And I find nothing here that requires an answer.

Objection VII: "All that remains for me is to ask how I received this idea of God. For I did not draw it from the senses; it never came upon me unexpectedly, as is usually the case with the ideas of sensible things when these things present themselves (or seem to present themselves) to the external sense organs. Nor was it made by me, for I plainly can neither subtract anything from it nor add anything to it. Thus the only option remaining is that this idea is innate in me, just as the idea of myself is innate in me."[79]

If there is no idea of God (and it has not been proved that there is one), this entire inquiry falls apart. Moreover, if it is my body that is in question, then the idea of myself originates in me from sight; if it is my soul that is in question, then there is absolutely no idea of the soul. Rather, we infer by means of reasoning that there is something inside the human body that

78. AT VII, 37.
79. AT VII, 51.

imparts to it the animal motion by which it senses and is moved. And this thing, whatever it is, we call the "soul," without having an idea of it.

Reply: If there is an idea of God (and it is obvious that there is), this entire objection falls apart. And when he adds that there is no idea of the soul, but rather that the soul is inferred by means of reasoning, this is the same thing as saying that there is no image of it depicted in the corporeal imagination, but that nevertheless there is such a thing as I have called an idea of it.

184   Objection VIII: "But there is another idea, one derived from astronomical reasoning, that is, it is elicited from certain notions innate in me. . . ."[80]

It seems there is at any given moment but a single idea of the sun, regardless of whether it is looked at with the eyes or is understood by reasoning that it is many times larger than it appears. For this latter is not an idea of the sun, but an inference by way of arguments that the idea of the sun would be many times larger were it seen at much closer quarters.

But at different times there can be different ideas of the sun: for example, if it is looked at on one occasion with the naked eye and on another occasion through a telescope. But arguments drawn from astronomy do not make the idea of the sun any greater or smaller; rather, they show that an idea of the sun that is drawn from the senses is deceptive.

Reply: Here too what is said not to be an idea of the sun, and yet is described, is precisely what I call an idea.

Objection IX: "Unquestionably, those ideas that display [*exhibent*] substances to me are something more and, if I may say so, contain within themselves more objective reality, than those which represent only modes or accidents. Again, the idea that enables me to understand a supreme deity,
185   eternal, infinite, omniscient, omnipotent, and creator of all things other than himself, clearly has more objective reality in it than do those ideas through which finite substances are displayed."[81]

I have frequently remarked above that there is no idea of God or of the soul. I now add that there is no idea of substance, for substance (given that it is matter subject to accidents and changes) is something concluded to solely by a process of reasoning; nevertheless, it is not conceived nor does it display any idea to us. If this is true, how can one say that the ideas that display substances to me are something greater and have more objective reality than those ideas that display accidents to me? Moreover, would M. Descartes

80. AT VII, 39.
81. AT VII, 40.

please give some thought once again to what he means by "more reality"? Does reality admit of degrees? Or, if he thinks that one thing is greater than another, would he please give some thought to how this could be explained to our understanding with the same level of astuteness required in all demonstrations, and such as he himself has used on other occasions?

Reply: I have frequently noted that I call an idea that very thing which is concluded to by means of reasoning, as well as anything else that is in any way perceived. Moreover, I have sufficiently explained how reality admits of degrees: namely, in precisely the way that a substance is a thing to a greater degree than is a mode. And if there are real qualities or incomplete substances, these are things to a greater degree than are modes, but to a lesser extent than are complete substances. And finally, if there is an infinite and independent substance, it is a thing to a greater degree than is a finite and dependent substance. But all of this is utterly self-evident.

Objection X: "Thus there remains only the idea of God. I must consider   186
whether there is anything in this idea that could not have originated from me. I understand by the word 'God' a certain substance that is infinite, independent, supremely intelligent, and supremely powerful, and that created me along with everything else that exists—if anything else exists. Indeed all these are such that the more carefully I focus my attention on them, the less possible it seems they could have arisen from myself alone. Thus, from what has been said above, I must conclude that God necessarily exists."[82]

On considering the attributes of God in order thence to have an idea of God and to see whether there is anything in it that could not have proceeded from ourselves, I find, unless I am mistaken, that what we think of that corresponds to the word "God" does not originate with us, nor need it originate with anything but external objects. For by the word "God" I understand a "substance," that is, I understand that God exists. But I understand this not through an idea but through a process of reasoning. And this substance I understand to be "infinite": that is, it is something whose boundaries or extremities I cannot conceive or imagine without imagining still more extremities beyond these. From this it follows that what emerges as the correlate of the word "infinite" is not the idea of divine infinity, but that of my own boundaries or limits. This substance I understand to be "independent," that is, I conceive of no cause from which God proceeds. Whence it is manifest that I have no idea corresponding to the word "independent" beyond the memory of my own ideas beginning at various times and their resulting dependencies.

Hence to say that God is "independent" is merely to say that God is   187

82. AT VII, 45.

among the number of those things of whose origin I form no image. In like manner, saying that God is "infinite" is tantamount to our saying that he is among the number of those things whose limits we do not conceive. And thus any idea of God is out of the question, for what sort of idea is it that has neither origin nor boundaries?

God is called "supremely understanding." I ask here: through what idea does M. Descartes understand God's act of understanding?

God is called "supremely powerful." Again, through what idea do we understand power which is of things yet to come, that is, of things that do not exist? Certainly I understand power from the image or memory of past actions, concluding to it thus: something did thus and so; therefore it was able to do it; and therefore, if it exists as the same thing, it will again be able to do thus and so, that is, it has the power to do something. Now these are all ideas that are capable of having arisen from external objects.

God is called "creator of all that exists." I can conjure up for myself some image of creation out of what I have observed, such as a man being born or his growing from something as small as a point to the shape and size he now possesses. No one has any other idea corresponding to the word "creator." However, to prove creation it is not enough to be able to imagine that the world was created. And thus, even if it were demonstrated that something "infinite, independent, supremely powerful, and so on" exists, it still does not follow that a creator exists, unless someone were to believe it is correct to infer from the fact that something exists which we believe to have created all other things, that the world has therefore been at some time created by him.

188   Moreover, when he says that the idea of God and of our soul is innate in us, I would like to know if the souls of those in a deep sleep are thinking. If they are not, then during that time they have no ideas. Whence no idea is innate, for what is innate is always present.

Reply: Nothing that we ascribe to God can originate from external objects, as from an exemplar, since nothing in God bears any resemblance to things found in external, that is, corporeal things. However, if we think of something that is unlike these external objects, it obviously does not originate from them but from the cause of that diversity in our thought.

And I ask here how our philosopher deduces [his conception of] God's understanding from external things. But I easily explain the idea I have of God's understanding by saying that by the word "idea" I understand everything that is the form of some perception. For who is there that does not perceive that he understands something? And thus who is there that does not have that form or idea of an act of understanding, and, by the indefinitely extending it, does not form an idea of the divine act of understanding? And the same applies to the rest of God's attributes.

But we used the idea of God that is in us to demonstrate God's existence, and such immense power is contained in this idea that we understand that, if in fact God does exist, it would be contradictory for something other than God to exist without having been created by him. And because of these considerations, it plainly follows, from the fact that his existence has been demonstrated, that it has also been demonstrated that the entire world, that is, all the things other than God that exist, have been created by him.

Finally, when we assert that some idea is innate in us, we do not have in mind that we always notice it (for in that event no idea would ever be innate), but only that we have in ourselves the power to elicit the idea.

189

Objection XI: "The whole force of the argument rests on the fact that I recognize that it would be impossible for me to exist, being of such a nature as I am (namely, having in me the idea of God), unless God did in fact exist. God, I say, that same being the idea of whom is in me. . . ."[83]

Since, therefore, it has not been demonstrated that we have an idea of God, and since the Christian religion requires us to believe that God is inconceivable (that is, as I see it, that we have no idea of him), it follows that the existence of God has not been demonstrated, much less the creation.

Reply: When it is asserted that God is inconceivable, this is understood with respect to a concept that adequately comprehends him. But I have repeated ad nauseam how it is we have an idea of God. And nothing at all is asserted here that weakens my demonstrations.

Against Meditation IV: Concerning the True and the False

190

Objection XII: "Thus I certainly understand that error as such is not something real[84] . . . but rather is merely a defect. And thus there is no need to account for my errors by positing a power[85] given to me by God for the purpose."[86]

It is certain that ignorance is merely a defect and that there is no need for some positive faculty of being ignorant. But it is not so obvious in the case of error. For it seems that stones and inanimate objects are incapable of erring simply because they lack the power of reasoning and imagining. Hence the obvious conclusion is that the faculty of reasoning, or at least that of imagination, is needed in order to err. But both of these are positive faculties bestowed upon all those and only those who err.

Moreover, M. Descartes asserts as follows: ". . . I note that these errors

---

83. AT VII, 51.
84. Hobbes omits "that depends upon God."
85. Hobbes substitutes *potestate* for *facultate*.
86. AT VII, 54

[that is to say, my errors] depend on the simultaneous concurrence of two causes: the faculty of knowing that is in me and the faculty of choosing, that is, the free choice of the will. . . ."[87] But this seems to contradict what had been said previously. It surely ought to be noted here that the freedom of the will has been assumed without proof, and in opposition to the position taken by the Calvinists.[88]

Reply: Even though in order to err one needs a faculty of reasoning, or rather of judging (that is, of affirming and denying), since error is a defect on the part of this faculty, still it does not therefore follow that this defect 191 is something real, any more than blindness is something real, although stones are not said to be blind simply because they are incapable of sight. And I marvel that as yet I have not come across a single legitimate argument in these objections. Now regarding freedom I made no assumptions here except what we all experience within ourselves. This is most evident by the light of nature, and I fail to understand why it is said that this passage is said to contradict what had gone before.

But even if perhaps there are many who, on considering God's fore-ordaining of things, cannot grasp how this is consistent with our freedom, still, there is no one who, on considering himself alone, fails to experience that being voluntary and being free are one and the same thing. But this is not the place for examining the opinions of others on this matter.

Objection XIII: "For example, during these last few days when I was examining whether anything in the world exists and noticed that, from the very fact that I was making this examination, it obviously followed that I exist. Nevertheless, I could not help judging that what I understood so clearly was true; not that I was coerced into making this judgment because of some external force, but because a great light in my intellect gave way to a great inclination of my will, and the less indifferent I was, the more spon-taneously and freely did I believe it."[89]

This expression, "a great light in my intellect," is metaphorical and is therefore unsuitable for use in an argument. However, anyone who is free 192 of doubt has pretensions of possessing such a light and has no less a tendency of the will to affirm what he does not doubt than does the person who really does have knowledge. Hence this light can be the reason why some-one obstinately defends or holds fast to an opinion, but not the reason why he knows his opinion to be true.

87. AT VII, 56. The bracketed text was added by Hobbes.

88. For a brief overview of the life and teachings of John Calvin, see Ronald J. Feenstra, "John Calvin," *Routledge Encyclopedia of Philosophy,* vol. 2, pp. 177–82 (New York: Routledge, 1998).

89. AT VII, 58–9.

Moreover, not only the knowledge that something is true, but also the belief or giving of one's assent has nothing to do with the will. For we believe whatever is proved by valid arguments or is related in a credible manner, whether we want to or not. It is true that affirming, denying, defending, and refuting propositions are acts of the will; but it does not therefore follow that internal assent depends on the will.

And thus the conclusion that follows is insufficiently demonstrated: ". . . inherent in this incorrect use of the free will is the privation that constitutes the very essence of error. . . ."[90]

Reply: There is no point to asking whether or not the expression "a great light" is suitable for use in an argument, so long as it is useful in providing explanations, as in fact it is. For everyone knows that by "the light in the intellect" is meant perspicuity of knowledge, which perhaps is not had by all who think they have it. But this does not preclude its being quite different from an obstinate opinion conceived without an evident perception.

However, when it is asserted here that we give our assent to things we clearly perceive, whether we want to or not, this is tantamount to saying that we seek a good that is clearly known, whether we want to or not. For the expression "or not" has no place in such matters, since it entails that we do and do not will the same thing.

Against Meditation V: Concerning the Essence of Material Things   *193*

Objection XIV: "For example, when I imagine a triangle, even if perhaps no such figure exists outside my thought anywhere in the world and never has, the triangle still has a certain determinate nature, essence, or form which is unchangeable and eternal, which I did not fabricate, and which does not depend on my mind. This is evident from the fact that various properties can be demonstrated regarding this triangle. . . ."[91]

Were the triangle to exist nowhere in the world, I fail to understand how it has a nature, for what exists nowhere does not exist and therefore has no being [*esse*] or nature. The triangle in the mind takes its origin from a triangle we have seen or else from one conjured up from ones we have seen. However, once we have named a thing "triangle" (whence we believe the idea of the triangle takes its origin), the name lingers on even if the triangle itself ceases to exist. Likewise, once we have conceived in our thought that all the angles of a triangle are equal to two right angles and have given this other name to the triangle: "having three angles equal to two right angles," even if an angle exists nowhere in the world, still the name remains, and the truth

90. AT VII, 60.
91. AT VII, 64.

of the following proposition is eternal: "a triangle is a thing that has three angles equal to two right angles." But the nature of a triangle will not be eternal, if perhaps every triangle were to perish.

Likewise, the proposition "man is an animal" is eternally true in virtue of the eternity of the names. However, were the human race to perish there would no longer be any human nature.

194 Whence it is evident that an essence, insofar as it is distinct from existence, is merely a joining of names by means of the verb "is." And therefore an essence without existence is a fiction of our own making. And it seems that as the mental image of a man is to a man, so essence is to existence, or as the proposition "Socrates is a man" is to the proposition "Socrates is or exists," so the essence of Socrates is to his existence. But when Socrates is non-existent, "Socrates is a man" signifies merely a joining of names, and the word "is" or "exists" basically means the image of the unity of a thing that has two names.

Reply: The distinction between essence and existence is known to all; and this talk about eternal names (as opposed to concepts or ideas of an eternal truth) has already been adequately refuted.

Against Meditation VI: Concerning the Existence of Material Things

Objection XV: "But since God has given me no faculty whatsoever for making this distinction [that is, whether or not ideas are emitted from bodies] but instead has given me a great inclination to believe that these ideas issue from corporeal things, I fail to see how God could be understood not to be a deceiver, if these ideas were to issue from a source other than corporeal things. And consequently corporeal things exist."[92]

195 It is a common belief that physicians who deceive the sick for reasons of health are not at fault—nor are fathers at fault who deceive their children for their own good—and that the misdeed involved in deception consists not in the falsity of what is said but in the harm done by those who deceive. Hence let M. Descartes consider whether this proposition is universally true: "in no instance can God deceive us." For if it is not universally true, then the conclusion "therefore corporeal things exist" does not follow.

Reply: My conclusion does not require that we could in no way be deceived (for I have readily granted that we are often deceived), but that we are not deceived when our error would attest to a desire to deceive on the part of God, something that is repugnant to him. Once again, here is another poor argument.

---

92. AT VII, 79. The bracketed text was added by Hobbes.

Final Objection: "For I now notice there is a considerable difference between these two [that is, between waking and dreaming]; dreams are never joined by the memory with all the other actions of life. . . ."[93]

I have a question regarding a person who dreams that he doubts whether he is dreaming or not. Could this person not dream that his dreams fit together with the ideas of things in a long series of past events? If he can, those things that seem to one who dreams to be the actions of his past life can be taken to be true no less than were he awake. Moreover, as M. Descartes himself asserts, since the certainty and truth of all knowledge depends entirely on the knowledge of the true God, either it is impossible for an atheist to infer on the basis of the memory of his past life that he is awake, or it is possible for someone to know that he is awake without the knowledge of the true God.

196

Reply: One who dreams cannot really connect the things he dreams with the ideas of past events, although he could dream that he is connecting them. For who denies that a person who is dreaming can be mistaken, and, on awaking some time later, easily discovers his mistake?

However, an atheist can infer that he is awake from the memory of his past life, but he cannot know that this sign is enough for him to be certain that he is not mistaken, unless he knows that he has been created by a God who does not deceive.

Fourth Set of Objections[94]

A Letter to the Distinguished Gentleman

Dear Sir:

It has not been your desire to bestow your blessings upon me without exacting a price. You demand repayment for a service most kind, and surely it is a heavy payment: you would have me become familiar with this absolutely brilliant work only on the condition that I make known my feelings about it. This is a harsh condition, compliance with which has been wrung from me by a craving to know things most fine, and I would be most delighted to protest against such a condition if, just as an exception

197

---

93. AT VII, 89. The bracketed text was added by Hobbes.

94. The author of the Fourth Set of Objections is the French philosopher and theologian Antoine Arnauld (1612–94). For a brief account of Arnauld's life and thought, see Stephen Nadler, "Antoine Arnauld," *Routledge Encyclopedia of Philosophy* (New York: Routledge, 1998), Vol. 1, pp. 443–8. Mersenne served as intermediary between Arnauld and Descartes.

is granted by the praetor[95] ("if an action has been performed under the influence of force or fear"),[96] I were able to obtain the following new exception: "if an action has been performed under the influence of pleasure."

What then is your wish? You do not await my judgment of the author, for you already know how highly I regard the supreme power of his intelligence [*ingenii*] and his singular erudition. Moreover, you are not unaware of how annoying the tasks are that take up my time; nor would it follow, were you to give me more credit than I deserve, that I am unaware of my own shortcomings. And yet what you present for examination requires both extraordinary intelligence [*ingenium*] and, above all, considerable serenity of mind in order for it to have the leisure to free itself from the clatter of all external things, which you know full well is impossible for the mind to accomplish without attentive meditation and deep contemplation upon itself. Still, if it is your wish, then I must obey. The fault for whatever mistake I make will lie with you, who are forcing me to write. Now although philosophy could claim the whole of this work for its own, nevertheless, since this exceedingly modest gentleman voluntarily places himself before a tribunal of theologians, I play a dual role here. First, I propose the objections that in my opinion could be raised by philosophers regarding the major questions as to the nature of our mind and of God. Next, I indicate those things at which a theologian could take offense in the work as a whole.

Concerning the Nature of the Human Mind

The first thing that arises here for us to marvel at is that the distinguished gentleman established as the principle of the whole of his philosophy the same one as established by St. Augustine—a man of most penetrating intelligence [*ingenii*] and greatly to be admired not only in theology but also in philosophy. For in *On the Free Choice of the Will,* Book II, Chapter 3, Alipius, during his debate with Evodius, was about to prove the existence of God when he asserted: " . . . first, to begin with things that are most evident, I ask you whether you yourself exist or whether perhaps you are afraid you might be mistaken in this line of questioning, since, in any event, if you did not exist you could never be mistaken?"[97] The words of our author are similar: "But there is some deceiver or other who is supremely powerful and

198

---

95. Arnauld may be referring to the praetor urbanus, who served as the chief interpreter of laws for the city of Rome.

96. The praetor was responsible for making prudential judgments in legal cases in which fear or intimidation played a significant role. See *The Civil Law, Including the Twelve Tables, the Institutes of Gaius, the Rules of Ulpian, the Opinions of Paulus, the Enactments of Justinian, and the Constitutions of Leo,* ed. and trans. by S. P. Scott (Cincinnati: The Central Trust Company, 1932), Vol. 3, pp. 56–66: The Digest of Pandicts, Book IV, Title II: "Where an Act is Performed on Account of Fear."

97. *On the Free Choice of the Will,* Book II, Chap. 3, sect. 7; PL 32, 1243.

supremely sly who is always deliberately deceiving me. Then too there is no doubt that I exist, if he is deceiving me."[98] But let us proceed and, more to the point, let us see how one could conclude from this principle that our mind is separate from the body.

I can doubt whether I have a body or even whether there are any bodies in the world. And yet it is not proper for me to doubt whether I am or exist during the time I am doubting or thinking.

Thus, I who am doubting and thinking am not a body; otherwise, in entertaining doubts about my body, I would be entertaining doubts about myself.

In fact, even if I were stubbornly to maintain that absolutely no bodies existed, nevertheless the thesis still stands: I am something. Therefore I am not a body.

This is a rather sharp bit of reasoning, but someone will raise the same objection that the author raises against himself: my doubting about a body or my denying that there is a body does not bring it about that no body exists. He says: "Perhaps then it is the case that these very things which I take to be nothing, because they are unknown to me, nevertheless are in fact no different from that me that I know. This I do not know, and I will not quarrel about it . . . I know that I exist; I ask now who is this 'I' whom I know. Most certainly, in the strict sense, the knowledge of this "I" does not depend upon things whose existence I do not yet know."[99]

But he admits that in the argument put forward in the *Discourse on* 199 *Method* the conclusion was deduced solely in order to exclude anything corporeal from the nature of the mind, and that this argument was put forward not according to the order of the truth of the matter[100] but only according to the order of his perception. Thus his point was that he knows utterly nothing that pertains to his essence except that he is a thinking thing. In saying this, it is obvious that his argument still remains mired in the same terms as before, and thus there remains the whole problem he promised to resolve. How does it follow, from the fact that he knows nothing else to pertain to his essence, that nothing else really does pertain to it? Nevertheless, I admit my slow-wittedness and confess that I could not find this addressed anywhere in the Second Meditation. But my best guess is that he attempts to prove this in the Sixth Meditation, since he judged that this proof depends upon a clear knowledge of God, which he had not yet acquired for himself in the Second Meditation. Thus he proves this conclusion in the following way:

98. AT VII, 25.

99. AT VII, 27–8.

100. Here Arnauld omits Descartes' parenthetical remark that "I was not dealing with it then" (AT VII, 8).

"...Because I know that all the things that I clearly and distinctly understand can be made by God such as I understand them, my ability clearly and distinctly to understand one thing without another suffices to make me certain that the one thing is different from the other, since they can be separated from each other, at least by God. The question as to the sort of power that might effect such a separation is not relevant to their being thought different . . . Thus, because on the one hand I have a clear and distinct idea of myself, insofar as I am merely a thinking thing and not an extended thing, and because on the other hand I have a distinct idea of a body, insofar as it is merely an extended thing and not a thinking thing, it is certain
200   that I am really distinct from my body and I can exist without it."[101]

We must stop here for a short time, since the whole problem seems to me to hinge on these few words. And first of all, in order to be true, the major premise of this syllogism should be understood to refer not to just any sort of knowledge of a thing, clear and distinct though it may be, but only to knowledge that is adequate. For the distinguished gentleman admits in his reply to the theologian[102] that for one thing to be conceived distinctly and separately from another by an act of abstraction on the part of the understanding inadequately conceiving the thing, a formal distinction is sufficient and a real distinction is not required.[103] From this he concludes in the same passage:

"But I completely understand what a body is when I think that it merely has extension and shape, is capable of moving, and so on, and I deny that there is anything whatsoever in it that belongs to the nature of the mind. Conversely, I understand that the mind is a complete thing that doubts, understands, wills, and so on, even though I deny that there is anything in it that is contained in the idea of a body."[104] Therefore there is a real distinction.

But if someone calls this minor premise into question, arguing it is merely a matter of the inadequacy of your conception of yourself when you conceive yourself as a thinking thing and not as an extended thing and, likewise, when you conceive yourself as an extended thing and not a thinking thing, we must see how it has been proved in the earlier phases of the argument. For I do not think this matter is so clear that it should be assumed to be an indemonstrable principle and something not to be proved.

Indeed, as to the first part of the above statement—namely, that you
201   completely understand what a body is in thinking that it is merely something having extension and shape, is capable of moving, and so on, and in denying that there is in it anything that belongs to the nature of the mind—

101. AT VII, 78.

102. Johan de Kater (Johannes Caterus), author of the *First Set of Objections.*

103. AT VII, 120.

104. AT VII, 121.

this adds very little to the discussion. For a person who contends that our mind is corporeal does not on that account think that every body is a mind. Were we to follow that line of reasoning, body would be related to mind the way genus is related to species. But a genus can be understood without a species, even if we were to deny to the genus all that is proper and peculiar to the species. Whence the logicians' commonplace: "the negation of the species does not negate the genus." Thus I can understand a figure without my understanding any of the attributes that are proper to a circle. Therefore it remains to be proved that the mind can be completely and adequately understood without the body.

I see no other argument in the entire work that is suitable for proving this except what was put forward at the very beginning: I can deny that there is any body or any extended thing, and yet I am certain I exist during the time I am denying this or am thinking. Therefore I am a thinking thing, not a body; and the body does not have a bearing on the knowledge I have of myself.

But so far as I can see, the only thing resulting from this is that some knowledge of myself can be obtained without the knowledge of the body. But it is not yet plainly evident to me that this knowledge is complete and adequate, such that I would be certain I am not mistaken when I exclude body from my essence. I shall use an example to make my point.

Suppose that someone knows [*noverit*] with certainty that an angle inscribed in a semicircle is a right angle and thus that this triangle formed from that angle and the diameter of the circle is right angled. Nevertheless, he may doubt and may not yet have grasped [*deprehenderit*] this fact with certainty. In fact, deluded by some fallacy, he denies that the square of the hypotenuse is equal to the sum of the squares of the sides. He will seem to have corroboration of his false belief by the very same line of reasoning advanced by the distinguished gentleman. "For while perceiving clearly and distinctly that the triangle is right angled, I still am in doubt whether the   *202* square of its hypotenuse is equal to the sum of the squares of its sides. Therefore," he says, "it does not belong to the essence of the triangle that the square of its hypotenuse is equal to the sum of the squares of its sides."

Moreover, even if I were to deny that the square of its hypotenuse is equal to the sum of the squares of its sides, still I continue to be certain that the triangle is right angled, and the clear and distinct knowledge remains in my mind that one of its angles is a right angle. This being the case, not even God could cause this triangle not to be right angled.

Therefore, a property about which I am in doubt or whose removal leaves me with the same idea of a thing does not belong to the essence of that thing.

Moreover, "because I know that all the things that I clearly and distinctly understand can be made by God such as I understand them, my ability clearly and distinctly to understand one thing without another suffices to make me certain that the one thing is different from the other, since they can be separated from each other, at least by God."[105] But I clearly and distinctly understand this triangle to be right angled, without my understanding the square of its hypotenuse to be equal to the sum of the squares of its sides. Therefore God, at least, can bring about a right triangle the square of whose hypotenuse is not equal to the sum of the squares of its sides.

I do not see what reply could be made here, except that the man in the example does not clearly and distinctly perceive a right triangle. But what is the basis for my claim that I perceive the nature of my mind more clearly than does the person in the example who perceives the nature of a triangle? For he is just as certain that a triangle inscribed in a semicircle has one right angle (which is what betokens a right triangle) as I am that from the fact that I think, it follows that I exist.

Thus, while the person in the example clearly and distinctly knows [*novit*] the triangle to be right angled, he is mistaken in judging that it does not belong to the nature of this triangle that the square of its hypotenuse 203   is equal, and so on. Just so, why am I not perhaps mistaken in judging that nothing else pertains to my nature which I clearly and distinctly know to be a thinking thing, except that I am a thinking thing, since perhaps it also belongs to my nature that I am an extended thing?

And certainly someone will declare that there is no cause for wonder if, when I conclude that I exist from the fact that I am thinking, the idea that I form of myself thus known represents to my soul nothing but myself as a thinking thing, which surely has been derived from my thought alone. As a result, it seems there can be derived from this idea no argument to the effect that nothing more pertains to my essence than what is contained in the idea.

Moreover, this argument appears to prove too much and leads us to the Platonic teaching (which nevertheless the author disproves) that nothing corporeal belongs to our essence, so that man is nothing but a soul, while a body is merely the vehicle for the soul—hence the definition of man as a soul using a body.

But if you answer that the body is not unconditionally excluded from my essence, but only insofar as I am precisely a thinking thing, it seems there is good reason for fear lest someone entertain the suspicion that perhaps the knowledge of myself insofar as I am a thinking thing is not the knowledge of something completely and adequately conceived, but only inadequately and with a certain abstraction on the part of the understanding.

Thus, geometricians conceive of a line as a length without width, and a surface as length and width together without depth, even though length does

105. AT VII, 78.

not exist without width nor width without depth. In like manner, someone could perhaps be in doubt whether every thinking thing is also an extended thing in which, nevertheless, in addition to the properties it has in common with other extended things (such as the capacity to take on various shapes, to move, and so on), there inheres a power of thinking peculiar to it. Whence it follows that although it could, by an abstraction on the part of the understanding, be taken for a thinking thing by virtue of this power alone, corporeal properties may really [*revera*] belong to a thinking thing. In like manner, even though quantity can be conceived in terms of length alone, in actual fact [*reipsa*] width and depth together belong to every quantity, along with length.

The difficulty is increased by the fact that this power of thinking appears to be attached to corporeal organs, since one could judge it to be dormant in infants and extinguished in the insane. And this is what unbelievers who have the soul's blood on their teeth most strongly urge.

Up to this point I have been considering the real distinction between our soul and the body. But since the distinguished gentleman undertook to demonstrate the immortality of the soul, it might be appropriate to ask whether immortality manifestly follows from this separation. For according to the principles of traditional [*vulgaris*] philosophy this does not follow at all, since philosophers have traditionally [*vulgo*] regarded the souls of brute animals to be distinct from their bodies, and yet these souls still perished with their bodies.

I had progressed this far in my reply and had intended to show how, according to our author's own principles (which I seem to have gathered from his method of philosophizing), the immortality of the mind is easily inferred from the real distinction between mind and body, when the results of the distinguished gentleman's late night studies were delivered to me. This work, in addition to shedding a great deal of light on the work as a whole, also offers the very same solution I was about to offer regarding the problem before us.

But as to the souls of brute animals, he hints in enough other passages that they have no soul. All they have is a body arranged in a certain manner and so composed of various organs that all the operations that we observe could take place in and through it.

But I fear it is possible this position might not gain acceptance in the minds of men if it is not bolstered by the strongest arguments. For on first blush it appears incredible how it could happen, without the intervention of any soul, that light reflected from the body of a wolf onto the eyes of a sheep should move the extremely thin fibers of the optic nerves, and that, as a result of this motion penetrating into the brain, animal spirits are diffused into the nerves in just the way required to cause the sheep to take flight.

At this juncture I will make one additional point, namely, that I thoroughly

approve of what the distinguished gentleman teaches regarding the distinction between imagination and thought [*cogitatione*] or understanding [*intelligentia*], and regarding the greater certainty of those things we grasp by
means of reason as opposed to the things we observe by means of the corporeal senses. For a long time ago I learned from St. Augustine, in his *On
the Greatness of the Soul,* Chapter 15,[106] that we must keep our distance from
those who are convinced that what we discern through our understanding
[*intelligentia*] is less certain than what presents itself to the corporeal eyes,
bothered as they always are with phlegm. Whence he also declares, in his
Soliloquies, Book I, Chapter 4,[107] that in matters pertaining to geometry he
found the senses to be like a boat. "For when," he says, "they had brought
me to the place I was bound for, I there took my leave of them; and, once
located on solid ground, I began to review these things in my thought, and
for a time my gait was unsteady. Thus it seemed to me a person could more
quickly navigate on land than he could perceive geometry by means of the
senses, even though the senses do seem to be of some help when we are first
learning geometry."

206   *Concerning God*

The first proof of the existence of God (the one the author spells out
in the Third Meditation) has two parts. The first part is that God exists if
indeed there is an idea of God in me. The second part is that I who have
such an idea could be derived only from God.

Regarding the first part, there is one thing that is not proved to me,
namely, that when the distinguished gentleman asserted that falsity properly
so-called can be found only in judgments, he nevertheless admits a bit later
that ideas can be false—not formally false mind you, but materially false.
This seems to me to be out of keeping with his first principles.

But I fear I should not be able to explain with enough lucidity my feelings on a matter that is decidedly obscure. An example will make it clearer.
The author asserts that if cold is but the privation of heat, the idea of cold
that represents it to me as if it were something positive will be materially
false.

Moreover, if cold is merely a privation, then there could not be an idea
of cold that represents it to me as something positive, and here the author
confuses a judgment with an idea.

For what is the idea of cold? Coldness itself, insofar as it exists objectively
in the understanding. But if cold is a privation, it cannot exist objectively in
the understanding by means of an idea whose objective existence is a positive

106. sec. 25; PL 32, 1049–50.
107. sec. 9; PL 32, 874.

being. Thus, if cold is but a privation, there could not be a positive idea of it, and hence there could never be an idea that is materially false.

This is confirmed by the same argument the distinguished gentleman uses to prove that the idea of an infinite cannot but be true. For although one could imagine that such a being does not exist, nevertheless one could   *207* not imagine that the idea of such a being presented nothing real to me.

We can readily say the same thing about every positive idea. For although one could imagine that cold, which I think is represented by a positive idea, is not something positive, still one cannot imagine that the positive idea presents to me nothing real and positive. This is because an idea is not said to be positive in virtue of the existence it has as a mode of thinking (for on that score all ideas would be positive), but rather in virtue of the objective existence it contains and that it presents to our mind. Therefore, though it is possible that this idea is not the idea of cold, it nevertheless cannot be a false one.

But, you may say, it is false precisely in virtue of its not being the idea of cold. Actually it is your judgment that is false, were you to judge it to be the idea of cold. But the idea, in and of itself,[108] is most true. In like manner, the idea of God surely ought not be called false, not even materially, even though someone could transfer it to something that is not God, as idolaters have done.

Finally, what does this idea of cold, which you say is materially false, display to your mind? A privation? Then it is true. A positive being? Then it is not the idea of cold. Again, what is the cause of this positive objective being, which, in your opinion, renders this idea materially false? It is I, you say, insofar as I am derived from nothing. Therefore, the positive objective existence of some idea can be derived from nothing, a conclusion that destroys the principal foundations of the distinguished gentleman.

But let us move on to the second part of the demonstration, where he asks whether I myself who have the idea of an infinite being could be derived from something other than an infinite being, and especially whether   *208* I am derived from myself. The distinguished gentleman contends that I could not be derived from myself, in view of the fact that, were I myself to give myself existence, I would also give myself all the perfections an idea of which I observe to be within me. But the theologian replies with the astute observation that "being derived from itself" [*esse a se*] ought to be taken not in a positive sense, but in a negative sense, to the effect that it means the same thing as "not derived from another." "But," he says, "if something is derived from itself (that is to say, not from something else), how do I prove that this thing encompasses all things and that it is infinite? I do not follow you now if you say: "if it is derived from itself, it would have easily given itself all

---

108. Reading *se* for *te* (AT VII, 207).

things. For neither is it derived from itself as from a cause, nor did it exist prior to itself such that it would choose beforehand what it would later be."

To refute this argument, the distinguished gentleman maintains that "being derived from itself" ought to be taken in a positive rather than a negative sense, even when it applies to God, to the effect that God "stands in the same relationship to himself as an efficient cause does to its effect." This seems to me to be a harsh statement and a false one at that.

Thus, while I am partly in agreement with the distinguished gentleman, I am partly in disagreement with him. For I confess I cannot be derived from myself except in a positive fashion, but I deny that the same may be said of God. In fact, I think it a manifest contradiction that something is derived from itself positively and, as it were, from a cause. Thus I bring about the same result as our author, but by way of quite another route, and it goes as follows:

209   For me to be derived from myself, I ought to be derived from myself in a positive fashion, and, as it were, from a cause. Therefore it is impossible for me to be derived from myself.

The major premise of this syllogism is proved by the gentleman's arguments that are drawn from the doctrine that, since the various parts of time can be separated from one another, the fact that I exist now does not entail my existing in the future, unless some cause, as it were, makes me over again at each individual moment.

As to the minor premise, I believe it to be so clear by the light of nature that it is largely a waste of time to try to prove it—a matter of proving the known by means of the less known. Moreover, the author seems to have recognized the truth of this, since he has not made bold to disavow it publicly. Please weigh the following statement made in reply to the theologian:[109]

". . . I did not say that it is impossible for something to be the efficient cause of itself. For although this is obviously the case when the meaning of "efficient cause" is restricted to those causes that are temporally prior to their effects or are different from them, still it does not seem that such a restriction is appropriate in this inquiry, . . . since the light of nature does not stipulate that the nature of an efficient cause requires that it be temporally prior to its effect."[110]

Well done, as far as the first part is concerned. But why has he left out the second part? And why has he not added that the very same light of nature does not stipulate that the essence [*ratio*] of an efficient cause requires that it be different from its effect, unless it is because the very same light of nature did not permit him to assert it?

And since every effect depends upon a cause and thus receives its exis-

109. Caterus.
110. AT VII, 108.

tence from a cause, is it not patently clear that the same thing cannot depend on itself or receive its existence from itself?   *210*

Moreover, every cause is the cause of an effect, and every effect the effect of a cause. Thus there is a reciprocal relationship between cause and effect. But a relationship must occur between two things.

Moreover, it is absurd to conceive of something receiving existence and yet having existence prior to the time we conceive it to have received existence. But this would be the case were we to ascribe the notions of cause and effect to the very same thing in respect to itself. For what is the notion of a cause? It is the giving of existence. And what is the notion of an effect? It is the receiving of existence. But the notion of a cause is prior by nature to that of an effect.

But we cannot conceive of something as a cause [*sub ratione causae*] (as something giving existence) unless we conceive of it as having existence; for no one gives what one does not have. Therefore we would first be conceiving a thing as having existence before conceiving of it as having received it; and yet in the case of whatever receives existence, receiving existence comes before having existence.

This argument can be put differently: no one gives what he does not have, therefore no one can give himself existence unless he already has it. But if he already has it, why would he give it to himself?

Finally, he claims that it is manifest by the light of nature that creation differs from preservation solely by virtue of a distinction of reason. But it is manifest by the very same light of nature that nothing can create itself. Therefore nothing can preserve itself.

But if we descend from the general thesis to the specific instance [*hypothesim*] of God, the matter will, in my judgment, be even more manifest: God cannot be derived from himself positively, but only negatively, that is, in the sense of not being derived from something else.

And first, it is manifest from the argument put forward by the distinguished   *211*
gentleman to prove that if a body is derived from itself, then it ought to be derived from itself in a positive fashion. For, as he says, the parts of time do not depend one on another. Thus, the fact that this body is presumed up until the present time to have been derived from itself (that is, it has no cause) does not suffice to make it exist in the future, unless there is some power in it that, as it were, continuously 'remakes' it.

But so far from this argument being relevant to the case of a supremely perfect or infinite being, the opposite could far rather be readily deduced, and for opposite reasons. For contained in the idea of an infinite being is the fact that its duration is also infinite, that is, it is bounded by no limits; and thus it is indivisible, permanent, and possessed of all things all at once [*tota simul*]. Temporal sequence cannot be conceived to be in this idea except erroneously and through the imperfection of our understanding.

Whence it manifestly follows that an infinite being cannot be conceived of as existing even for a moment without at the same time being conceived of as always having existed and as existing in the future for eternity (which is what the author himself teaches in another passage). Hence it is pointless to ask why it would continue to exist.

Further—as is frequently taught by St. Augustine (than whom no one after the time of the sacred authors has ever spoken more nobly and sublimely about God)—in God there is no past or future, but an eternal present. And from this it appears quite evident that it is only with absurdity that one can ask why God continues to exist, since this question obviously involves a temporal sequence of before and after, of past and future, and this ought to be excluded from the notion of an infinite being.

212   Moreover, God cannot be thought of as being derived from himself positively [*a se positive*], as if he had initially produced himself, for in that case he would have existed before he existed. Rather, God can be thought to be derived from himself solely in virtue of the fact that he really does preserve himself, as the author frequently states.

But preservation is no more consonant with an infinite being than is an initial production. For what, pray, is preservation, except a certain continuous remaking of something? Thus every instance of preservation presupposes an initial production; and for this reason the term "continuation," like the term "preservation," implies a certain potentiality. But an infinite being is the purest actuality, without any potentiality.

Let us conclude then that God can be conceived to be derived from himself [*esse a seipso*] in a positive fashion only by reason of the imperfection of our understanding, which conceives of God after the manner of created things. This will be established even more firmly by means of another argument.

The efficient cause of something is sought only with respect to a thing's existence, not its essence. For example, on seeing a triangle, I may seek the efficient cause that brought about the existence of this triangle, but it would be absurd for me to seek the efficient cause of the fact that the triangle has three angles equal to two right angles. Saying that an efficient cause is the reason for this is not a proper answer to someone making an inquiry; all that can be said is that it is simply the nature of a triangle to have such a property. Thus it is that mathematicians do not demonstrate by way of efficient or final causes, since they do not concern themselves with the existence of their object. But it no less belongs to the essence of an infinite being that it exist and even, if you will, that it continues in existence, than it is of the essence of a triangle that it have three angles equal to two right angles. Therefore, just as one cannot give an answer by way of efficient causality to the person asking why a triangle has three angles equal to two right angles but must say only that such is the eternal and unchangeable nature of a triangle, just so,

to the person asking why God exists or why God continues to exist, the 213
advice should be given that no efficient cause (either inside or outside God),
no "quasi-efficient" cause (for I am in disagreement about things, not words)
is to be sought. Rather, this alone should be claimed as the reason: that such
is the nature of a supremely perfect being.

The distinguished gentleman states that the light of nature dictates that
there exists nothing about which it is inappropriate to ask why it exists or to
inquire into its efficient cause, or, if it has none, to demand to know why it
does not need one.[111] Against this, my answer to the person asking why God
exists is that one should not reply in terms of an efficient cause. Rather, one
should say merely that it is because he is God, that is, an infinite being. And
if someone were to ask for the efficient cause of God, we should answer that
God needs no efficient cause. And were the inquirer once again to ask why
God does not need an efficient cause, we should answer that it is because he
is an infinite being, whose existence is his essence; for the only things that
need an efficient cause are those in which it is appropriate to distinguish
their actual existence from their essence.

Thus is overthrown all that the author adds just after the passages cited:
"Thus," he says, "if I thought that nothing could in any way be related to
itself the way an efficient cause is related to its effect, it is out of the question that I then conclude that something is the first cause. On the contrary,
I would again ask for the cause of that which was being called the 'first
cause,' and thus I would never arrive at any first cause of all things."[112]

On the contrary, were I to think we should seek the efficient (or quasi-
efficient) cause of any given thing, I would seek a cause of each individual
thing that was different from that thing, since it is most evident to me that 214
in no way can something be in the same relation to itself as an efficient
cause is to its effect.

The author, in my opinion, should be put on notice so that he can consider these things attentively and diligently, since I certainly know there is
hardly a theologian who would not take exception to the statement that God
is derived from himself in a positive fashion, and, as it were, from a cause.

My only remaining concern is whether the author does not commit a
vicious circle when he says that we have no other basis on which to establish that what we clearly and distinctly perceive is true, than that God exists.

But we can be certain that God exists only because we clearly and evidently perceive this fact. Therefore, before we are certain that God exists, we
ought to be certain that whatever we clearly and evidently perceive is true.

I add something that had escaped me. What the distinguished gentleman
affirms as certain seems to me to be false, namely, that there can be nothing

111. AT VII, 108.
112. AT VII, 108.

in him, insofar as he is a thinking thing, of which he is unaware. For this "him, insofar as it is a thinking thing," he understands to be merely his mind, insofar as it is distinct from his body. But who does not realize that there can be a great many things in the mind of which the mind is unaware? The mind of an infant in its mother's womb has the power to think, but it is not aware of it. I pass over countless examples similar to this one.

Concerning Matters That Can Attract the Attention of Theologians

To put an end to a discussion that has at times become tedious, it is preferable here to aim for brevity and merely show what these matters are rather than debate them in greater detail.

First, I fear that some people may take offense at this rather wide-open style of philosophizing in which everything is called into doubt. And surely the author himself admits in his *Discourse on Method*[113] that this style is dangerous to people of ordinary intelligence [*mediocribus ingeniis*]. Still, I confess that this concern is lessened in the Synopsis.[114]

All the same, this Meditation ought to be bolstered with a brief preface in which the author indicates that these things are not being seriously doubted at all. Rather, the purpose of doubting is to set aside for a short time whatever provides the least (or, as the author says elsewhere, "hyperbolic") occasion for doubting whether something so firm and stable might be found that not even the most perverse person should have even the slightest grounds for doubting it. Thus, in place of the words: "since I was ignorant of the author of my origin," I would advise replacing them with: "I pretended to be ignorant. . . ."[115]

In the Fourth Meditation ("Concerning the True and the False"), I would urgently entreat the author, for reasons too numerous to list, to indicate two things either in this Meditation or in the Synopsis.

The first is that when he inquires into the cause of error, he exhaustively treats the kind of error committed in sorting out truth and falsity but not the kind of error that occurs in the pursuit of good and evil.

For the former kind of error suffices for the author's plan and purpose, and the remarks made here regarding the cause of error may give rise to the gravest objections, were these remarks to be extended to apply to the domain of the latter kind of error. Thus, unless I am mistaken, prudence and the order to be used in teaching (about which our author is most zealous) demand that whatever is not relevant and can provide an opportunity for squabbling should be left out. Otherwise the reader may be hampered in perceiving

215

216

113. AT VI, 15.
114. AT VII, 12.
115. AT VII, 77.

what is important by being drawn into senseless brawls regarding things that are nonessential.

The second thing that I would like to point out to our author is that, in asserting that we should not give our assent to anything unless we know it clearly and distinctly, he is dealing only with things that pertain to the academic disciplines and that fall within the grasp of human understanding; he is not, however, dealing with matters of faith and the conduct of life. This is why he condemns the rashness of the opinionated, but not the conviction of prudent believers.

For, as St. Augustine wisely reminds us in his *On the Usefulness of Believing*, Chapter 15: "In the souls of men there are three activities that seem similar to one another and most suitable for being distinguished from one another: understanding, believing, and being opinionated."[116]

A person understands something if he grasps it by means of a sure argument. A person believes something if, having been influenced by some weighty authority, he thinks it to be true, even though he does not grasp it by means of a sure argument. And a person is opinionated who thinks he knows something which he does not know.

"But being opinionated is the most detestable of all, and for two reasons. First, if a person is convinced he already knows something, he cannot learn it about if in fact there is something to be learned; and second, the rashness itself is a sign of an ill-tempered soul. . . .

"Thus what we know we owe to reason; what we believe we owe to authority; what we are opinionated about we owe to error. . . . These things have been said so that we might understand that, when holding fast to our faith even in those things we do not yet grasp, we are innocent of the rashness of the opinionated. . . .

"For those who claim that we should believe only what we know are on their guard only against the accusation of being opinionated—a trait that is admittedly base and wretched. But were one to consider carefully that there is a great deal of difference between someone who thinks he knows something and someone who understands that he does not know something and yet believes it on the strength of some authority, then he will indeed avoid the charge of error, poor breeding, and arrogance."[117]

And a bit later in Chapter 12, St. Augustine adds: "A great many arguments can be brought forward to show that absolutely nothing in human society would remain safe were we to have set down as a precept that we should believe only what we could grasp with full discernment." Thus far to this point we have the teachings of St. Augustine.

---

116. *On the Usefulness of Believing,* Chap. 11, sec. 25; PL 42, 83. Arnauld's citation of Chapter 15 is incorrect.

117. *Ibid.,* Chap. 12, sec. 26; PL 42, 84.

The distinguished gentleman will easily judge for himself, and in accord with his own sense of prudence, how important it is to draw the above distinction, lest the many who in these times are prone to impiety might be able to abuse his words in order to overturn the faith.

But what I foresee will be most especially offensive to theologians is that according to the teachings of the distinguished gentleman the dogmas taught by the Church regarding the most holy mysteries of the altar seem incapable of remaining whole and intact.

For we believe on faith that once the substance of the bread has been removed from the Eucharistic bread only the accidents remain there. These latter are: extension, shape, color, odor, taste, and the other sensible qualities.

The distinguished gentleman believes there are no sensible qualities but merely the various motions of the small bodies that surround us, by means of which we perceive the various impressions which we in turn call by the names "color," "taste," and "odor." Thus there remain shape, extension, and the ability to move about. But the author denies that these features [*facultates*] can be understood without the substance in which they inhere; moreover, he holds that they cannot exist without it, a point he also repeats in his reply to the theologian.

And he acknowledges only a formal distinction between these affections and substance. But this sort of distinction seems insufficient for distinguishing those affections that are also separated from one another by divine intervention.

I have no doubt but that the distinguished gentleman's piety is such that he will carefully and attentively ponder this and will judge that he must apply himself with the greatest of zeal, lest, when he meditates upon championing the cause of God against the impious, he appear to have somehow created a danger to the very faith established by God's authority, by whose grace the gentleman hopes to win that eternal life about which he has undertaken to convince mankind.

Reply to the Fourth Set of Objections

I could not have hoped for a more insightful and at the same time a more courteous judge of my work, or for anyone more enterprising than the person whose observations you[118] sent me. For he treats me with such considerateness that I easily perceive that he supports me and my cause. And yet he has considered in such careful detail the positions he opposes and has scrutinized them so carefully that I expect nothing remains that has escaped his keen intelligence [*aciem*]. Moreover, so insightfully does he argue against

---

118. Mersenne.

those positions he judged to be less in need of proof [*minus probanda*] that I have no fear that anyone should think he would have indulged me by hiding anything. Thus, I am not so much bothered by his objections as I am pleased with his not having raised further objections. 219

Reply to the First Part: Concerning the Nature of the Human Mind

I will not take the time here to thank the distinguished gentleman for bringing the authority of St. Augustine to my aid and for putting forward my arguments in a manner that suggests he fears they might not appear powerful enough to others.

But first I will assert that where I began to show how, from the fact that I know [*cognoscam*] that nothing else belongs to my essence (that is, to the essence of the mind alone) beyond my being a thinking thing, it follows that nothing else really belongs to it. The passage in question is precisely where I proved that God exists—that very God, I say, who can bring about all that I clearly and distinctly know [*cognosco*] to be possible.

For perhaps there may be many things in me of which I am as yet unaware [*nondum adverto*] (for example, in this passage I was in fact assuming that I was as yet unaware that the mind has the power to move the body or that it is substantially united to the body). Nevertheless, since what I do notice is sufficient for me to subsist with it alone, I am certain that I could have been created by God without those other things of which I am unaware, and therefore that these other things do not belong to the essence of the mind.

If a thing can exist without some other things, then it seems to me that the latter are not included in the thing's essence; and although mind is of the essence of man, still it is not, strictly speaking, of the essence of the mind that it be united to a human body.

Mention must also be made of the sense in which I understand that a real distinction is not to be inferred from the fact that one thing is conceived without the other by an act of abstraction on the part of the understanding inadequately conceiving the thing, but only from the fact that each of the two is completely understood without the other, that is, each is understood to be a complete thing.[119] 220

For I do not think an adequate knowledge of the thing is required here, as the distinguished gentleman assumes. Rather, the difference consists in the fact that an adequate knowledge of the thing necessitates there being contained in that knowledge absolutely all the properties that are in the thing known. And thus God alone knows that he has an adequate knowledge of all things.

However, even if perhaps a created understanding really has an adequate

119. AT VII, 200.

knowledge of many things, still it can never know that it has this knowledge unless God were to reveal this fact in a special way. For all that is needed for the understanding to have an adequate knowledge of something is that the power of knowing, which is in the understanding, be capable of having this thing for an object. And this can easily happen. But for the understanding to know that it has adequate knowledge or that God has placed nothing else in the thing except what the understanding knows [*cognoscit*] to be there, it would have to equal the infinite power of God, and it is obviously self-contradictory for such a thing to occur.

But now, in order to know that a real distinction obtains between two things, our knowledge of these two things need not be adequate, unless we were capable of knowing it to be adequate. But we can never know this, as has just been stated. Therefore our knowledge need not be adequate.

221 Thus, when I said it is not sufficient for making a real distinction that one thing is understood without the other by an act of abstraction on the part of the understanding inadequately conceiving the thing, I did not think it possible to infer from this that an adequate knowledge is required for a real distinction, but merely a knowledge that was not rendered inadequate by us through an act of abstraction on the part of the understanding.

For it is one thing for our knowledge to be wholly adequate (a matter whose truth we can never know for certain unless God revealed it to us), and quite another for our knowledge to be sufficiently adequate for us to perceive that we have not rendered it inadequate through an act of abstraction on the part of the understanding.

In the same way, when I declared that a thing must be understood completely, I did not mean that the act of understanding should be adequate, but only that the thing ought to be understood well enough to know that it is complete.

I thought this was sufficiently obvious from passages both prior to and subsequent to the passage in question. For shortly before our passage I had drawn a distinction between complete and incomplete beings; and I declared that for things to be really distinct from one another, each thing must be understood to be a being in its own right and different from every other being.[120]

But later, upon declaring that I completely understand what a body is, I immediately added that I also understand that the mind is something complete.[121] I took these two statements to mean the same thing; that is, I took "understanding a thing completely" and "understanding a thing to be something complete" to mean precisely the same thing.

But here one can rightly ask what I understand by "something complete"

---

120. AT VII, 120.
121. AT VII, 121.

and how I prove that what suffices for a real distinction is that two things are understood as complete, with each of them being understood one without the other.

Now in answer to the first question, by "something complete" I simply understand a substance endowed with those forms or attributes which suffice to let me recognize that it is a substance. *222*

For we do not know substances immediately, as I have noted elsewhere.[122] Rather, we know them from the mere fact that we perceive certain forms or attributes that need to inhere in something if they are to exist. We call that thing in which they inhere a "substance."

But if afterwards we wanted to strip that very same substance from those attributes by whose means we know it, we would destroy all our knowledge of it. As a result we could of course utter some words about it, but we would not clearly and distinctly perceive the meanings of these words.

I am not ignoring the fact that there are certain substances that traditionally are called "incomplete." But if they are called incomplete because they are incapable of existing alone in their own right, I confess it seems to me contradictory that they are substances (that is, things subsisting in their own right) and at the same time that they are incomplete (that is, things incapable of subsisting in their own right). But things can be called incomplete substances in the sense that they are seen in relation to some other substance with which they constitute a unity in its own right, although insofar as they are substances, there is surely nothing incomplete about them.

Thus, a hand is an incomplete substance when it is considered in relation to the entire body of which it is a part; but it is a complete substance when it is considered by itself. And in the same way, mind and body are incomplete substances when they are considered in relation to the human being that together they constitute; but if they are considered by themselves, they are complete.

For just as being extended and divisible, having a shape, and so on, are forms or attributes by means of which I recognize that substance we call "body"; just so, performing acts of understanding, willing, doubting, and so on, are forms by means of which I recognize a substance we call "mind." Nor do I understand a thinking substance to be any less a complete thing than I do an extended substance. *223*

And there is no way anyone can maintain what the distinguished gentleman adds, namely, that perhaps body is related to mind the way genus is related to species. For although a genus can be understood without this or that specific difference, nevertheless a species can in no way be thought without a genus.

For we readily understand, for example, a figure without any thought

122. See Descartes' discussion of the piece of wax in Meditation Two, AT VII, 30–1.

being given to a circle (although this act of understanding is distinct only if it is seen in relation to some particular kind of figure, and it is of something complete only if it embraces the nature of a body). But we do not understand the specific difference of the circle without at the same time thinking of figure.

But the mind can be perceived distinctly and completely (that is, to a degree sufficient for it to be taken to be something complete) without any of those forms or attributes by means of which we acknowledge the body to be a substance, as I think I have sufficiently shown in the Second Meditation. And the body is understood distinctly and as something complete, without any of the attributes that belong to the mind.

Nevertheless, the distinguished gentleman argues here that even though some knowledge of myself could arise without any knowledge of the body, still one should not conclude from this that this knowledge is complete and adequate, so as to make me certain I am not mistaken when I exclude body from my essence. And he makes his point by means of the example of a triangle inscribed in a semicircle, a figure we can clearly and distinctly understand to be right angled, even though we may not know or may even deny that the square of its hypotenuse is equal to the sum of the squares of its sides. Nevertheless, we ought not on this account infer that there could be a [right][123] triangle the square of whose hypotenuse is not equal to the sum of the squares of its sides.

But as far as this example is concerned, it differs in many respects from the matter being discussed.

For first, although perhaps a triangle can be taken in the concrete [*in concreto*] for a substance having a triangular shape, certainly the property of having the square of its hypotenuse equal to the sum of the squares of its sides is not a substance. Nor can either the triangle or this property be understood to be something complete in the way in which mind and body are so understood; nor indeed can either of them be called a "thing" in the sense in which I used the term when I said it is sufficient that I could understand one thing (namely something complete) without the other, and so on, as is manifest from the remarks that followed: "Moreover, I find in myself faculties. . . ."[124] For I did not say that these faculties were things; on the contrary, I carefully distinguished them from things or substances.

Second, although we can clearly and distinctly understand that a triangle inscribed in a semicircle is right angled without noticing that the square of its hypotenuse is equal to the sum of the square of its sides, nevertheless we cannot clearly understand the triangle in which the square of its hypotenuse

---

123. While this word is lacking in the Latin, the French version adds it (AT XI, 174); moreover, the sense of the passage clearly requires it.

124. AT VII, 78.

is equal to the sum of the squares of its sides without at the same time notic-   *225*
ing that it is right angled. But we can clearly and distinctly perceive the
mind without the body and the body without the mind.

Third, although we could have a concept of a triangle inscribed in a
semicircle that does not contain the concept of the equality of the square of
its hypotenuse and the sum of the squares of its sides, nevertheless we could
not have a concept of the triangle such that no proportion between the
square of its hypotenuse and the sum of the squares of its sides is understood
to belong to this triangle. And thus, while we do not know the nature of this
proportion, we can deny of the triangle only what we clearly understand
not to belong to it. However, we can never have this understanding with
respect to the proportion when it is one of equality. But obviously nothing
that belongs to the mind is included in the concept of the body, and nothing that belongs to the body is included in the concept of the mind.

And so, even though I asserted that it is sufficient that I could clearly and
distinctly understand one thing without the other, and so on, one cannot on
that account add: but I clearly and distinctly understand this triangle, and so
on. First, because the proportion between the square of the hypotenuse and
the sum of the squares of the sides is not something complete. Second, because
this proportion of equality is clearly understood only in the case of a right
triangle. Third, because a triangle can in no way be distinctly understood,
were we to deny the proportion existing between the sum of the squares of
its sides and the square of its hypotenuse.

But now I must declare how it is that from the mere fact that I could
clearly and distinctly understand one substance without the other, I am cer-   *226*
tain that the one excludes the other.

My explanation is that the very notion of a substance is just this: what
can exist in its own right [*per se*], that is, without the help of any other substance. Nor has anyone who perceives two substances by means of two different concepts failed to judge them to be really distinct.

Thus, had I not been seeking certainty greater than is commonplace, I
would have been content to have shown in the Second Meditation that the
mind is understood to be something that subsists, even though absolutely
nothing belonging to the body is ascribed to it, and, conversely, that the body
also is understood to be something that subsists, even though nothing that
belongs to the mind is ascribed to it. And I would have added nothing further in proof of the real distinction between the mind and the body, since
we ordinarily judge that all things are related to one another in fact [*in ordine
ad veritatem*] in the same way they are related to one another from the per-
spective of our perception of them [*in ordine ad nostram perceptionem*]. But
because one of those hyperbolic doubts I put forward in the First Meditation went so far as to make me unable to be certain about this very thing
(namely, that things are really [*juxta veritatem*] such as we perceive them),

so long as I was supposing that I was ignorant of the cause of my being [*authorem meae originis*]. For this reason everything I wrote regarding God and truth in the Third, Fourth, and Fifth Meditations adds weight to the conclusion regarding the real distinction between the mind and the body, which I eventually completed in the Sixth Meditation.

227   However, the distinguished gentleman declares that he understands a triangle inscribed in a semicircle without his knowing that the square of its hypotenuse is equal to the sum of the squares of its sides. It is indeed the case that this triangle is capable of being understood even if no thought is given to the proportion that exists between the square of its hypotenuse and the sum of the squares of its sides. But it cannot be understood that this proportion should be denied of the triangle. On the contrary, in regard to the mind, we understand not only that it exists without a body but also that all the attributes belonging to a body can be denied of it. For it is of the nature of substances that they mutually exclude one another.

Nor does the distinguished gentleman offer anything in refutation of me when he added that there is no cause for wonder if, when I conclude that I exist from the fact that I am thinking, the idea that I form in this way merely represents me as a thinking thing. For in like manner, when I examine the nature of the body, I find absolutely nothing in it that has the smell of thought about it [*redoleat*]. And there can be no greater argument for a distinction between two things than the fact that, on turning our attention to either of the two, we discern absolutely nothing in the one that is not different from what is in the other.

Moreover, I fail to see why it is that this argument "proves too much." For to show that one thing is really distinct from another thing, nothing more can be said except that the one thing could be separated from the other through divine power. And it seemed to me that I took sufficient care lest anyone therefore think that man is merely "a soul using a body." For in

228   that very same Sixth Meditation, where I dealt with the distinction between the mind and the body, I also proved at the same time that the mind is substantially united to the body. And I do not recall having read anywhere any arguments proving this that were more powerful than the ones I used. And the person who claims that a man's arm is a substance really distinct from the rest of his body does not on that account deny that the arm belongs to the nature of the whole man; nor does the person who claims that the arm belongs to the nature of the whole man provide on that account any occasion for suspecting that it cannot subsist in its own right. In like manner, it seems to me I have proved neither too much (by showing that mind can exist without body) nor too little (by asserting that it is substantially united to the body), since this substantial unity does not stand in the way of having a clear and distinct concept of the mind alone as something complete. And therefore this concept differs markedly from the concept of a surface

or a line, which cannot thus be understood to be complete things unless depth is also ascribed to them, in addition to length and width.

Finally, although the power of thinking is dormant in infants and disturbed (though surely not extinguished) in the insane, this fact ought not make one think that the power of thinking is joined to the corporeal organs in such a way that without them it could not exist. For from the fact that we often experience our power of thinking to be impeded by these organs it does not at all follow that this power is produced by them; and there are no grounds, or hardly any, on the basis of which this conclusion can be proved.

Nevertheless, I do not deny that the close conjunction of mind and body (something we constantly experience with ourselves) is the reason why we   *229* do not notice the real distinction of the mind and the body unless we attentively meditate on it. However, in my opinion, those who frequently ponder what is stated in the Second Meditation will be easily persuaded that the mind is distinct from the body, and not merely by a mere construction or abstraction on the part of the understanding. Rather, it is known as something distinct because it really is distinct.

I have no answer to give to the comments the distinguished gentleman adds here regarding the immortality of the soul, since they are not in conflict with me. But as far as the souls of brute animals are concerned, this is not the place to consider them. In addition, unless I were to discuss the whole of my physics, I could not say more about them than what I already described in Part V of the *Discourse on Method*. Nevertheless, lest I say nothing at all on the matter, it seems to me that what is especially noteworthy is that there can be no motion—either in the bodies of brute animals or in our own—unless absolutely all the organs or instruments are present, with whose help these motions could also be brought out in a machine. Thus, not even in ourselves does the mind immediately move the external members; rather, it merely directs the spirits coursing from the heart through the brain and into the muscles, causing them to perform certain motions. This is because by themselves these spirits may be applied with equal facility to the performance of many different actions. But most of the motions that take place in us in no way depend on the mind: for example, heartbeat, digestion, growth, and breathing while we are asleep, and even, while we are awake, such actions as walking, singing, and the like, since these latter take place in   *230* the mind without the mind taking any note of them. And when people fall from a height and extend their arms toward the ground to protect their head, they obviously do this without any advice from their reason, but merely because the sight of the impending fall extends all the way to the brain and sends animal spirits into the nerves in the manner necessary to produce this motion without the mind giving its assent, as if it were produced in a machine. And since we certainly experience this in ourselves, why should we marvel so if light reflected off the body of a wolf onto the eyes of a sheep were to have the same power to excite in the sheep the motion of flight?

But now, if we were to desire to use reason to determine whether certain motions of brute animals resemble those performed in us with the help of the mind or whether they resemble merely those motions that depend merely upon the influence of the spirits and the disposition of the organs, we must consider the differences that obtain between them: namely, those differences I described in Part V of the *Discourse on Method*,[125] for I do not think any others are going to be discovered. Then it will be readily apparent that all the actions of brute animals resemble only those of our actions which take place without any help from the mind. Thus we are forced to conclude that absolutely no principle of motion in brute animals is known to us except the mere disposition of the organs and the continuous flow of the spirits that are produced by the heat of the heart as it thins the blood. And at the same time we will notice that up to this point nothing has given us an occasion for attributing anything else to brute animals except the mere fact that by not distinguishing these two principles of motion when we previously observed that one principle depends solely on spirits and organs (in brute animals as well as in ourselves), we unadvisedly believed that the other principle (which consists of mind or thought) also was present in brute animals. And obviously whatever we were so convinced of from our youth— even if afterwards it be shown by arguments to be false—is still not easily removed from our stock of opinions, unless we give our attention to these proofs frequently and over a long period of time.

231

Reply to the Second Part: Concerning God

Up to this point I have attempted to refute the distinguished gentleman's arguments and to withstand his attack. From here on, as is the custom for those who struggle with those stronger than themselves, I will not place myself in direct opposition to him; rather, I will dodge his blows.

He brings up only three points in this part, and these can be readily accepted if they are taken in the sense in which he understands them. But I understood what I wrote in a different sense, which also seems to me to be true.

The first point is that certain ideas are materially false. As I understand it, these ideas are such that they present matter for error to the power of judgment. But the gentleman, by considering these ideas taken formally, argues that no falsity is in them.

The second point is that God is derived from himself positively and, as it were, from a cause. Here I had in mind merely that the reason why God

125. AT VI, 57–9.

does not need any efficient cause in order to exist is founded on something positive, namely, on the very immensity of God, than which there can be nothing more positive. The gentleman proves that God can never be produced or preserved by himself through some positive influence of an efficient cause. I too am in agreement with all of this.

The third and final point is that there can be nothing in our mind of which we are unaware. I understood this with respect to operations, whereas the gentleman, who understands this with respect to powers, denies this.

But let us carefully explain each of these one by one. When the gentleman says that if cold were merely a privation,[126] there could not be an idea [of cold] that represents it as something positive, it is obvious that he is merely dealing with the idea taken formally. For since ideas are themselves forms of a certain sort and are not made up of any matter, whenever we consider them insofar as they represent something, we are taking them not materially but formally. But if we view them not insofar as they represent this or that thing but merely insofar as they are operations of the understanding, then we could surely say that we are taking them materially. But in that case they would bear absolutely no relationship to the truth or falsity of their objects. Hence it seems to me that we can call these ideas materially false only in the sense I have already described: namely, whether cold be something positive or a privation, I do not on that account have a different idea of it; rather, it remains the same in me as the one I have always had. And I say that this idea provides me with matter for error if it is true that cold is a privation and does not have as much reality as heat, because, in considering either of the ideas of heat or cold just as I received them both from the senses, I cannot observe any more reality being shown me by the one idea than by the other.

And it is obviously not the case that I have confused judgment with an idea, for I have said that material falsity is to be found in the latter, whereas only formal falsity can exist in the former.

However, when the distinguished gentleman says that the idea of cold is coldness itself insofar as it exists objectively in the understanding, I think a distinction is in order. For it often happens in the case of obscure and confused ideas (and those of heat and cold should be numbered among them) that they are referred to something other than that of which they really are ideas. Thus, were cold merely a privation, the idea of cold would not be coldness itself as it exists objectively in the understanding, but something else which is wrongly taken for that privation: namely, a certain sensation having no existence outside the understanding.

But the same analysis does not hold in the case of the idea of God, or at least when the idea is clear and distinct, since it cannot be said to be referred

126. AT VII, 206.

to something with which it is not in conformity. But as to confused ideas of gods which are concocted by idolaters. I fail to see why they too cannot be called materially false, insofar as these ideas provide matter for their false judgments. Nevertheless, surely those ideas that offer the faculty of judgment little or no occasion for error are presumably less worthy of being called materially false than are those that offer it considerable occasion for error; however, it is easy to exemplify the fact that some ideas offer a greater occa-

234 sion for error than others. For this occasion does not exist in confused ideas formed at the whim of the mind (such as the ideas of false gods) to the extent that it does in ideas that come to us confused from the senses (such as the ideas of heat and cold), if, as I said, it is in fact true that they display nothing real. But the greatest occasion of all for error is in ideas that arise from the sensitive appetite. For example, does not the idea of thirst in the man with dropsy in fact offer him matter for error when it provides him an occasion for judging that drinking something will do him good, when in fact it will do him harm?

But the distinguished gentleman asks what it is that is shown to me by this idea of cold, which I have said to be materially false. He says: if it shows a privation, then it is true; if it shows a positive being, then it is not the idea of cold.[127] Quite true. However, the sole reason for my calling this idea materially false is that, since it is obscure and confused, I could not determine whether or not what it shows me is something positive outside my sensation. Thus I have an occasion for judging that it is something positive, although perhaps it is merely a privation.

Hence one should not ask what the cause is of this positive objective being that causes this idea to be materially false, since I am not claiming that this materially false idea is caused by some positive being but rather that it is caused solely by the obscurity that nevertheless does have something positive as its subject, namely, the sensation itself.

And surely this positive being is in me insofar as I am a true thing; but the obscurity, which alone provides me an occasion for judging that this idea

235 of the sensation of cold represents something external to me that is called "cold," does not have a real cause but arises solely from the fact that my nature is not perfect in every respect.

My basic principles are in no way weakened by this objection. However, since I never spent very much time reading the books of the philosophers, it might have been a cause for worry that I did not sufficiently take note of their manner of speaking when I asserted that ideas that provide the power of judgment with matter for error are materially false, had it not been for the fact that I found the word "materially" used in the same sense as my own in the first author that came into my hands: namely in Francisco Suárez'

127. AT VII, 207.

Metaphysical Disputations, Disp. IX, sect. 2, no. 4.[128] But let us move on to the most significant items about which the distinguished gentleman registers his disapproval. However, in my opinion, these things seem least deserving of disapproval: namely, in the passage where I said that it is fitting for us to think that in a sense God stands in the same relationship to himself as an efficient cause does to its effect. For in that very passage I denied what the distinguished gentleman says is a harsh saying, and a false one at that: namely, that God is the efficient cause of himself. For in asserting that "in a certain sense, God stands in the same relationship to himself as an efficient cause,"[129] I did not take the two relationships to be identical. And in saying by way of preface that "it is wholly fitting for us to think . . ." I meant that my sole explanation for these things is the imperfection of the human understanding. However, I asserted this throughout the rest of the passage; for right at the very beginning, where I said that there exists nothing about which it is inappropriate to inquire into its efficient cause, I added "or, if it does not have one, to demand why it does not need one."[130] These words are a sufficient indication that I believed there exists something that needs no efficient cause. But what, besides God, can be of this sort? And a short time later I said that "in God there is such great and inexhaustible power that he never needed the help of anything in order to exist. Moreover, God does not now need a cause in order to be preserved; thus, in a manner of speaking, God is the cause of himself."[131] Here the expression "cause of himself" can in no way be understood to mean to an efficient cause; rather, it is merely a matter of the inexhaustible power of God being the cause or the reason why he needs no cause. And since this inexhaustible power or immensity of essence is incomparably positive, I said that the cause or the reason why God does not need a cause is a positive one. This could not be said of anything finite, even if it is supremely perfect in its own kind. But if a finite thing were said to be derived from itself, this could only be understood in a negative sense, since no reason derived from its positive nature could be put forward, on the basis of which we might understand that it does not need an efficient cause.

236

And in like manner, in all the other passages in which I compared the formal cause or reason derived from God's essence (on account of which God does not need a cause, either in order to exist or to be preserved) with the efficient cause (without which finite things cannot come into existence), I always did this in such wise that the difference between the formal cause and the efficient cause may come to be known from my own very words. Nowhere have I said that God preserves himself by means of some

128. Francisco Suárez, *Opera Omnia,* vol. 25, p. 322 (Paris: Ludovicus Vivès, 1856–78).
129. AT VII, 111.
130. AT VII, 108.
131. AT VII, 109.

237   positive influence, as is the case with created things preserved by him; on the
contrary, I merely said that the immensity of power or essence, on account
of which he needs no one to preserve him, is something positive.

And thus I can readily agree with everything the distinguished gentleman puts forward to prove that God is not the efficient cause of himself and
that he preserves himself neither by means of any positive influence nor by
means of a continuous reproduction of himself. This is the only thing that
is achieved from his arguments. However, as I hope is the case, even he will
not deny that this immensity of the power on account of which God does
not need a cause in order to exist, is in God something positive, and that
nothing similarly positive can be understood in anything else on account
of which it would not require an efficient cause in order to exist. This is all
I meant when I said that with the exception of God alone, nothing can be
understood to be derived from itself unless this is understood in a negative
sense. Nor was there any need for me to assume any more than this in order
to resolve the difficulty that had been put forward.

However, since the distinguished gentleman warns me here with such
seriousness that "there can scarcely be found a theologian who would not
take exception to the proposition that God is derived from himself in a positive fashion and, as it were, from a cause,"[132] I will explain a bit more carefully why this way of speaking seems to me to be extremely helpful and even
necessary in treating this question, and also why it seems to me to be quite
removed from suspicion of being likely to cause someone to take offense.

I am aware that theologians of the Latin Church do not use the word
causa [cause] in speaking of divine matters, when they are discussing the
procession of persons in the Most Holy Trinity. And whereas theologians of
the Greek Church use the words αἴτιον [cause] and ἀρχὴν [principle] inter-
changeably, theologians of the Latin Church prefer to use only the word
principium [principle], taking it in its most general sense, lest from their man-
238   ner of speaking they provide anyone an occasion on this basis for judging
the Son to be less than the Father. But where no such danger of error is possible, and the discussion concerns not God considered as triune but only as
one, I fail to see why the word "cause" should be shunned to such a degree,
especially when we arrive at a point where it seems quite helpful and almost
necessary to use it.

However, there can be no greater use for this term than if it aids in demonstrating the existence of God, and no greater necessity for it than if the existence of God manifestly could not be proved without it.

But I think it is obvious to everyone that a consideration of efficient causes
is the primary and principal, not to say the only means, of proving the existence of God. However, we cannot pursue this proof with care unless we

132. AT VII, 214.

give our mind the freedom to inquire about the efficient causes of all things, including even God himself, for by what right would we thence exclude God before we have proved that he exists? We must therefore ask with respect to every single thing whether it is derived from itself or from something else. And the existence of God can indeed be inferred by this means, even if we do not provide an explicit account of how one is to understand that "something is derived from itself." For those who follow exclusively the lead of the light of nature immediately at this juncture form a certain concept common to both efficient and formal cause alike, i.e., what is derived from something else [*est ab alio*] is derived from it as it were from an efficient cause; but whatever is derived from itself [*est a se*] is derived, as it were, from a formal cause, that is, because it has an essence of such a type that it does not need an efficient cause.

For this reason I did not explain this doctrine in my *Meditations;* rather I   *239*
assumed it to be self-evident.

But when those who are accustomed to judging that nothing can be the efficient cause of itself and to distinguishing carefully an efficient cause from a formal cause see the question being raised as to whether something is derived from itself, it easily happens that while thinking that this expression refers only to an efficient cause properly so-called, they do not think the expression "derived from itself" should be understood to mean "as from a cause," but only negatively as meaning "without a cause," with the result that there arises something concerning which we must not ask why it exists. Were this rendering of the expression "derived from itself" to be accepted, there could not be an argument [*ratio*] from effects to prove the existence of God, as the author of the First Set of Objections has shown.[133] Therefore this rendering is in no way to be accepted.

However, to give an apt reply to this, I think it is necessary to point out that there is a middle ground between an efficient cause properly so-called and no cause at all: namely, the positive essence of a thing, to which we can extend the concept of an efficient cause in the same way we are accustomed in geometry to extend the concept of an exceedingly long arc to the concept of a straight line or the concept of a rectilinear polygon with an indefinite number of sides to the concept of a circle. And I fail to see how this can be explained any better than by saying that in this query the meaning of "efficient cause" should not be restricted to those causes which are temporally prior to their effects or are different from them. For, first, the ques-   *240*
tion would be pointless, since everyone knows that the same thing cannot exist prior to itself or be different from itself. Second, we could remove one of these two conditions from its concept and yet the notion of an efficient cause would remain intact.

133. AT VII, 95.

For the fact that an efficient cause need not be temporally prior is evident from the fact that it has the defining characteristic [*rationem*] of a cause only during the time it is producing an effect, as has been said.

But from the fact that the other condition as well cannot be set aside, one ought to infer only that it is not an efficient cause taken in the strict sense, and I grant this. However, one ought not infer that it is in no sense a positive cause which can be compared by way of analogy to an efficient cause; and this is all that is called for in my argument. For by the very same light of nature by which I perceive that I would have given myself all the perfections of which there is an idea in me (if indeed I had given myself existence), I also perceive that nothing can give itself existence in that restricted sense in which the term "efficient cause" is typically used, namely, in such a way that the same thing, insofar as it gives itself existence, is different from itself, insofar as it receives existence, since being the same thing and not being the same thing (that is, being different from itself) are contradictory.

And thus, when the question arises whether something can give itself existence, one must understand this to be equivalent to asking whether the nature or essence of anything is such that it needs no efficient cause in order to exist.

And when one adds that if there were such a thing, it would give itself all the perfections of which there is some idea in it, if the meaning of this
241 is that this thing cannot fail to have in actuality all the perfections that it knows. The reason for this is that we perceive by the light of nature that a thing whose essence is so immense that it does not need an efficient cause in order to exist also does not need an efficient cause in order to possess all the perfections that it knows, and that its own proper essence gives it in an eminent fashion all that we can think an efficient cause is capable of giving to any other things.

And the words "if it does not yet have them, it will give them to itself,"[134] are helpful only in explaining the matter, since we perceive by the same light of nature that this thing cannot now have the power and the will to give itself anything new, but that its essence is such that it possesses from eternity all that we can now think it would give itself, if it did not already possess it.

Nevertheless, all these modes of speaking, which are taken from the analogy of an efficient cause, are particularly necessary in order to direct the light of nature in such wise that we pay particular attention to them. This takes place in precisely the same way in which Archimedes, by comparing the sphere and other curvilinear figures with rectilinear figures, demonstrated various properties of the sphere and other curvilinear figures that otherwise could hardly have been understood. And just as no one raises objections regarding proofs of this sort, even if during the course of them one is required

134. AT VII, 208, which refers back to Meditation Three (AT VII, 48).

to consider a sphere to be similar to a polyhedron, I likewise think I cannot be blamed here for using the analogy of an efficient cause in order to explain those things that pertain to a formal cause, that is, to the very essence of God.

And there is no possible danger of error in this matter, since that one single aspect which is a property of an efficient cause and which cannot be extended to a formal cause contains a manifest contradiction and thus is incapable of being believed by anyone, namely, that something is different from itself or that it simultaneously is and is not the same thing.

Moreover, one should note that we have ascribed to God the dignity inherent in being a cause in such wise that no indignity inherent in being an effect would follow thence in him. For just as theologians, in saying that the Father is the *principium* [principle] of the Son, do not on that account grant that the Son came from a principle; just so, although I have granted that God can in a certain sense be called the cause of himself, nevertheless nowhere have I in the same way called him an effect of himself. For it is customary to use the word "effect" primarily in relation to an efficient cause, and to regard it as less noble than its efficient cause, although it is often more noble than other causes.

However, when I here take the entire essence of a thing for its formal cause, I am merely following in the footsteps of Aristotle, for in his *Posterior Analytics,* Book II, Chapter 11,[135] having passed over the material cause, he calls the αἰτία [cause] the τὸ τί ἦν εἶναι [the what it was to be] or, as philosophers writing in Latin traditionally render it, the *causa formalis* [formal cause], and he extends this to all the essences of all things, since at this point he is dealing not with the causes of a physical composite (any more than I am here) but more generally with the causes from which some knowledge could be sought.

But it was hardly possible for me to discuss this matter without ascribing the term "cause" to God. This can be shown from the fact that, when the distinguished gentleman attempted to do the same thing I did by a different route, he nevertheless was completely unsuccessful, at least as I see it. For after using a number of words he shows that God is not the efficient cause of himself, since the defining characteristic [*ratio*] of "efficient cause" requires it to be different from its effect. Then he shows that God is not derived from himself in a positive sense, where one understands the word "positive" to mean the positive influence of a cause. Next he shows that God does not truly preserve himself, if by "preservation" one means the continuous production of a thing. All of this I readily grant. At length he tries to prove that God cannot be said to be the efficient cause of himself because, he says, the efficient cause of a thing is sought only with respect to the thing's existence, but not at all with respect to its essence. But existing is no less of the essence

242

243

---

135. 94b21–3.

of an infinite being than having three angles equal to two right angles is of the essence of a triangle. Thus, if one is asked why God exists, one should no more answer by way of an efficient cause than one should do if asked why the three angles of a triangle are equal to two right angles. This syllogism can easily be turned against the distinguished gentleman in the following way: even if an efficient cause is not sought with respect to essence, still it can be sought with respect to existence; but in God essence and existence are not distinguished; therefore one can seek an efficient cause of God.

But in order to reconcile these two positions, someone who seeks to know why God exists should be told that one surely ought not respond in terms of an efficient cause in the strict sense but only in terms of the very essence or formal cause of the thing. And precisely because in God existence is not distinguished from essence, the formal cause is strikingly analogous to an efficient cause and thus can be called a "quasi-efficient cause."

Finally, he adds that the reply to be made to someone who is seeking the efficient cause of God is that he has no need of one; and to someone 244 quizzing us further as to why God does not need one, the reply should be that this is because God is an infinite being whose existence is his essence. For the only things that need an efficient cause are those in which its actual existence can be distinguished from its essence. On the basis of these considerations he says he overturns what I had said, namely, that were I to think that nothing could somehow be related to itself the same way that an efficient cause is related to an effect, I would never, in inquiring into the causes of things, arrive at any first cause of all things. Nevertheless, it appears to me that my position has not been overturned nor has it been shaken or weakened. Moreover, on this depends the principal force not just of my argument but of absolutely all the arguments that can be put forward to prove the existence of God from effects. Yet virtually every theologian holds that no proof can be put forward unless it is from effects.

And thus when he disallows the analogy of an efficient cause being ascribed to God's relationship to himself, far from making the argument for God's existence transparent he instead prevents readers from understanding it, especially at the end where he concludes that were he to think that an efficient or quasi-efficient cause were to be sought for anything, he would be seeking a cause of that thing which is different from it. For how would those who do not yet know God inquire into the efficient cause of other things so as in this way to arrive at a knowledge of God, unless they thought that one could seek the efficient cause of anything whatever? And finally, how 245 would they make an end of their search for God as the first cause if they thought that for any given thing one must look for a cause that is different from it?

The distinguished gentleman certainly appears to be doing the very same thing here that he would do were he to follow Archimedes (who spoke of the properties that he had demonstrated of a sphere by means of an analogy with rectilinear figures) and were to say, "If I thought that a sphere could not be taken for a rectilinear or quasi-rectilinear figure having an infinite number of sides, I would attach no force to this demonstration, since strictly speaking the argument holds not for a sphere as a curvilinear figure but merely for a sphere as a rectilinear figure having an infinite number of sides." It is, I say, as if the distinguished gentleman, while not wanting to characterize the sphere thus and nevertheless desirous of retaining Archimedes' demonstration, were to say, "If I thought that the conclusion Archimedes drew there was supposed to be understood with respect to a rectilinear figure having an infinite number of sides, I would not admit this conclusion with respect to the sphere, since I am both certain and convinced that a sphere is in no way a rectilinear figure." Obviously in making these remarks he would not be doing the same thing as Archimedes had done; on the contrary, he would definitely prevent himself and others from correctly understanding Archimedes' demonstration.

I have pursued these matters here at somewhat greater length than perhaps the subject required, in order to show that it is a matter of greatest importance to take care lest there be found in my writings the least thing that theologians may justly find objectionable.

Finally, as to the fact that I did not commit a vicious circle when I said that it is manifest to us that the things we clearly and distinctly perceive are true only because God exists; and that it is manifest to us that God exists only because we perceive this fact clearly, I have already given a sufficient explanation in the Reply to the Second Set of Objections, sections 3 and 4,[136] where I drew a distinction between what we are actually perceiving clearly and what we recall having clearly perceived sometime earlier. For first of all it is manifest to us that God exists, since we are attending to the arguments that prove this; but later on, it is enough for us to recall our having clearly perceived something in order to be certain that it is true. This would not suffice, unless we knew that God exists and does not deceive us.

Now as to the doctrine that there can be nothing in the mind, insofar as it is a thinking thing, of which it is not aware, this appears to me self-evident, because we understand that nothing is in the mind, so viewed, that is not a thought or is not dependent upon thought. For otherwise it would not belong to the mind insofar as it is a thinking thing. Nor can there exist in us any thought of which we are not aware at the very same moment it is in us. For this reason I have no doubt that the mind begins to think immediately upon its being infused into the body of an infant, and at the same time is aware of its thought, even if later on it does not recall what it was

246

---

136. AT VII, 140, 142.

thinking of, because the images [*species*] of these thoughts do not inhere in the memory.

However, it should be noted that although we surely are always actually aware of the acts or operations of our mind, this is not always the case with regard to faculties or powers, except potentially. In other words, when we prepare ourselves to use some faculty, if this faculty is in the mind, we are immediately and actually aware of it. And therefore we can deny that it is in the mind if we are unable to become aware of it.

Reply To Those Matters That Can Attract the Attention of Theologians

I have opposed the distinguished gentleman's first group of arguments and have dodged the second group. At this time I completely agree with the arguments that follow, with the exception of the last one, concerning which I trust I will be able easily to bring it about that he will agree with me.

Thus, I fully grant that the things contained in the First Meditation, and even in the others, are not suited to the range of every intelligence [*ingenium*]. And whenever the occasion presented itself I attested to this and will do so in the future. And this was the only reason why I did not treat these things in the *Discourse on Method,* which had been written in French, but reserved them instead for these *Meditations,* which I warned early on should be read only by those who have both intelligence [*ingeniosis*] and learning [*doctis*]. Nor should one claim that I would have done better had I refrained from writing about things the vast majority of people ought to refrain from reading. For so necessary do I take these things to be that I am convinced that without them nothing firm and lasting can ever be established in philosophy. And although fire and iron cannot be handled safely either by people who are careless or by children, still, because such things are useful for everyday life, no one believes that on that account we should do without them.

But it is consistent with my works as a whole that, first, in the Fourth Meditation[137] I dealt only with the sort of error which is committed in determining what is true and what is false, but not with the sort of error that occurs in the pursuit of good and evil; and that, second, I always excluded those things that belong to the realm of faith and the practical conduct of life when I asserted that we should give our assent only to things we know clearly. And I also expressly made this point in my Reply to the Second Set of Objections, section 5,[138] and I gave advance warning of this in the Synopsis.[139] The reason for saying this is to declare how highly I value the distinguished gentleman's opinion and how welcome I find his advice.

137. AT VII, 215.
138. AT VII, 149.
139. AT VII, 15.

What remains is the Sacrament of the Eucharist, with which the distinguished gentleman believes my opinions are not in conformity, because, he says, "we believe on faith that once the substance of the bread has been removed from the Eucharistic bread, only the accidents remain there."[140] However, he thinks that I do not acknowledge any real accidents but only modes which cannot be "understood without the substance in which they inhere, and hence that they cannot exist without it."

I can escape this objection quite easily by saying that to date I have never denied real accidents, for although in the *Dioptrics* and *Meteorology* I did not employ them to explain the things I was dealing with, nevertheless I stated in no uncertain terms in *Meteorology,* page 164,[141] that I did not deny them. But in these *Meditations* I was supposing that they were in fact not yet known 249 to me, but I was not on that account supposing that there were no real accidents. For the analytic style of writing that I followed allows the supposing at various times of certain things that have not yet been sufficiently examined, as is evident in the First Meditation, where I assumed many things that I disavowed later on in subsequent Meditations. And surely I had no intention here of firmly establishing anything regarding the nature of accidents; rather, I put forward merely those things about them that were apparent at first glance. Finally, one should not infer from my having stated that modes cannot be understood without some substance in which they inhere that I denied that they can be posited apart from their substance through divine power, since I totally affirm and believe that God can do many things which we are incapable of understanding.

However, to proceed here more freely, I will not conceal the fact that I am convinced that everything affecting our senses is simply and solely the surface which is the boundary of the dimensions of the body that is being sensed. For it is only at the surface that contact takes place. And not just I, but nearly all philosophers, including Aristotle himself,[142] affirm that sensation takes place only through contact. Thus, for example, bread and wine are sensed only insofar as their surface is touched either immediately by the sense organ or through the interposition of air or some other bodies, as I hold, or, as many philosophers claim, through the interposition of intentional species [*speciebus intentionalibus*].

However, we should note that this surface should not be reckoned exclusively on the basis of the body's external shape that our fingers touch. Rather we should also consider all those tiny holes that are found both 250 between the ground particles of wheat out of which the bread is made and between the particles of alcohol, water, vinegar, and dregs or tartar, which

---

140. AT VII, 217.

141. AT VI, 239.

142. *De Anima,* Book 3, Chap. 13, 435b2.

in combination produce wine; and the same thing holds for the very small particles of other bodies. For obviously, since they have various shapes and motions, these small particles can never be so tightly joined together that they fail to leave many spaces between them that are not empty but are filled with air or some other matter. Thus when it is held up close to the eye we see in a piece of bread rather large spaces of this sort that can be filled not just with air but with water or wine or other liquids. And since the bread always remains exactly the same, even if the air or some other matter contained in its pores is altered, it is evident that these things do not belong to its substance. Thus the surface of the bread is not the one that surrounds the piece of bread as a whole and that uses the shortest perimeter, but the one that immediately circumscribes each of its particles.

We should note too that not only is this entire surface moved when the whole piece of bread is carried from place to place, it is also moved when some of the particles of the piece of bread are agitated by the air or by some other bodies entering its pores. Thus, if certain bodies are of such a nature that either some or all their parts are constantly being moved (which I believe is true for most of the parts of bread and for all of the parts of wine), we must also understand that their surfaces are in a certain continuous motion.

Finally, it should be noted that by the "surface" of the bread or wine or some other body I do not here understand any part of the substance or surely of the quantity of the same body, nor even a part of the surrounding bodies, but only that boundary which is conceived to be between the individual particles and the bodies that surround them and whose only being is purely modal.

Contact takes place only at this boundary, and a thing is sensed only through contact. Moreover, the substances of the bread and wine are said to be changed into the substance of something else in such a way that this new substance is completely contained within the same boundaries within which the other substances were previously contained (that is, it exists in precisely the same place where the bread and wine previously existed), or rather— since these boundaries are constantly being moved—where they would be now, were they still present. It necessarily follows from these considerations that this new substance must affect all our senses in precisely the same way in which the bread and wine would have affected them had no transubstantiation taken place.

But the Church teaches in the Council of Trent, Session 13, canons 2 and 4,[143] that there takes place a conversion of the entire substance of the

251

143. *Canons and Decrees of the Council of Trent: Original Text with English Translation,* by Rev. H. J. Schroeder, O.P. (Saint Louis: Herder Book Company, 1941), pp. 351–2 (Latin) and pp. 74–5 (English).

bread into the substance of the body of Christ our Lord, while the species of the bread remains. I fail to see here what could be understood by the "species of the bread," except that surface which is in between the individual particles of the bread and the bodies surrounding them.

For as has already been stated, it is only at this surface that contact occurs; and, as Aristotle himself acknowledges, all the senses, and not just the sense we specifically refer to as "touch," sense by means of touching. See his *De Anima,* Book 3, Chapter 13: καὶ τὰ ἄλλα αἰσθητήρια ἀφῇ αἰσθάνεται.[144]

Now everyone is of the opinion that "species" means precisely what is *252* needed in order to affect the senses. Moreover, everyone who believes that the bread is converted into the body of Christ at the same time thinks that this body of Christ is contained within the exact same surface as the bread would be, were it present. This is the case despite the fact that the body of Christ is there not in the proper sense of being in a place, "but sacramentally, and with that type of existence which, although we are hard put to express it in words, and yet, when our thought is illumined by faith, we can take to be possible for God, and we ought to believe this most resolutely."[145] All of these matters are explained so aptly and correctly by means of my principles that not only do I have no fear that it will cause orthodox theologians to take even the slightest offense but, on the contrary, I anticipate instead that they will thank me greatly for putting forward in my physics opinions that are in far greater agreement with theology than the traditional ones. For certainly, as far as I know, the Church has never taught anywhere that the species of the bread and wine that remain in the Sacrament of the Eucharist are certain real accidents that miraculously subsist by themselves when the substance in which they inhered is taken away.[146]

But perhaps the theologians who first attempted to elucidate this question in a philosophical manner were so firmly persuaded that these accidents *253* which move the senses are something real and different from a substance, that they did not notice that their position could ever be doubted. Thus, without any investigation of the matter and without any valid argument, they supposed the species of the bread to be real accidents of the same type. From this

---

144. 435b2: "and all the senses sense by means of touch."

145. Council of Trent, Session 13. Descartes cites the passage verbatim, except for the omission of the words "present to us in his substance" after "sacramentally." See *Canons and Decrees of the Council of Trent: Original Text with English Translation,* p. 350 (Latin) and p. 73 (English).

146. The paragraphs that follow were not in the first edition of the *Meditations, Objections and Replies.* The first edition of the *Replies to the Fourth Set of Objections* ends here with the following sentence: "I am omitting the other things that might be needed here until I demonstrate all these things more fully in my Summa of Philosophy (which I have here in front of me); from these things are deduced the solutions that satisfactorily address each of the objections normally occurring in this subject matter."

point on they were completely involved in explaining how these accidents could exist without a subject. But they encountered so many difficulties in this project that, like wayfarers who wandered into a stretch of bad road and an utterly impassable terrain, they should have judged from their predicament alone that they had strayed from the right path.

For first of all they seem inconsistent, or at least those do who do grant that all perception of the senses takes place by means of contact, when they assume that something in the objects other than their variously disposed surfaces is needed in order to move the senses, since it is self-evident that only a surface is needed for bringing about contact. But if they do not grant this, they cannot bring to bear a single thing to this question that has any semblance of truth.

Next, the human mind cannot think of the accidents of bread as being real and yet as existing without the substance of the bread without at the same time conceiving of these accidents after the manner of a substance. Thus there appears to be a contradiction entailed in believing both that the entire substance of the bread is changed, as the Church believes, and at the same time that something real remains which was previously in the bread. For nothing real can be understood to remain except what subsists, and although it is called an accident, it nevertheless is conceived as a substance. And thus, saying that real accidents remain is in fact the same thing as saying that the entire substance of the bread is indeed changed, but that nevertheless the part of the substance which is called a real accident remains. And this, if not in words then certainly in concept, entails a contradiction.

254

And this appears to be the main reason why some have disagreed with the Roman Catholic Church on this point. But who denies that when we are free and no theological or philosophical argument compels us to embrace other opinions, those beliefs are most especially to be embraced that could provide others neither the occasion nor the pretext for turning away from the truth of the faith? However, I believe I have shown with sufficient transparency that the opinion which posits real accidents is not in conformity with theological considerations. And in my Summa of Philosophy,[147] which I now have here in front of me, it will be clearly demonstrated that this opinion is in total opposition to philosophical considerations. In that work I will show how color, taste, weight, and whatever else moves the senses depend solely on the outermost surface of bodies.

Finally, we cannot suppose there to be real accidents unless something new and quite incomprehensible is gratuitously added to the miracle of transubstantiation (which can only be inferred from the words of consecration). Through this addition these real accidents exist without the substance

---

147. Descartes here refers to his *Principles of Philosophy,* published in 1644.

of the bread in such a manner that they do not meanwhile themselves become substances. But this is in conflict not only with human reason but also with the axiom of the theologians who declare that these words of consecration bring about only what they signify and who refuse to deem something a miracle when it can be explained by natural reason. All these problems are completely removed by virtue of my explanation of this matter. For, far from my position needing some miracle in order to preserve accidents after the removal of the substance; on the contrary, my position stipulates that they cannot be removed without a new miracle (namely, the one through which the dimensions are changed). Word has it that occasionally it has happened that in place of the consecrated bread, flesh or a child appeared in the hands of the priest, but this is never believed to have taken place through the cessation of a miracle, but rather through a completely new miracle.

Moreover, there is nothing incomprehensible or difficult in supposing that God, the creator of all things, could change one substance into another and that this subsequent substance remains completely within the same surface within which the previous substance was contained. Nor again can one say that anything is more in conformity with reason or is more commonly accepted among the philosophers than the fact that not just every sense but generally every action of a body upon another body takes place by means of contact and that this contact can occur only at the surface. Whence it plainly follows that a given surface must always act and be acted upon in the same way, even though the substance that was beneath it is changed.

For this reason, if it is fitting to write here without giving offense, I have dared to hope the time will sometime come when the opinion that posits real accidents will be rejected by theologians as irrational, incomprehensible, and harmful to the faith, and that my opinion will be accepted in its place as certain and indubitable. I believed this should not be concealed here, so that I might do battle as best I can with the slanderous talk of those who wish to appear more learned than others and thus endure nothing more unwillingly than when something new in the sciences is put forward for which they cannot claim for themselves any previous knowledge.

It is often the case that the more they believe it to be true and of great importance, the more bitterly do they rail against it. And what they cannot refute with arguments they maintain is in opposition to the Holy Scriptures and the truths of faith, without giving any reason. They are indeed impious when they desire to use the authority of the Church in order to overturn the truth in this matter. But I turn my appeal from these people to the pious and orthodox theologians to whose judgments and criticism I most freely submit.

255

256

Announcement by the Author[148] Regarding the Fifth Set of Objections[149]

Before publishing the first edition of these Meditations[150] I wanted to have them examined not only by the Doctors of the Sorbonne but also by all other learned men who would take the trouble to do so. Thus I hoped that by having these objections and my replies printed as a continuation of the *Meditations,* each of them following the order in which they were produced, this would serve to render the truth more evident. And although the *Fifth Objections* did not seem to be the most important of those sent to me, and they were rather lengthy, I did not fail to have them printed in their proper order,[151] out of courtesy to their author. I even allowed him to see the proofs, so that nothing should be set down as his of which he did not approve.

199 But he has since produced a large volume[152] containing these same objections, together with several new counter-objections [*instances*] or answers to my replies; and he there complains about my having published them, as if I had done it against his wishes, and says he sent them to me only for my private instruction. As a result, I shall from now on gladly comply with his desire and relieve this volume of their presence. This was the reason why, on learning that Clerselier was taking the trouble to translate the other objections, I asked him to omit these.[153] And in order that he may have no cause to regret their absence, I should inform the reader here that I have lately read them a second time and also read all the new counter-objections in the large volume containing them, with the purpose of extracting from them all the points I should judge to stand in need of reply; but I have been unable to discover a single one to which, in my opinion, those who understand at all the meaning of my *Meditations* would not be able to reply without my help. As to those who judge books only by their size or by their title, I have no ambition to seek their approbation.

148. The "author" is Descartes himself.

149. This item and the following, that is, the letter to Claude Clerselier of January 12, 1646, were both published in the 1647 French edition of the *Meditations, Objections, and Replies.*

150. That is, the Latin edition of 1641.

151. By which Descartes means that he published Gassendi's objections as he received them, placed them after the *Fourth Set* by Arnauld, and published his *Replies* after the *Fifth Set,* as opposed to interspersing them within the text as a point-by-point rebuttal, as he did with the *Third Set* by Hobbes and, in the second edition of the *Meditations,* with the *Seventh Set* by Bourdin.

152. Pierre Gassendi, *Disquisitio metaphyica* (Amsterdam, 1644).

153. In fact, Clerselier printed this author's note and the letter that follows, together with his own translator's announcement, in place of the *Fifth Set of Objections and Replies,* but he included the *Fifth Set* as an Appendix at the end of the volume.

Letter from Descartes to Clerselier Serving as a Reply to a Selection of the Principal Counter-Objections Made by Gassendi against the Preceding Replies.[154]

Sir,

I am greatly indebted to you in that, noticing that I have neglected to reply to the large volume of counter-objections the author of the *Fifth Objections* wrote in answer to my *Replies,* you asked some of your friends to collect together the strongest arguments from this book and sent me the selection they made. In this you have shown more attention for my reputa- tion than I myself; for I assure you that it is a matter of indifference to me whether I am esteemed or despised by the people whom such arguments might have persuaded. The brightest of my friends who read his book declared to me that they have found nothing in it to capture their attention, and they are the only people I desire to satisfy. I know that most men seize on appearance more readily than the truth and judge more often badly than well. This is why I hold that their approbation is not worth the trouble I would incur in doing everything that might be useful to secure it. But none-theless I am pleased with the selection you sent me, and I feel myself obliged to reply to it, more in order to express my gratitude to your friends for their work than because I need to defend myself. For I believe that those who have taken the trouble to compose it must now judge, as I do, that all the objections this book contains are based solely on some terms being mis-understood or some assumptions that are false. But though all the objections they have noted are of that sort, they have been so diligent that they even added objections I do not remember having previously read there.

They notice three criticisms directed against the First Meditation: (1) "that I require something impossible in wanting people to give up every kind of preconceived opinion"; (2) "that in thinking we have given all of them up we acquire other more harmful preconceived opinions"; and (3) "that the method I have proposed of doubting everything cannot serve in discover-ing any truth."

The first of these criticisms is due to the author of this book not having considered that the word "preconceived" does not apply to all the notions in our mind, of which I agree it is impossible for us to divest ourselves, but only to all those opinions we believe as a result of previous judgments we have made. And since making or not making a judgment is an act of the will, as I have explained in the appropriate place, it is evident that it is something

---

154. That is, against the *Replies to the Fifth Set of Objections.*

within our power; for in order to rid ourselves of all preconceived opinions, nothing needs to be done except to resolve to affirm or deny none of the matters we have previously affirmed or denied, unless after a fresh examination. But yet we do not on that account cease to retain all these same notions in memory. Nevertheless I have said that there was a difficultly in expelling from our own belief everything we had put there previously, partly because we need to have some reason for doubting before determining to do so—that was why I propounded the main reasons for doubting in my First Meditation—and partly also because whatever resolution we have formed to deny or affirm nothing, it is easy to forget it afterwards if we did not impress it firmly on our memory; and this was why I recommended that we should think about it with care.

The second objection involves nothing more than a manifestly false assumption; for though I said that we must even compel ourselves to deny the things we had previously affirmed with too great assurance, I expressly
205   limited the period during which we should so behave to the time in which we bend our thought to the discovery of something more certain than what we had been able thus to deny; and during this time it is evident that we could not entertain any preconception that might be more harmful.

The third criticism contains a mere quibble. Although it is true that doubt alone does not suffice to establish any truth, this does not prevent it from being useful in preparing the mind for establishing truth afterwards. It is the sole purpose for which I have used it.

Your friends note six objections to Meditation Two. The first is that in the statement, "I think, therefore I am," the author of these counter-objections claims that I imply the assumption of this major premise, "he who thinks, exists," and that I have thus already espoused a preconceived opinion. Here he once more mishandles the term "preconceived": for though we may apply this term to that proposition when it is brought forward without scrutiny, and we believe it true merely because we remember having made this same judgment previously, we cannot maintain on every occasion that it is a preconceived opinion. For when we examine it, it appears so evident to the understanding that we cannot prevent ourselves from believing it, even though it may perhaps be the first time in our life we have thought of it— and consequently it would not be something preconceived. But the greater error here is that this author assumes that the knowledge of particular propositions must always be deduced from universal ones, following the order of syllogisms in Dialectics. This shows that he is but little acquainted
206   with the way by which truth should be investigated. For it is certain that in order to discover the truth we should always start with particular notions, in order to arrive at general ones subsequently, though we can also do the reverse: after having found the universals, deduce other particular truths from them. Thus in teaching a child the elements of geometry we will certainly

not make him understand in general that "when equals are taken from equals the remainders are equal" or that "the whole is greater than its parts" unless we show him examples in particular cases. For, failing to guard against this error, our author has been led astray into the many false reasonings with which he has enlarged his book. He has merely constructed false major premises according to his whim, as though I had deduced from them the truths I have explained.

The second objection that your friends note is: "in order to know that one thinks, we must know what thought is, which I certainly do not know," they say, "because I have denied everything." But I have denied nothing but preconceived opinions and by no means notions like these, which are known without any affirmation or negation.

The third is: "that thought cannot be without an object, for example, the body." Here we must keep clear of the ambiguity in the word "thought," which can be taken for the thing that thinks and for that thing's activity. Now I deny that the thing that thinks needs any object other than itself in order to exercise its activity, though it can also reach out to material things when it examines them.

The fourth: "that even though I have a thought of myself, I do not know   *207* whether that thought is a corporeal action or a self-moving atom, rather than an immaterial substance." Here the ambiguity in the word "thought" is repeated, and apart from this, I see nothing but a question without basis, somewhat of this kind: you judge that you are a man, because you perceive in yourself all the things on account of which you give the name "men" to those who possess them; but how do you know that you are not an elephant rather than a man, for some other reasons you cannot perceive? After the substance that thinks has judged that it is intellectual because it has noted in itself all the properties of intellectual substances, and has been unable to recognize any of those belonging to body, once more it is asked how it knows that it is not a body rather than an immaterial substance.

The fifth objection is similar: "that though I find nothing extended in my thought, it does not follow that it is not at all extended, because my thought is not the rule of the truth of things." And likewise the sixth: "that possibly the distinction discovered by my thought between thought and body is false." But here we must particularly notice the ambiguity in the words "my thought is not the rule of the truth of things." For if the claim is that my thought should not be the rule for others, requiring them to believe something because I think it true, I entirely agree. But that is not at all to the   *208* point here. For I have never wanted to force anyone to follow my authority; on the contrary, I have announced in various places that we should never allow ourselves to be persuaded except by the evidence of reasons. Further, if the word "thought" is taken indifferently for any kind of operation of the soul, it is certain that we can have many thoughts, from which we can infer nothing about the truth of things outside of us. But that also is not to the point here, where the question concerns only thoughts that are clear and distinct perceptions, and judgments each of us can make for himself as a result of these perceptions. This is why, in the sense in which these words should be understood here, I say that each person's thought—that is, the perception or knowledge he has of a thing—must be for him the rule for the truth of that thing; that is, that all the judgments he makes must conform to that perception in order to be correct. Even with respect to the truths of the faith, we should perceive some reason persuading us that they have been revealed by God, before determining ourselves to believe them; and though ignorant people do well to follow the judgment of more capable ones with respect to those things difficult to know, it must nevertheless be their own perception that tells them that they are ignorant and that those whose judgments they want to follow are perhaps less ignorant, otherwise they would be wrong to follow them and would be acting more like automata or like beasts rather than men. Hence it is the most absurd and

209   extravagant error that a philosopher can commit, to wish to make judgments that do not correspond to his perception of things. Yet I fail to see how our author can excuse himself from having fallen into this blunder in most of his objections; for he does not want each individual to abide by his own perception but claims that we should rather believe the opinions or fancies he pleases to propose for us, even though we do not perceive them at all.

Your friends have noted in opposition to the Third Meditation: (1) "that not everyone experiences in himself the idea of God"; (2) "that if I had this idea I should comprehend it"; (3) "that several people have read my arguments without being persuaded by them"; and (4) "that it does not follow from the fact that I know myself to be imperfect, that God exists." But, if we take the word "idea" in the way I quite expressly said I took it, without getting out of the difficulty by the equivocation of those who restrict it to the images of material things formed in the imagination, we will be unable to deny having some idea of God, except by saying that we do not understand the meaning of the words "the most perfect thing that we can conceive"; for that is what all men call "God." But to go so far as to say one does not understand the meaning of the words that are the commonest in the mouths of men is to have recourse to strange extremes in order to find objections. Besides, it is the most impious confession one can make, to say of oneself, in the sense in which I have taken the word "idea," that one has no idea of God; for this is not merely to say that one does not know God by means

210   of natural reason, but also that neither by faith nor by any other means could one have any knowledge of him, because if one has no idea, that is, no perception corresponding to the meaning of the word "God," it is no use saying that one believes that God exists; it would be the same as saying that one

believes that *nothing* exists, thus remaining in the abyss of impiety and the depths of ignorance.

What they add—"that if I had this idea I should comprehend it"—is claimed without basis. For, because the word "comprehend" implies some limitation, a finite mind could not comprehend God, who is infinite; but this does not prevent him from perceiving [*apercevoir*] God, just as one can touch a mountain without being able to embrace it.

What they say about my arguments—"that several people have read [them] without being persuaded by them"—can easily be rebutted, for there are others who have understood them and have been satisfied with them. For we should believe what a single person who says, without intending to lie, that he has seen or understood something, rather than a thousand others who deny it, for the mere reason that they could not have seen it or understood it. Thus in the discovery of the Antipodes,[155] the report of a few sailors who had circumnavigated the earth was believed rather than the thousands of philosophers who did not believe the earth to be round. And, while they cite here the *Elements* of Euclid as confirmation, saying that everyone finds them easy to understand, I beg them to consider that among those thought the most learned in the philosophy of the Schools, there is not one in a hundred who understands them, and that there is not one in ten thousand who understands all the demonstrations of Apollonius or Archimedes, even though they are as evident and as certain as those of Euclid.   *211*

Finally, they prove nothing when they say "that it does not follow from the fact that I know myself to be imperfect, that God exists." For I do not immediately deduce the conclusion from that alone, without further considerations; they merely remind me of the trickery of this author who has the habit of truncating my arguments and reporting only parts of them in order to make them seem imperfect.

I see nothing in what they have noted with respect to the three other Meditations, to which I have not amply replied elsewhere, as for example, to their objection: (1) "that I was guilty of circularity in proving the existence of God from certain notions in us, and afterwards saying that we can be certain of nothing unless we already know that God exists"; (2) "that knowledge of God's existence is useless in acquiring knowledge of the truths of mathematics"; and (3) "that God may be a deceiver." On this subject, consult my reply to the *Second Set of Objections,* sections 3 and 4, and the end of the second part of the reply to the *Fourth.*[156]

But at the end they add a thought that, to my knowledge, is not to be found in this author's book of counter-objections, though it is very similar   *212*

---

155. Located approximately 350 miles southeast of New Zealand, the Antipodes Islands were not discovered until early in the 19th century.

156. See AT VII, 141–6 and 245 on.

to his criticisms: "many excellent minds," they say, "believe they clearly see that mathematical extension, which I posit as the principle of my physics, is nothing other than my thought, and that it has and can have no subsistence outside of my mind, being merely an abstraction I form from physical body; that consequently the whole of my physics must be imaginary and fictitious, as is all pure mathematics; and that the real physics of things God has created requires a real, solid, and non-imaginary matter." Here we have the objection of objections, the summation of the whole doctrine of these excellent minds cited here. Everything that we can understand and conceive, is, according to their story, but imaginations and fictions of our mind that can have no subsistence; from this it follows that nothing of what we can understand, conceive, or imagine must be admitted as true, that is, that we must entirely close the door against reason and content ourselves with being monkeys or parrots and no longer men, if we wish to place ourselves on a level with these excellent minds. For if the things we conceive must be esteemed to be false merely because we can conceive them, what is there left for us but to accept as true the things we do not conceive and to fashion our system of belief out of them, imitating others without knowing why we imitate them, like monkeys, and uttering only words we do not understand, like parrots? But I have much with which to console myself, since here my
213   critics have joined my physics with pure mathematics, which I desire above all that it resemble.

There are two questions added at the end, namely, how the soul moves the body if it is not material and how it can receive the forms [*espèces*] of corporeal objects. These give me here merely the opportunity of declaring that our author had no right, under pretext of objecting to me, to propound a quantity of such questions, the solutions of which are not necessary for the proof of what I have written. The most ignorant people can raise more such questions in a quarter of an hour than the wisest would be able to solve in a lifetime. Thus I do not feel called upon to answer any of them. And these questions presuppose, among other things, an explanation of the union between soul and body, which I have not yet treated. But I will tell you, for your own benefit, that the whole difficulty involved in these questions arises entirely from a false assumption that can by no manner of means be proved, namely, that if the soul and the body are two substances of diverse nature, that prevents them from being capable of acting on one another; for, on the contrary, those who admit the existence of real accidents, like heat, weight, and similar things, do not doubt that these accidents can act on the body, and yet there is more difference between them and it—that is, between accidents and a substance—than there is between two substances.

For the rest, since I have pen in hand, I shall note here two of the ambi-
214   guities I have found in this book of counter-objections, because they seem to me able most easily to entrap a less attentive reader; and I desire in this

way to testify to you that if I had found anything else I believed worthy of reply I would not have neglected to deal with it.

The first is on page 63,[157] where because I have said in one place, that   *215* while the soul doubts the existence of all material things it knows itself precisely, "in the strict sense (*praecise tantum*)," only as an immaterial substance; and seven or eight lines lower down, in order to show that, by these words "in the strict sense," I do not mean an entire exclusion or negation, but only an abstraction from material things, I said that in spite of that, I was not sure that there was nothing corporeal in the soul, although nothing of such a nature was known in it; my opponents treat me so unjustly as to wish to persuade the reader that in saying "in the strict sense," I wanted to exclude the body and have thus contradicted myself afterwards in saying that I did not want to exclude it. I make no reply to the subsequent accusation of having assumed something in the Sixth Meditation that I had not previously proved and of having thus committed a fallacy. It is easy to recognize the falsity of this accusation, which is only too common in the whole of this book and might make me suspect that its author had not acted in good faith, if I had   *216* not known his character and did not believe he has been the first to be entrapped by so false a belief.

The other ambiguity is on page 84,[158] where he wants to make "to

157. *Metaphysical Disquisitions*, pp. 62–4, part 3 of the *Counter-Objection* following Doubt 4 against Meditation Two and the Reply (AT IXa, 214–5). The relevant portion of the passage is as follows: ". . . after you said, 'I am then in a strict sense only a thing that thinks,' you declared that you do not know, and do not here dispute, 'whether you are that complex system of members, called the human body, or a subtle air infused into those members, or fire, or vapor, or breath, etc.' From this, two conclusions follow. One is that when we arrive at your proof in Meditation Six, you will be convicted of having failed to prove at any point that you are not a complex system of members, or subtle air, or vapor, etc., and that you will not be able to take that as granted or proved. Secondly, it will follow that it was unjustifiable to draw the conclusion: 'I am then in a strict sense only a thing that thinks.' What does that word 'only' mean? Is it not restriction to something thinking solely, and exclusive of all other things, among which we find a system of members, a subtle air, fire, vapour, etc.?"

158. *Metaphysical Disquisitions*, p. 84, part 1 of the *Counter-Objection* following Doubt 8 against Meditation Two and the Reply (AT IXa, 216): "You say 'that you have not abstracted the concept of wax from the concept of its accidents.' I concede you good faith in the matter! Are not these your very words: 'I distinguish the wax from its external forms, and consider it in naked isolation, as it were divested of the garments that cover it'? What else is the abstraction of the concept of one thing from the concept of others but the considering of it apart from them? What else but to consider it in naked isolation, with the covering vestments stripped off? Is there any other way of abstracting the concept of human nature from the concepts of individual men, than by distinguishing it from the so-called individuating differences and considering it in isolation and stripped of that which invests it? But it is a task I little relish to argue about a point, ignorance of which would ensure logic student's beating from his teachers. You say 'that you rather wished to show how the substance of wax is manifested by its accidents.' It was that you wished to point out, that which you clearly announced. Is not this a neat way of getting out of the difficulty? And when you wished to point it out, what means did you employ for doing so, or how did you make the wax manifest, if not by looking to its accidents, first as to its garments and then stripping these off and considering it in isolation?"

abstract" and "to distinguish" mean the same, though all the time there is a great difference between them: for in distinguishing a substance from its accidents, we must consider both one and the other, and this helps greatly in coming to know it; whereas if instead we only separate by abstraction this substance from its accidents, that is, if we consider it quite alone without thinking of them, that prevents us from knowing it well, because it is by its accidents that the nature of substance is manifested.

217   Here, Sir, is all of what I believe I should reply to the large book of counter-objections; for, although perhaps I should better content the author's friends if I refuted all of his counter-objections one after the other, I believe I should not satisfy my own friends, who would have cause to reprove me for having occupied time with something so little in need and of thus putting my leisure at the disposal of all those who might care to squander theirs in proposing useless questions to me. But I thank you for the attention you have given me. Adieu.

412   ## Sixth Set of Objections

After a very careful and thorough reading of your *Meditations* and the replies you made to the objections that have so far been raised, we find there still remain some concerns that you would do well to remove.

413   The first concern is that from the fact that we think it does not seem entirely certain that we exist. For in order for you to be certain that you think, you ought to know what it is to think, or what thought is, or again what your existence is. And since you do not yet know what these things are, how can you know that you think or that you exist? Therefore, when you say "I think," and when you add "therefore I am," you really do not know what you are saying. In fact, you are utterly ignorant of what you are saying or thinking, since this seems to require you to know that you know what you are saying, and this in turn requires you to be cognizant of the fact that you know that you know what you are saying, and so on ad infinitum. Thus it is evident that you cannot know whether you exist or even whether you think.

However, turning to the second concern, when you say that you think and that you exist, someone might argue that you are mistaken, that you are not thinking but are merely being moved, and that you are merely a corporeal motion, since no one has as yet been able to grasp that argument of yours whereby you think you have demonstrated that what you call thought cannot be a corporeal motion. Have you therefore used your method of analysis to dissect all the motions of your subtle matter in such a way that you are certain that you could show us, who pay very close attention and who are, we think, rather intelligent people, that it is self-contradictory for our thoughts to be dispersed among those corporeal motions?

The third concern is quite similar. Several Church fathers, along with the Platonists, believed that angels are corporeal (and thus the Lateran Council[159] concluded that angels can be represented pictorially). They believed precisely the same thing regarding the rational soul, with some church fathers actually of the opinion that the soul is transmitted to one by one's parents; nevertheless they declared that both angels and the human soul think. Thus they seem to have believed that this could take place through corporeal motions, or even that angels were themselves corporeal motions; and in no way did they distinguish thought from these motions. This point can be confirmed by the thoughts of apes, dogs, and other animals. For dogs bark while sleeping as if they were chasing after hares or robbers. And when they are awake they know they are running, just as when they are asleep they know they are barking, even though we do not acknowledge, as you do, that there is something in them that is distinct from their bodies. But if you deny that a dog knows that it runs or thinks, leaving aside the fact that you assert this without proof, the dog itself might perhaps form a similar opinion about us, namely, that we do not know whether we are running or thinking while we run or think. For you do not see the dog's internal mode of operating any more than the dog observes yours; and there are great men who today ascribe the power of reasoning to brute animals, or who in previous times have done so. So foreign is it to us to believe that all of the functions of these animals can be adequately explained by means of the science of mechanics (that is, without reference to sense, life, and soul), that we are willing to risk everything in order to prove that this position is both impossible[160] and worthy of ridicule. And finally there are plenty of people who will say that man himself has neither sense nor intellect and that he can do everything by means of mechanical devices and without any mind, given the fact that an ape, a dog, and an elephant can perform all their activities in this way. For if the paltry reasoning power of brute animals differs from the reasoning power of men, it differs merely in degree and does not form the basis for an essential difference.

The fourth concern is with regard to the knowledge possessed by an atheist. When the atheist declares "if equals are subtracted from equals the

414

---

159. There have been five Lateran Councils; most likely the council referred to here is the Fourth Lateran Council (1215). This council issued a summary of orthodox doctrines entitled *Firmiter,* directed against the Albigensians, among others. This summary affirmed that all beings, both spiritual and corporeal, i.e., those angelic and earthly, were created by God and that the creation of human beings was subsequent to that of angels. There is no suggestion whatever in this summary that angels are material; in fact, *Firmiter* very clearly assumes a distinction between spiritual creatures and corporeal creatures. Nor, for that matter, is there any discussion of the iconography of angels.

160. For some reason the authors of the *Sixth Set of Objections* used the Greek *adunaton* rather than one of the obvious Latin terms. Perhaps this was in imitation of Aristotle, who used this term throughout his works to characterize the views of opponents.

remainders will be equal" or "the three angles of a rectilinear triangle are equal to two right angles," and a thousand similar examples, he claims that his knowledge is certain and even, according to your rule, most evident. For he cannot think of these statements without believing them to be most certain. The atheist contends that this is so true that even if God did not exist and were not possible, as he believes, he would be no less certain of these truths than were God really to exist. And he denies that any grounds for doubting can be brought forward to him which would at all distress him or cause him to be in doubt. What then do you bring forward? That God, if he exists, can deceive him? But he will deny that he can be deceived in these matters even if God exerts the full thrust of his omnipotence to this purpose.

From this there arises a fifth concern which is rooted in that deception which you wholly deny of God. A great many theologians believe that the damned, both angels and men, are continually being deceived by the idea placed in them by God of a fire that torments them, so that they give the firmest credence and believe they see most clearly and perceive that they really are being tormented by fire even though there is no fire. This being the case, is it not possible that God can deceive us with similar ideas and find continual amusement at our expense by sending species or ideas into our souls? Thus we think we see clearly and perceive with each of our senses things that nevertheless are not outside us, so that neither the heavens nor the earth exist, nor do we have arms, feet, eyes, and so on. God could surely do this without injustice or wickedness, since he is the supreme lord of all things and has absolute power in the management of his possessions, especially since this contributes to checking men's pride and punishing them for their sins, whether this be because of original sin or because of some other causes which are hidden from us. These points seem definitely to be confirmed in those passages in Scripture which show us that we can know nothing. For example, the passage in Paul, 1 Corinthians 8:2: "If anyone," he says, "thinks he knows anything, he has not yet known as he ought to know." And in the passage in Ecclesiastes 8:17: "I understood that of all the works of God man can find no reason for the things that happen under the sun; and the more someone labors to seek it out the less he will find; even if a wise man were to say that he knows, he will not be able to find it." However, the entire book makes it apparent that the wise man speaks as he does on account of carefully thought out reasons and not impetuously or thoughtlessly, especially when a question is raised regarding the mind, which you contend is immortal. For Ecclesiastes 3:19 declares that "the death of a man is the same as the death of beasts." But lest you reply that this is to be understood only in respect to the body, the author of Ecclesiastes adds that "man has no preeminence over a beast." And speaking of this very spirit of man he denies that there is anyone who knows whether it goes upward (that is, whether it is immortal) or goes downward with the spirits of animals (that is, whether it perishes). Nor is it appropriate for you to maintain that this is being uttered in the persona of an unbeliever; were that the case, the writer ought to have warned us about this and to have refuted what he had alleged. Nor again is it appropriate for you to deny that you should reply to these things on the grounds that Scripture is a matter for theologians. For since you are a Christian, it is fitting for you to be prepared to reply to all those who raise an objection against the faith, but especially against those views you desire to maintain, and to do as satisfactory a job as you possibly can.

The sixth concern arises from the indifference of judgment or freedom, which you refuse to ascribe to the perfection of the will but only to its imperfection, so that indifference is eliminated whenever the mind clearly perceives what is to be believed or done or left undone. Do you not see that by maintaining these positions you are destroying God's freedom, since you *417* are removing from his will that indifference as to whether he will establish this world rather than some other world or no world at all, even though it is a matter of faith that from all eternity God was indifferent as to whether he should establish one world or countless worlds or even no worlds at all? But who doubts that God has always seen with the clearest intuition all that is to be done or left undone? The clearest vision and perception of things does not therefore eliminate the indifference of choice. And if indifference cannot be compatible with human freedom, neither will it be compatible with divine freedom, since the essences of things are, like numbers, indivisible and immutable. Thus indifference is included no less in the divine freedom of choice than in human freedom of choice.

The seventh concern deals with the surface on which, or by means of which, you say all sensations take place. For we do not understand how it could happen that it is neither a part of the bodies which are sensed nor a part of the air and the vapors, given that you deny that it is any part or even the outer surface of these things. Nor, for that matter, do we grasp your claim that there are no real accidents which pertain to some body or substance and which could exist by divine power without any subject, and which really do exist in the Sacrament of the Altar. Nevertheless, there is no reason for our professors to be perturbed by your views until they see whether you are going to prove them in your treatise on physics, which you give us cause to anticipate and which they scarcely believe will put these views forward so clearly that they can or must be embraced, with earlier teachings being rejected.

The eighth concern arises from your reply to the *Fifth Set of Objections*. How can the truths of geometry or metaphysics, such as the ones you call to mind, be immutable and eternal and yet not be independent of God?[161] *418* For what type of cause is it according to which these truths depend upon

---

161. See AT VII, 380.

God? Could God have brought it about that there never was such a thing as the nature of a triangle? And how, pray tell, could God bring it about from all eternity that it was not true that twice 4 is 8 or that a triangle does not have three angles? Therefore either these truths depend solely on an intellect that is thinking of them or on existing things, or else they are independent, since it seems God could not have brought it about that any of these essences or truths were not from all eternity.

Finally, the ninth concern is especially troubling to us. You claim that one should not place any trust in the operations of the senses and that the certainty of the intellect is far greater than that of the senses. For how can the intellect enjoy any certainty unless it has previously acquired it from properly disposed senses? Moreover, how can the intellect correct an error on the part of one of the senses unless some other sense first corrects the error? On account of refraction, a stick submerged in water appears bent, even though it is straight. What is going to correct this error? The intellect? Hardly. It is the sense of touch. And the same determination must obtain in the other instances. Thus if you employ all the senses when they are in good working order and are always presenting the same data, you will achieve the greatest certainty of which man is naturally capable. But this certainty will often elude you if you place your trust in the operation of the mind, which is often mistaken in matters about which it believed doubt to be impossible.

These are the main concerns that give us pause. Please also append to these a certain procedure, along with certain identifying characteristics, that would render us most certain that when we understand so completely one thing apart from another, it is certain that the one is so distinct from the other that they could subsist separately, at least by the power of God. In other words, how can we with certainty know clearly and distinctly that this distinction made by the intellect does not arise exclusively from the intellect itself but proceeds from things themselves? For when we contemplate the immensity of God without thinking about his justice, or when we contemplate his existence without thinking about the Son or the Holy Spirit, do we not completely perceive this existence, or God as existing, apart from these persons—which some unbeliever could deny, just as you deny that mind or thought pertains to the body? Thus just as one argues poorly when one concludes that the Son and the Holy Spirit are essentially distinct from God the Father or can be separated from him, so too no one will grant you that thought or the human mind are distinct from the body, even though you conceive the one apart from the other and utterly deny the one of the other, and even though you do not think that this takes place through some act of abstraction on the part of your mind. Surely, if you handle these concerns in a satisfactory manner, then, as far as we are concerned, absolutely nothing else remains that would displease our theologians.

Appendix

A few questions raised by others are appended here, so that you might reply to these together with the immediately preceding ones, since they address the same argument. Certain very learned and insightful people wished to have the following three points explained more carefully:

1) How do I know with certainty that I have a clear idea of my soul?
2) How do I know with certainty that this idea is completely different from anything else?
3) How do I know with certainty that this idea contains absolutely nothing   *420* corporeal?[162]

Reply to the Sixth Set of Objections

1. It is indeed true that no one can be certain that he thinks or that he exists unless he knows what thought is and what existence is. This is not to say that it requires a knowledge which is reflective or which is acquired through demonstration, much less a knowledge of reflective knowledge, through which one knows that one knows, and again knows that one knows that one knows, and so on ad infinitum. This sort of knowledge can never be had about anything. Rather, it is quite sufficient that one knows it by that inner knowledge which always precedes reflective knowledge. This inner knowledge, in the case of thought and existence, is innate in all men in such a way that we could not really be without it, even if perhaps we are overwhelmed by preconceived opinions and are attentive more to words than to their meanings, and thus could imagine that we do not have such knowledge. Thus when someone notices that he is thinking and that it follows from this that he exists, even though perhaps he had never before sought to know what thought is or what existence is, still he cannot fail to have a sufficient knowledge of each of these, so that on this score he is satisfied.

2. Nor too is it possible, when someone notices that he thinks and understands what it is to be moved, that he would believe himself to be mistaken and that he is not thinking but only being moved. For since the idea or notion he has of thought is plainly different from that of corporeal motion,   *423* it is necessary for him to understand the one to be different from the other. However, on account of his habit of ascribing to one and the same subject many different properties among which no connection is known, it could happen that he doubts or even that he affirms that he is one and the same thing which thinks and which moves from place to place. And one should

---

162. The *Sixth Set of Objections* continues with a letter from "Various Philosophers and Geometers to Descartes."

note that there are two ways in which things of which we have different ideas can be taken to be one and the same thing: namely, either by a unity and identity of nature or merely by a unity of composition. Thus, for example, we surely do not have the same idea of figure and motion, just as we do not have the same idea of the act of understanding and the act of willing, nor of bones and flesh, nor of thought and an extended thing. But nevertheless we clearly perceive that the very same substance which is able to take on a shape is also capable of being moved, and thus that what has a shape and what is capable of being moved are one and the same thing by virtue of a unity of nature. Likewise, a thing that understands and a thing that wills are also one and the same by virtue of a unity of nature. However we are not perceiving the same aspect about a thing that we consider under the form of bone and that we consider under the form of flesh. For this reason we cannot take them to be one and the same thing by virtue of a unity of nature, but only by virtue of a unity of composition, that is, insofar as it is one and the same animal that has bones and flesh. But the question before us now is whether we perceive that a thing that thinks and an extended thing are one and the same by virtue of a unity of nature. In other words, do we find between thought and extension the same sort of affinity or connection that we observe between shape and motion or between the act of understanding and the act of willing? Or rather, are they said to be one and the same merely by virtue of a unity of composition, insofar as they both are found in the same man, just as bones and flesh are found in the same animal? I accept the latter view, since I observe a distinction or difference in every respect between the nature of an extended thing and that of a thing that thinks, which is no less than the difference I observe between bones and flesh.

424

However, you say in addition that no one has as yet been able to grasp my demonstration. Lest this conflict, which involves an appeal to authority, be detrimental to the truth, I am forced to reply that while not very many people have as yet examined the demonstration, still there are several who affirm that they understand it. And just as a lone witness who has sailed to America and declares that he has seen the Antipodes warrants greater credence than a thousand others who deny them on the grounds that they have no acquaintance with them; so likewise, in the case of those who appropriately examine the weightiness of arguments, greater authority attaches to the one person who says he correctly understands some demonstration than to the thousand others who, without providing any proof, claim that this very same demonstration cannot be understood by anyone. For although they themselves do not understand it, this is no impediment to others being able to understand it. Indeed, by drawing this conclusion on the grounds they do, they show they do not reason with sufficient care and thus do not warrant having very much faith placed in them.

Finally, there is the question of whether I have used my method of analysis to dissect all the motions of my subtle matter in such a way that I am certain that I could show people who pay very close attention and who are, to their way of thinking, rather intelligent, that it is self-contradictory for our thoughts to be dispersed among corporeal motions. This, as I interpret it, is to say that thoughts and corporeal motions are one and the same. My answer to this is that it is indeed most certain to me, but I do not promise that others will be persuaded of it, however attentive and astute they may think they are, at least not so long as they turn their attention not to things purely intelligible but only to things imaginable, as those people appear to have done who imagined that the distinction between thought and motion is to be understood by way of a dissection of some subtle matter. For this distinction is to be understood solely from the fact that the notion of a thing that thinks and that of an extended or mobile thing are utterly different and independent of one another, and that it is self-contradictory for these things, which are clearly understood by us to be different and independent, not to be able to be established separately, at least by God. Thus, however often we find them in one and the same subject (as, for example, thought and corporeal motion in the same man), we should on that account believe that there they are one and the same not by virtue of a unity of nature, but only by virtue of a unity of composition.

3. What is asserted here regarding the Platonists and their followers has already been rejected by the entire Catholic Church and commonly by all the philosophers. Now the Lateran Council did indeed conclude that angels could be depicted pictorially, nevertheless it did not on that account grant that angels are corporeal. And even if they really were believed to be corporeal, their minds certainly cannot be understood to be any more inseparable from angelic bodies than men's minds are from human bodies. And surely, were we here to entertain the notion that a human soul is transmitted to one by one's parents, we could not therefore conclude that it was corporeal, but only that it proceeds from the parents' soul, just as the body arises from the parents' body. As far as dogs and apes are concerned, even if I were to grant that there is thought in them, it would not in any way follow from this that the human mind is not distinct from the body but rather that in other animals too their minds are distinct from their bodies. This was the position espoused by these very same Platonists, whose authority was just now being praised. In this they were following the Pythagoreans, as is evident from their belief in metempsychosis. However, not only have I declared that there is no thought whatever in brute animals, as is here being assumed by my critics, I also proved it by means of the strongest of arguments, arguments that to date have not been refuted by anyone. But actually those who claim that dogs while awake know they are running and even while asleep that they are barking (as if these people were well acquainted with the animals'

hearts) assert this but do not prove it. For even if they add that they do not believe that the operations of beasts can be explained by means of the science of mechanics without reference to sense, life, and soul (this I take to mean "without reference to thought," for I have not denied that there is in brute animals something commonly called "life," or a corporeal soul, or an organic sense), to the extent that these people are "willing to risk everything proving that this position is both impossible and worthy of ridicule," still, this should not be taken to be a proof. And the same can be said with regard to any other assertion, however true it may be. In fact, people do not usually take risks unless their arguments lack probative force. And since at one time great men mocked claims about the existence of the Antipodes in nearly the same way, I believe we should not immediately take to be false what others mock.

Finally there is the added remark: "there are plenty of people who will say that man himself has neither sense nor intellect and that he can do 427 everything by means of mechanical devices and without any mind, given the fact that an ape, a dog, and an elephant can perform all their operations in this way. . . ." Yet surely this argument fails to prove anything except perhaps that certain men conceive everything so confusedly and adhere so tenaciously to prematurely formed beliefs (which they understand in merely a verbal fashion) that, rather than change them, they deny regarding themselves what they cannot help always experiencing within themselves. For surely we cannot avoid always experiencing within ourselves that we think. It may be shown that brute animals can perform all their operations without any thought, but one should not on that account conclude that therefore one also does not think. The only exception would be someone who has persuaded himself beforehand that he functions in no way different from brute animals and who, for the sole reason that he ascribes thought to animals, so stolidly adheres to the statement that "men and brute animals function in the same way," that, on being shown that brute animals do not think, he prefers to rid himself of that thought of his, of which he cannot fail to be aware, rather than change his opinion that he functions in the same way as brute animals. Nevertheless, I am not easily convinced that there are many men of this sort. But indeed if it be granted that thought is not distinct from corporeal motion, there are many more to be found who contend, with much better reason, that it is the same thing that is in brute animals and in us, since they observe all the corporeal motions in animals that they find in us. And they add that a difference that is merely a matter of degree does not alter the essence, even though they think perhaps there is less reasoning power in beasts than there is in us; nevertheless, they quite properly infer that the minds of animals are manifestly in precisely the same species as our own minds.

428   4. As to the knowledge possessed by an atheist, it is easy to demonstrate

that it is not immutable and certain. For, as I have already asserted, the less powerful the atheist imputes the author of his being to be, the greater will be the occasion he will have for questioning whether perhaps he is of so imperfect a nature that he is deceived even in things that seem to him most evident. And he will never be able to free himself of this doubt unless he first recognizes that he has been created by a true God who cannot deceive.

5. The statement that it is self-contradictory for men to be deceived by God is clearly demonstrated from the fact that the form of deception is non-being, toward which a supreme being cannot tend. And on this point all theologians are in agreement, and on it depends all the certainty of the Christian faith. For why should we believe in things revealed by God if we thought that sometimes we are deceived by him? And although theologians commonly affirm that the damned are tormented by the fire of hell, still they do not on that account believe that the damned are "being deceived by a false idea that God has implanted in them of a tormenting fire," but rather that the damned are truly being tormented by a fire, for "just as the incorporeal spirit of a living man is naturally confined in a body, so too after death it can easily be confined in corporeal fire through divine power, and so on." See the Master, *IV Sent.*, Dist. 44.[163]

However, as to the Scripture passages, I do not think it is my place to answer questions about them, except when they appear to be in opposition to some opinion that is unique to me. For when the Scriptures are brought to bear against beliefs that are common among all Christians, such as are those that are here being attacked, namely, that something can be known and that human souls are not like those of animals, I should I be fearful of the charge of arrogance if I did not prefer to be satisfied with the replies that have already been discovered by others, rather than think up new ones. For I have never involved myself in theological studies except insofar as they contributed to my private instruction, nor do I experience within me sufficient divine grace to believe myself called to these sacred studies. And thus I proclaim that I will not make any replies in the future regarding objections such as these. However, I will not yet adhere to this change in policy, lest perhaps I provide people an occasion for believing that I am silent because I could not provide a sufficiently appropriate explanation for the passages cited. [. . .][164]

6. As for freedom of the will, the account to be given in the case of God is vastly different from the one to be given in our own case. For it is self-

429

---

163. Peter Lombard (c. 1100–60) acquired the title "Master of the Sentences" in virtue of his *Four Books of Sentences,* which he compiled between 1148 and 1151. This systematically organized collection of quotations from church fathers and later theologians became a standard theological text for nearly 500 years.

164. Descartes continues with explanations of the biblical passages.

432 contradictory for the will of God not to have been indifferent from all eternity to everything that has happened or ever will happen, since it is impossible to imagine the idea of anything good or true, anything to be believed or to be done or to be left undone being in the divine intellect prior to his will having determined itself to bring these things about such as they are. Nor am I speaking here of temporal priority; rather, there is not even a priority of order or of nature or of a distinction of reason reasoned,[165] as they say, as if this idea of the good impelled God to choose one thing rather than another. Thus, for example, God did not will to create the world in time because he saw that it would be better this way than were he to have created it from all eternity. Nor did he will that the three angles of a triangle should be equal to two right angles because he knew that it could not be otherwise, and so on. On the contrary, it is because he willed to create the world in time that it is better than were he to have created it from all eternity. And the fact that it is true and inalterable that the three angles of a triangle should necessarily equal two right angles is owing to the fact that God willed it to be so; and the same for the other cases. Nor is there any problem in the fact that it could be said that the merits of the saints are the cause of their gaining eternal life, for their merits are not a cause in the sense that they determine God to will something, but merely in the sense that they are the cause of an effect of which God has from all eternity willed their merits to be the cause. And thus God's supreme indifference is the supreme proof of his omnipotence. But as for man, since he finds that the nature of every good and every truth is already determined by God and that his will could not be directed toward something else, it is evident that he embraces the good and the true the more willingly, and hence also the more freely, according as he sees it more clearly; and that he is never indifferent except when

433 he does not know which alternative is better or truer, or certainly when he does not see it so plainly that he cannot be in doubt regarding it. And thus there is a vast difference between the indifference that pertains to human freedom and the indifference that pertains to divine freedom. Nor is it of any relevance here that the essences of things are said to be indivisible. For first of all, no essence can pertain univocally to God and to a creature. And second, indifference does not pertain to the essence of human freedom, since not only are we free when ignorance of what is right renders us indifferent, but we are also free (and especially so) when a clear perception impels us to pursue something.

7. I conceive of the surface by which I think our senses are affected no

---

165. This is a term used by some medieval writers to designate mental distinctions, or "distinctions of reason," for which there is no foundation or basis in reality; rather, such a distinction arises exclusively through reflective activity on the part of the intellect. See Francisco Suárez, *Metaphysical Disputations,* Disp. VII, 1, sec. 4–5.

differently than all mathematicians and philosophers normally conceive it, or at least ought to conceive it. They distinguish it from the body and suppose that it lacks any depth. However, the word "surface" is taken in two senses by mathematicians. In one sense, they use it to refer to a body to whose length and breadth alone they direct their attention and that is viewed without reference to its having any depth, although they are not denying that it does have some or other depth. In the second sense, they use it merely to refer to a mode of a body, that is, when all its depth is denied. And for this reason, in order to avoid ambiguity, I asserted that I was speaking of that surface which is merely a mode and hence cannot be a part of a body; for a body is a substance, and a mode cannot be a part of a substance. But I did not deny that the surface is the outer limit of a body; on the contrary, it can just as appropriately be called the outer limit of the contained body as much as of the body that contains, in the sense in which those bodies are said to be contiguous whose outer limits are touching one another. For surely, when   *434*
two bodies touch one another, each one's outer limit is one and the same;[166] and this extremity is a part of neither body but is the same mode of each body and can remain if these bodies are removed, provided only that other bodies having precisely the same size and shape replace them. In fact, that sort of place which Aristotelians call the "surface of a surrounding body"[167] cannot be understood to be a surface in any other sense except in the one in which it is not a substance but a mode. For the position of a tower is not changed even if the air surrounding the tower is changed or even if some other body is substituted in its place; thus the surface, which is here taken to be the place, is a part of neither the surrounding air nor the tower.

However, in order to reject[168] the reality of accidents, it does not appear to me necessary to demand additional proofs over and above those I have already treated. For first, since every sensation takes place through touch, nothing but the surface of bodies can be sensed. But if there are real accidents, they ought to be something different from that surface, which is merely a mode. Therefore, if they exist they cannot be sensed. But has anyone ever believed they existed if he did not think they are sensed? Second, it is altogether contradictory that there should be real accidents, since anything real can exist separately from any other subject. But whatever can exist thus separated is a substance, not an accident. Nor is there relevance to the   *435*
claim that real accidents can be separated from their subjects not naturally but only through divine power, for "taking place naturally" merely means

166. Aristotle, *Physics,* Book 4, Chap. 4, 211a34.

167. Ibid., 212a6–6a.

168. Literally, to "drive off the stage by clapping." A literal, but more contemporary translation might be to "hiss off the stage." Descartes' use of such a scornful term does little to conceal his utter contempt for the medieval Aristotelian doctrine of accidents—or for Aristotelianism generally.

"taking place through the ordinary power of God," which in no way differs from God's extraordinary power and whose impact on the world is no different. Thus if everything that can exist naturally without a subject is a substance, then whatever can exist without a subject—even if through God's power, however extraordinary it may be—must also be called a substance. Indeed I do admit that one substance can inhere[169] in another substance; but when this happens it is not the substance itself that has the form of an accident, but merely the mode of its inherence. For example, when clothing[170] inheres in a man, it is not the clothing itself but merely the man's state of being clothed that is an accident. But since the chief reason which moved philosophers to posit real accidents was that they thought that perceptions of the senses could not be explained without them. I promised that in my writings in physics I would describe this in minute detail, addressing each of the senses one by one. This is not to say that I wanted any of my views to be taken on faith; rather I thought that right-thinking people would easily surmise what I could achieve regarding the other senses, given what I have already explained in the *Dioptrics* in regard to sight.

8. It is evident to anyone who takes note of the immensity of God that there can be absolutely nothing that does not depend on him. This is true not merely for everything that subsists, but for all order, every law, and every rational basis for what is true and good. For otherwise, as was said a short while ago, God would plainly not have been indifferent to creating the things he created. For if some rational basis for what is good were to have existed prior to God's preordaining of things, this would have determined him to what was best to do. On the contrary, however, because God has determined himself toward those things that ought now to be made, they are for that reason, as Genesis has it, "very good."[171] In other words, the reason for their goodness depends on the fact that God willed to make them so. Nor is it necessary to inquire in regard to the types of cause it is by which this goodness, or the other truths—both mathematical as well as metaphysical— depend upon God. For since those who enumerated the types of causes perhaps did not pay attention to this type of causing, it is hardly any wonder that they gave no name to it. In fact, however, they did give a name to it: it could be called an "efficient cause," and for the same reason that a king is the one who puts a law "into effect," even though the law is not itself something existing physically but is merely a "moral being," as they say. Nor too

436

---

169. *accidere.*

170. *Habitus* is the state of being surrounded by a noncausal, nonmeasuring environment. It is one of the ten predicaments or predicate categories of medieval Aristotelian logic. The standard medieval example of a *habitus* is the state of being clothed. See Thomas Aquinas, *Commentary on Aristotle's Metaphysics,* Book 5, lesson 9, sec. 892; Book 11, lesson 12, sec. 2377.

171. Gen. 1:31.

is it necessary to ask how God could have been able to bring it about from all eternity that it not be true that twice 4 is 8, and so on. For I admit that this cannot be understood by us. On the other hand, however, I rightly understand that there can be nothing in any class of being which does not depend upon God, and that it would have been easy for God to establish certain things such that we men would not understand that these things could be otherwise than they are. Thus it would be illogical to doubt something we correctly understand because of something we neither understand nor observe any reason why we should understand it. Hence we should not think that eternal truths depend upon the human intellect or upon other existing things. Rather they depend on God alone, who, as supreme legislator, has established them from all eternity.

9. For us to observe correctly what sort of certainty belongs to sense, we must distinguish three levels, as it were, within it. To the first pertains only that by which the corporeal organ is immediately affected by external objects. And this can only be the motion of the particles of the organ in question   *437* and the change in configuration and position resulting from that motion. The second level includes everything that immediately results in the mind from its being united to the corporeal organ that is thus affected. And such are the perceptions of sorrow, tickling, thirst, hunger, colors, sound, taste, smell, heat, cold, and the like, which arise from the union and, as it were, the intermingling of mind and body, as was asserted in the Sixth Meditation. Finally, the third level includes all those judgments we have been accustomed to make from our youth regarding things outside us, on the occasion of motions in the corporeal organs.

For example, when I see a stick, one should not think that some "intentional species" wing their way from the stick to the eye, but merely that rays of light reflected from the stick excite certain motions in the optic nerve and, by this means, in the brain, as I have explained at sufficient length in the *Dioptrics*. And it is in this motion of the brain, which we have in common with brute animals, that the first level of sensing consists. But from this there follows the second level of sensing that extends only to the perception of color or light reflected from the stick. It arises from the fact that the mind is so intimately conjoined with the brain that it is affected by the motions which take place in it; and nothing else is to be assigned to sense, if we wish to distinguish it carefully from the intellect. For it is on the basis of this sensation of color by which I am affected that I judge a stick existing outside me has color, and it is on the basis of the extension of this color, its boundaries and relation of its position to the parts of my brain that I draw conclusions regarding the stick's size, shape, and distance. And this is the case even though people commonly attribute these two activities to sense, and were I therefore here to assign them to the third level of sensing, still it is manifest that   *438* it depends upon the intellect alone. And I have demonstrated in the *Dioptrics* that size, distance, and shape can be perceived only by reasoning from one of these aspects to another. But the difference lies solely in the fact that when we make judgments now for the first time on account of some new observation, we attribute them to the intellect. But as to those judgments we made from our earliest years—made in precisely the same way as the ones we make now—concerning things which affected our senses or even things to which we concluded by means of a process of reasoning, we assigned them to sense. And we made this assignment because habit makes us reason and judge very quickly, or rather we recall judgments we had for a long time been making regarding similar things, and thus we fail to distinguish these operations from a simple perception of sense.

Thus it is evident that when we declare that the certainty of the intellect is far greater than that of the senses, we mean merely that the judgments we make as adults as a result of new observations are more certain than those we formed in early childhood without any reflection at all. No doubt this is true. For it is obvious that it is not a question here of the first and second levels of sensing, since there cannot be any falsity in it. Hence when it is asserted that a stick in water appears broken on account of refraction, this is the same as saying that how it appears to us is the basis on which a child would judge it to be broken and even the basis on which we make the same judgment in accordance with the preconceived opinions with which we have become accustomed from our youth. But I cannot grant what is added here, namely, that this error is corrected by touch and not by the intellect. The reason is that even though it is through touch that we judge the stick to be straight (this judgment taking place in the same way as that to which we have been accustomed from infancy and which therefore is called "sense"), nevertheless this does not suffice to correct an error of sight. On the contrary, in addition we need to have some power of reasoning to teach us that in this matter we ought to give more credence to a judgment based on touch than to a judgment elicited from sight. Since this power of reasoning has not been in us from our infancy, it must be ascribed not to sense but to the intellect alone. And therefore in this very case it is the intellect alone that corrects an error of sense; and no instance can ever be brought forward in which error results from our trusting the operation of the mind more than sense.

10. Since the difficulties that remain are put forward more as doubts than as objections, I am not so arrogant that I would dare to reply that I will provide a satisfactory account for those difficulties concerning which to this day I see men of great intelligence and learning have doubts. Still, so that I might perform to my capacity and that I not fail in my cause, I will candidly state how it happened that I completely freed myself from these same doubts. For thus I will be delighted if perhaps these same things be used by others; but if not, at least I will not be aware of any rashness on my part.

When I first made a real distinction between the human mind and the   *440*
body on the basis of arguments displayed in these *Meditations* and inferred
that the mind is more known than the body, and so on, I surely was compelled to give my assent because I observed nothing in them that was inco-
herent or that was not deduced from evident principles according to the
rules of logic. But I confess I was not for that reason fully convinced; and
the same thing happened to me that happens to astronomers who, after having been won over by arguments that the sun is several times larger than the
earth, still cannot bring themselves to judge that the sun is not smaller than
the earth when they are actually turning their eyes toward it. But I advanced
further and passed over to a consideration of physical things by placing my
trust in the same basic principles. I did this first by attending to the ideas or
notions of anything at all that I found within myself. I diligently distinguished
them one from the other so that all my judgments would be congruent with
them. As a result, I observed that absolutely nothing belongs to the concept
of a body except that it is something which has length, breadth, and depth,
and that it is capable of various shapes and motions. I also found that these
shapes and motions are merely modes which no power could cause to exist
apart from a body. But colors, smells, tastes, and the like are merely certain
sensations existing in my thought, differing no less from bodies than does
pain from the shape or motion of the weapon that is inflicting the pain.
Finally, I observed that heaviness, hardness, the power of heating, attracting,
and purging, and all the other qualities we experience in bodies consist
exclusively in motion or the privation of motion and the configuration and
arrangement of their parts.

Since these opinions differ considerably from those that I had previously   *441*
held regarding physical things, I then began to consider the reasons why I had
previously believed otherwise. And I observed that the chief reason was that,
beginning from infancy, I had made various judgments regarding physical
things, insofar as they aided in the preservation of the life I was entering,
and I later retained the same opinions I had previously conceived. And since
at that age the mind used the corporeal organs less properly and was very
firmly attached to them, it did not do any thinking apart from them and
perceived things only in a confused fashion. And although it was conscious
of its own nature and possessed within itself an idea of thought as well as an
idea of extension, nevertheless, since it understood nothing without also at
the same time imagining something, it took them both to be one and the
same, referring to the body all the notions it had of things that are related
to the intellect. And since I never freed myself later in life from these preconceived opinions, I did not know anything at all with enough distinctness,
and I assumed that everything was corporeal, even though I assumed that
the ideas or concepts of these very things which I took to be corporeal were
often such that they referred to minds rather than to bodies.

For I conceived of heaviness, for example, as if it were a certain real quality that is present in solid bodies. Although I called it a "quality," referring it
to the bodies in which it inhered, nevertheless, by adding that it was "real,"
I actually thought it was a substance. In the same way, clothing, taken in
442   itself, is a substance, even though when referred to the man who is clothed,
it is a quality. And again, the mind, even though it is really a substance, can
nevertheless still be called a quality of the body to which it is joined. And
although I imagined that heaviness is diffused throughout the entire body
that is heavy, still I did not ascribe to it that very same extension which constitutes the nature of a body. For the true extension of a body is such that it
excludes any mutual penetrability of its parts. However, I thought there was
as much heaviness in a ten-foot-long piece of wood as there was in a one-
foot-long bar of gold or some other metal. In fact I judged that all the heaviness could be contracted to a mathematical point. Indeed, I also saw that
heaviness, while remaining coextensive with the body that is heavy, could
exert its entire force in any part of the body. For if the body were suspended
by a rope, it could pull on the rope with all its force just as if this heaviness
were only in the part touching the rope and were not diffused throughout
the remaining parts—regardless of the part to which the rope might be
attached. And it is in precisely this way that surely I now understand the
mind to be coextensive with the body, the whole of the mind in the whole
body, and the whole mind in every one of its parts. But it appears that the
belief that this idea of heaviness was drawn from the one I had of the mind
is chiefly attributable to the fact that I believed that heaviness carried bodies
toward the center of the earth as if it contained within itself some knowledge. For this certainly could not take place without knowledge, nor could
any knowledge occur unless it be in a mind. Nevertheless, I also used to attribute a few other properties to heaviness that cannot be understood to be
attributable in the same way to a mind: for example, that it is divisible,
measurable, and so on.

443   But after I had taken sufficient note of these things, I carefully distinguished the idea of the mind from the ideas of the body and corporeal
motion, and I came to realize that all the other ideas of real qualities or substantial forms which I had formerly possessed had been put together or
fabricated by me from those previously mentioned ideas. Thus I easily freed
myself from all the doubts that have been proposed here. For first of all, I
had no doubt about whether I possessed a clear idea of my mind, inasmuch
as I had an intimate awareness of it. Nor did I have any doubt about whether
this idea was utterly different from the ideas of other things and about
whether it contained anything corporeal. For although I had sought true
ideas of these other things as well, and I seemed to know all of them in a
general sort of way, still I utterly failed to find anything in them that was not
completely different from the idea of the mind. And I saw that there is a far

greater distinction between things such as mind and body, which appeared distinct even though I thought attentively about both of them, than there is between things that are such that when we think of both of them we do not see that one of these can exist apart from the other—despite the fact that we can understand one while not thinking about the other. Thus the immensity of God can readily be understood even if no attention is given to his justice; but if attention is given to both, it is utterly self-contradictory for us to think that God is immense but not just. Moreover, the existence of God can also be rightly understood, even if one were ignorant of the persons of the Holy Trinity, inasmuch as they can be perceived only by a mind illumined by faith. But when they have been perceived, I deny that a real distinction can be understood to obtain among them by reason of the divine *444* essence, although it may be allowed by reason of their relations to one another.

And finally I was not fearful about my being obsessed about my method of analysis or about having made an error when, because I saw that there are certain bodies that do not think, or rather because I clearly understood that certain bodies can exist without thought, I preferred to argue that thought does not belong to the nature of the body rather than conclude that thought is a mode of the body on the grounds that there are certain other bodies— human bodies, for example—which do think. For I have never really seen or perceived that human bodies think, but merely that it was the same men who possess both thought and a body. And I observed that this occurs as a result of combining a thing that thinks with a something corporeal, because, in examining by itself a thing that thinks, I observed nothing in it that belonged to the body, just as I observed no thought in corporeal nature, when I considered it by itself. On the contrary, however, in examining all the modes of body and mind, I observed absolutely nothing whose concept did not depend on the concept of the thing of which it was a mode. Because we often see two things joined together, one should not conclude that they are one and the same. But because we sometimes observe one of them apart from the other, it is quite appropriate to draw the inference that they are different. Nor should the power of God deter us from drawing this infer- ence, since it is no less contradictory in its very concept that what we clearly perceive to be two different things should become one and the same, intrin- *445* sically and not through a combination, than that things which are in no way distinct should be separated. And thus if God were to bestow upon certain bodies the power of thinking (as in fact he has done in the case of human bodies), he can decouple this very power from them, and thus it is no less really distinct from them.

Nor do I marvel at the fact that at one time, before I had freed myself from the preconceived opinions of the senses, it surely was the case that I perceived rightly that 2 and 3 make 5, and that when equals are subtracted from equals the remainders are equal, and many similar examples, since nevertheless I did not believe that the soul of a man is distinct from his body. For it is easy for me to observe that it did not happen that while I was still just a young child I would make a false judgment regarding those propositions that everyone equally admits, for at that time they were not yet of any use to me; nor do children learn to count 2 and 3 before they are capable of judging whether they make 5, and so on. On the contrary, however, from my infancy I had conceived of mind and body as one single thing, for my observation that I was composed of mind and body was confused. And it occurs in nearly every instance of imperfect knowledge that many things are grasped simultaneously as if they were one thing, but that later on must be distinguished by means of a more careful scrutiny.[172]

172. Descartes ends the *Reply to the Sixth Set of Objections* by answering the letter from "Various Philosophers and Geometers."

INDEX

Page numbers refer to the Adam and Tannery edition of *Oeuvres de Descartes,* volume VII (and are shown on this book's margins), except for the few references to the *Letter Serving as a Reply to Gassendi,* which come from volume IX and are so indicated.